International Human Rights

BLACK LETTER OUTLINES

International Human Rights

THIRD EDITION

Linda A. Malone
Distinguished Professor of Law and Visiting Scholar
Environmental Law Institute
Washington, D.C.

BLACK LETTER SERIES®

WEST
ACADEMIC
PUBLISHING

Summary of Contents

Table of Contents

Capsule Summary

I. HISTORY OF THE RIGHTS OF INDIVIDUALS

Under modern international law of human rights, individuals are protected *without regard to their status as nationals or aliens*.

A. TRADITIONAL CONCEPT

1. Historically, the state's treatment of individuals was considered a domestic affair, not a matter for international law.

2. Exceptions include a Roman recognition of a state's obligation to aliens, 19th century European "minority treaties" protecting ethnic minorities, rules of war traceable to the 17th and 18th centuries, and the gradual internationalization of rights with respect to slavery.

B. EARLY TWENTIETH CENTURY

1. The International Labor Organization (ILO), established after WWI, recognized international human rights by setting forth basic universal standards for labor and social welfare.

2. Many Post-WWI treaties protected national, religious, linguistic and ethnic minorities.

C. POST-WORLD WAR II

The world's reaction to the Holocaust and other Nazi atrocities during WWII resulted in the modern concept of international human rights law. The Nuremberg tribunal demonstrated the international concern for human rights, which was key to the formation of the United Nations in 1945.

II. HUMAN RIGHTS & THE UNITED NATIONS

The UN Charter in 1945 was the first attempt to provide comprehensive protection for all individuals. The Charter, Universal Declaration of Human Rights, International Covenant on Civil and Political Rights (with Optional Protocol) and International Covenant on Economic, Social and Cultural Rights form the "International Bill of Human Rights." The dual purposes of the United Nations are to protect human rights and accomplish international peace. (pp. 17–18) The United Nations' mission to protect human rights is acknowledged in the Universal Declaration of Human Rights (p. 18) and codified in the International Bill of Rights. (p. 17)

A. THE UN CHARTER

1. Article 55 provides for the observance of "human rights and fundamental freedoms for all without distinction as to race, sex, language or religion," while

Article 56 states that "all members pledge themselves to take joint and separate action . . . [for] the purposes set forth in Article 55."

2. In *Sei Fuji v. California*, the California Supreme Court held that Articles 55 and 56 are not self-executing.

B. THE UNIVERSAL DECLARATION OF HUMAN RIGHTS

The Declaration was intended to define the rights protected in Articles 55 and 56, but it is not legally binding *per se*. It may, however, be considered binding as a new rule of *customary international law*.

1. Civil and Political Rights included prohibitions of slavery, torture, various kinds of discrimination, arbitrary arrests, and interferences with privacy as well as protections of rights to a fair trial, marriage, property ownership, political asylum, equal access to public positions, and freedoms of religion, expression, movement, peaceful assembly and association.

2. Economic, Social and Cultural Rights include rights to social security, employment, education, health care, etc.

In March of 2011, Assistant Secretary of State Michael Posner stated that the U.S. policy towards economic, social, and cultural rights will be guided by five principles:

a. Such rights should be expressly set forth or derived from the Universal Declaration and the International Covenant on Economic, Social, and Cultural Rights.

b. The U.S. will only endorse language that reaffirms the "progressive realization" of these rights and prohibits discrimination.

c. Language must be compatible with domestic and constitutional frameworks.

d. Highlight the U.S. policy of providing food, housing, medicine, and other basic requirements to people in need.

e. Emphasize the interdependence of all rights and recognize the need for accountability and transparency in their implementation, through democratic participation of the people.

Generally the U.S. plans to be more proactive and stop tacitly allowing oppressive states to substitute economic well-being for human rights. John R. Cook, *Contemporary Practice of the United States*, 105 AM. J. INT'L L. 590, 590–92 (2011).

3. Limitations on human rights are recognized through exceptions for the maintenance of public order and preservation of state security.

C. UN HUMAN RIGHTS COVENANTS

1. The International Covenant on Civil and Political Rights deals with the rights mentioned above in greater detail. It also provides for the Human Rights Committee, which oversees compliance through periodic state reports.

2. The International Covenant on Economic, Social and Cultural Rights likewise details the above rights. States are only required to "take steps" towards accomplishing the goals contained in the Covenant.

D. UN HUMAN RIGHTS INSTITUTIONS

The UN Charter authorizes various bodies to articulate and oversee compliance with human rights, including the Human Rights Council, the Human Rights Committee, the UN High Commissioner for Human Rights, the Commission on the Status of Women, as well as the Security Council, General Assembly, Economic and Social Council, and the Commission on Crime Prevention and Criminal Justice.

III. FUNDAMENTAL HUMAN RIGHTS

A. RIGHT OF PEOPLE TO SELF-DETERMINATION

1. Self-determination is the right of people in a territory to decide the political and legal status of that territory.

2. "People" contains both objective and subjective elements. Objectively, it is an ethnic group linked by a common history. Subjectively, it is a group identifying itself as a "people".

3. There is still much disagreement on the right of groups to secede, the reunification of groups in divided states, and the right of minorities to preserve separate identities within a state. The rights of **indigenous peoples** present conflicts with respect to territorial claims, state sovereignty, and traditional institutions.

B. PROHIBITION OF SLAVERY

The prohibition of slavery is a fundamental norm as a matter of customary international law from which no derogation is permitted.

C. GENOCIDE

1. "Genocide" is an act "committed with the intent to destroy . . . a national, ethnical, racial, or religious group, as such."

2. Genocide is a crime for which individuals are punishable; charges include conspiracy, incitement, attempt, and complicity to genocide.

3. Before the advent of the International Criminal Court (ICC) in 2002, punishment was left to domestic courts and, more recently, tribunals established by the UN.

D. CRIMES AGAINST HUMANITY

The Nuremberg Charter charged Nazi leaders with "crimes against humanity" by invoking the customary law of human rights.

E. PROHIBITIONS OF DISCRIMINATION

1. **Racial** discrimination is "any distinction . . . based on race, color, descent . . . impairing the recognition . . . on equal footing, of human rights and fundamental freedoms." A UN committee has jurisdiction to hear complaints, but its power to act is limited to reports and recommendations. Apartheid is considered a crime against humanity.

2. **Sexual** discrimination is "any distinction . . . on the basis of sex . . . impairing or nullifying the recognition . . . of human rights and fundamental freedoms." A UN convention attempts to eliminate prejudices and customs based on the idea of the inferiority or superiority of either of the sexes.

3. **Religious** freedom is limited only by the necessity "to protect public safety, order, health or morals or the fundamental rights and freedoms of others."

4. **Torture**, including attempt and complicity to torture, are *always* prohibited. It does not include pain or suffering incidental to lawful sanctions. The Committee Against Torture has the unusual power to initiate inquiries.

5. **Refugees**, at present, have no right to be granted asylum under customary international law, although this is subject to criticism. A state has the right to grant asylum, but an admitted refugee may only be deported for reasons of national security. Diplomatic asylum is granting refuge in the territory of another state creating a right of safe conduct from the foreign state.

6. **Children** enjoy the full range of rights granted to adults, but are additionally protected from various forms of sexual exploitation. A UN committee oversees compliance through state reports. The U.S. has not ratified the Children's Convention.

IV. NEWLY EMERGING RIGHTS & FUNDAMENTAL RIGHTS RECOGNIZED AS CUSTOMARY INTERNATIONAL LAW

Many rights contained in international agreements are also recognized as customary international law. A right may be elevated to international custom through virtually universal adherence, widespread participation or support and frequent invocation or application.

V. DEROGATION FROM PROTECTION OF RIGHTS

Treaties often allow derogation from the rights in times of "war or other public emergencies." Certain rights may not be derogated from, even during public emergencies. A state intending to derogate must inform other state parties, provide reasons for the derogation, and communicate the date on which the derogation terminates. The European Court of Human Rights gives states latitude in determining whether there is a "public emergency", but is more demanding in holding it accountable to other obligations under international law.

VI. THE INTERNATIONAL COURTS

A. THE INTERNATIONAL COURT OF JUSTICE (ICJ) IS THE PRINCIPAL JUDICIAL ORGAN OF THE UN

1. All UN members are parties to the ICJ Statute and must consent to jurisdiction.

2. Fifteen judges are elected with regard for balanced distribution.

3. The ICJ has contentious (binding) and advisory (non binding) jurisdiction.

4. The ICJ has compulsory jurisdiction for: the interpretation of a treaty, a question of international law, the existence of any fact which would constitute a breach of international obligation and the extent of any reparations resulting from the breach. A state may make reservations to the ICJ's compulsory jurisdiction.

5. The Security Council decides how to enforce the judgments of the Court.

B. THE INTERNATIONAL CRIMINAL COURT (ICC) HAS JURISDICTION OVER GENOCIDE, WAR CRIMES, & CRIMES AGAINST HUMANITY

The ICC may only address a case if states with jurisdiction are unable or unwilling to prosecute. The U.S. has refused to become a party to the treaty.

C. THE COURT OF JUSTICE OF THE EUROPEAN UNION IS THE JUDICIAL ORGAN OF THE EU

1. It acts as a referee between disputing member states and guards against infringement of individual rights by the EU institutions.

2. Usually there is a judge from each member state and the Court issues a single "judgment of the court" after secret deliberations, protecting them from the pressure of national interest.

3. Jurisdiction is conferred on it by treaties, with the power to hear direct actions or make preliminary rulings.

4. The Court's primary legislation includes the EU's constitutive treaties, while secondary legislation consists of the laws created by EU institutions.

VII. REGIONAL ORGANIZATIONS

The UN encourages regional organizations to settle local disputes before referring them to the Security Council, but the Security Council must authorize any enforcement actions. The Council often chooses to defer to the jurisdiction of regional organizations.

A. THE ORGANIZATION OF AMERICAN STATES (OAS)

The main functions of the OAS are to strengthen security, ensure peaceful dispute resolution, and promote economic, social, and cultural development. The OAS has drafted many human rights treaties, but is only mildly successful in their ratification.

B. THE COUNCIL OF EUROPE

The Council has been influential in incorporating human rights obligations into the economic focus of the EU.

C. THE AFRICAN UNION (AU)

The AU is concerned primarily with noninterference and dispute resolution, but plays a limited role in dealing with human rights conflicts regionally.

VIII. REGIONAL HUMAN RIGHTS LAW & INSTITUTIONS

A. THE EUROPEAN SYSTEM

Europe has the longest standing and most well developed regional system of human rights law.

1. The European Convention on Human Rights is similar to the International Covenant, but fails to recognize a people's right to self determination, the rights of certain minorities, and children's rights. The European Social Charter recognizes a wider range of rights, but has not been ratified by all the states.

2. The European Commission of Human Rights hears cases between states (compulsory jurisdiction) and with respect to individuals (optional jurisdiction). The European Court of Human Rights has optional jurisdiction, but its judgments are binding and the Court may award damages.

3. Originally, the European Court of Human Rights could only hear cases after the review of the Commission, but now all applicants have direct access to the Court. The Court is the first permanent, full time human rights court and the execution of its judgments is overseen by the Committee of Ministers of the Council of Europe.

B. THE INTER-AMERICAN SYSTEM

1. The American Declaration of the Rights and Duties of Man defines the fundamental rights of the individual mandated of all members of the OAS Charter.

2. The Inter-American Commission on Human Rights (IACHR) evolved from a body empowered to prepare reports and make recommendations to the formal organ of the OAS to further the American Declaration.

3. The American Convention on Human Rights (which the U.S. has not yet ratified) is similar to the European Convention except that it does not include a wide range of economic or social rights. It differs from other international regimes by making the right of individual petition mandatory and interstate petitions optional for the IACHR, which is authorized to consider charges of rights violation under the Convention.

4. IACHR has both contentious and advisory jurisdiction. Contentious jurisdiction is optional, but the Court's judgment is final, binding and enforced by the OAS. Advisory jurisdiction is not binding and allows the Court to give its opinions interpreting the Convention and other American human rights treaties.

C. THE AFRICAN SYSTEM

The African Charter on Human and People's Rights guarantees a wide range of rights and established a Commission to hear petitions. The African Court of Justice and Human Rights was created by a protocol in 2009, but awaits fifteen signatures to go into effect.

D. EMERGING SYSTEMS

Nations in the Arab world and Asia do not have the strong regional human rights systems available in Europe and the Americas.

As of 2009, however, significant progress had been made toward recognizing regional action in the human rights arena through the establishing of several charters and organizations.

The ASEAN Intergovernmental Commission on Human Rights was established in 2009, and the ASEAN Human Rights Declaration was adopted in 2012. While many Western countries support the declaration in theory, many, including the U.S. have been critical of the language used in the declaration, expressing concern that it is inconsistent with international standards.

IX. HUMANITARIAN INTERVENTION BY THE UN

A. HISTORIC DEVELOPMENT OF THE SECURITY COUNCIL (UNSC)

1. The Security Council was established in the UN Charter in 1945 with fifteen members, five permanent.

2. The UNSC has the authority to take enforcement action to "maintain or restore international peace and security." It often must balance respecting state sovereignty with promoting human rights.

3. Any member of the UN may bring any dispute to the Security Council and a non member may bring a dispute if it agrees to the obligations of the settlement. All members of the UN must accept and carry out the decisions of the UNSC.

B. CHAPTER VI: PACIFIC SETTLEMENT

The first step of the Security Council is to seek a peaceful means of reconciliation, usually mediation and preventative diplomacy.

C. CHAPTER VII: ACTION WITH RESPECT TO THREATS TO THE PEACE, BREACHES OF THE PEACE, & ACTS OF AGGRESSION

1. When the Council has determined that one of the three above has occurred and peaceful measures would be inadequate, it may take actions such as demonstrations, blockades, or military operations to restore the peace. The Council may not order states to participate in military action.

2. The UN gradually adopted Chapter VII to provide a legal basis for humanitarian intervention.

3. Specific Enforcement Actions Under Chapter VII:

   a. 1991: The UN established "safe havens" in northern **Iraq** to allow Kurdish exiles to return under international protection.

   b. 1992: The UN first sent a team to observe the administration of humanitarian aid in **Somalia** and later authorized a U.S. led military operation to deliver aid to Somalis.

c.   In response to the bombing of villages in the Republic of **Bosnia and Herzegovina**, the UN authorized "all necessary means" to enforce "No-Fly Zones" over the area.

d.   1994: The failure of the international community to respond to the genocide in **Rwanda** prompted intense investigations as to how this inaction could be avoided in the future.

e.   1994: The UN authorized "all necessary means" to return the democratically elected President in **Haiti**. Generally, however, how a government assumes power is not a matter of international law absent human rights violations.

f.   International Tribunal in Former Yugoslavia (ICTY) and Rwanda (ICTR) were established with jurisdiction over international criminal offenses such as genocide and crimes against humanity.

X. HUMANITARIAN INTERVENTION BY STATES

A. PRO-INTERVENTIONIST

Collective or individual humanitarian intervention may be defended as not being force *directed against* the territorial integrity or political independence of the state concerned.

B. ANTI-INTERVENTIONIST

1.   Armed intervention is necessarily force against a state's territorial integrity and none of the narrow exceptions for the use of force include humanitarian intervention.

2.   The Security Council was subject to much criticism of its handling of the Northern Alliance Treaty Organization (NATO) bombings in Kosovo and may re-evaluate the scope of humanitarian intervention. The recent humanitarian situation in the Sudan may give the international community a chance to redefine its role in intervention.

XI. THE HUMANITARIAN LAW OF ARMED CONFLICT

A. SOURCES OF THE LAW OF ARMED CONFLICT

Customary law and international treaties such as The Hague and Geneva Conventions are the primary sources of armed conflict law.

B. PROTECTIONS PROVIDED BY THE HAGUE & GENEVA CONVENTIONS

1. Protection of the Individual

a.   Combatants (not only members of armed forces) are generally only protected by limitations on weapons and tactics.

b.   Wounded, sick, or surrendered combatants are protected from further attack and must be provided with medical care.

    c. POWs must be treated humanely (no torture, experimentation, or invasions of personal dignity) and released upon the conclusion of active hostilities.

    d. Civilians under enemy occupation must have various protected zones and delineated rights under an occupied government.

  2. Protection of Property

    a. Military installations are subject to attack, but the commander of attacking forces must notify the enemy.

    b. Undefended buildings or towns are not to be attacked.

    c. Medical facilities, works of art, and "cultural property" have special protection.

C. CONFLICTS ENCOMPASSED BY THE GENEVA CONVENTIONS & PROTOCOLS

  1. The Conventions in their entirety apply to international conflicts.

  2. Only article 3, concerning the humane treatment of non combatants, applied to civil wars until Protocol II was adopted in 1977, detailing more provisions for conflicts between a state's and dissident forces.

  3. Protocol I makes the Geneva conventions apply to wars of self determination.

D. SANCTIONS & ENFORCEMENT

  1. The Hague Conventions are regarded as customary international law following the Nuremberg Tribunal.

  2. The Geneva Conventions contain provisions allowing individuals to be criminally prosecuted for violations although they are not entirely self-administered; the parties' interests are safeguarded by a neutral power or humanitarian organization.

    Protocol I expands the substantive rules and procedural mechanisms of the Convention for repression of breaches.

  3. The Charter of the International Military Tribunal at Nuremberg provided for individual criminal responsibility for crimes against peace, crimes against humanity, or war crimes.

  4. Anyone participating in the execution of a common plan for these crimes is responsible for all acts performed by any persons in the execution of the plan. The fact that an individual was acting pursuant to orders is not a defense, but may be a mitigating factor.

E. "UNLAWFUL COMBATANT" STATUS & MILITARY COMMISSIONS

  1. Different humanitarian law provisions may apply depending on how a conflict and its combatants are characterized.

  2. The U.S. setup for military commissions, which came into being for "unlawful combatants" following the September 11, 2001 attacks, has been found lacking in providing for habeas corpus protection for prisoners held at Guantanamo Bay, Cuba.

XII. SOURCES OF HUMAN RIGHTS LAW

Customary international law is important for its application to states not parties to treaties, as well as its ability to supplement areas not addressed in treaties. It is difficult to establish, however, because of a lack of consistency in state practices and because it is ascertained by subjective analysis.

A. TWO APPROACHES TO CUSTOMARY INTERNATIONAL LAW

1. Objectivist/Sociological: universal and therefore binding on every state.

2. Participatory/Voluntarist: applies only to those states that participated in the custom.

B. ESTABLISHMENT OF AN INTERNATIONAL CUSTOM

1. Quantitative factors include past state practice and duration of the state practice. To establish custom definitively, the practice must be followed consistently by a number of states representing diverse geographic, economic, and social characteristics. Customary law may also be limited to a region or locality.

2. A qualitative factor is *opinio juris*, the sense that there is a legal obligation compelling states to follow a certain practice.

C. RESOLUTIONS AND RECOMMENDATIONS OF INTERNATIONAL ORGANIZATIONS

Resolutions are not legally binding, but are frequently used as evidence of customary international law.

D. APPLICATION OF INTERNATIONAL CUSTOMARY LAW

Customary law enjoys universal application, with two exceptions: clear and consistent objection and historic departure from a rule.

E. RELATIONSHIP BETWEEN TREATIES & CUSTOMARY INTERNATIONAL LAW

Treaties may be given equal weight with custom, prevail over custom, be proof of custom, or codify custom. Generally, they are given equal weight.

XIII. GENERAL PRINCIPLES OF LAW

A general principle of law is one so fundamental that it is a basic tenet in virtually every major legal system. The principles fill in the gaps left by treaties and customary law, but these gaps **are** becoming fewer. General principles continue to be applied in procedural matters and problems of international judicial administration.

XIV. EXTRADITION

A. OBLIGATION TO EXTRADITE

In the absence of a treaty, there is no obligation to extradite. Some treaties provide that a state cannot extradite its own nationals.

B. EXTRADITABLE OFFENSES

Treaties often provide for extradition on grounds of double criminality, when the alleged conduct is an offense in both the requisitioning and asylum state. A few treaties list extraditable offenses.

C. STANDARD TREATY LIMITATIONS ON EXTRADITION

1. Extradition may not be granted if the fugitive will be subject to discrimination.

2. The request for extradition might require sufficient prima facie evidence of guilt.

3. Most treaties contain exemptions for extradition for political offenses. Purely political offenses include treason or espionage. Related political offenses have varying degrees of connection between the crime and the political act. There is a growing trend to exempt acts of terrorism from treatment as political offenses.

4. The requisitioning nation cannot prosecute an extradited person for offenses other than those stated as the grounds for extradition.

5. The crime must have been committed within the territorial jurisdiction of the requisitioning state.

6. Exceptions for crimes of a religious, fiscal, or military nature are often included.

D. METHODS TO AVOID EXTRADITION TREATIES

A potential asylum state may deny a fugitive permission to enter or deport the individual as an undesirable alien. Occasionally, states recover fugitives by abduction from the asylum state.

XV. ENFORCEMENT OF HUMAN RIGHTS LAW IN THE U.S. & OTHER DOMESTIC COURTS

Because the United States has failed to ratify so many human rights treaties, enforcement of human rights largely depends on the incorporation of custom into U.S. law by the courts.

A. THE ALIEN TORT CLAIMS ACT

The Statute gives the district court jurisdiction over civil actions by an alien for a tort committed in violation of the law of nations or a U.S. treaty. The Supreme Court held that there is a presumption against extraterritorial application of U.S. law under the ATCA. It did not, however, address whether corporations are immune from tort liability, as the statute was presumed not to apply.

B. U.S. TREATY LAW

1.   The Supremacy Clause declares treaties to be on par with federal legislation. In the event of a conflict, the last in time prevails.

2.   Self-executing treaties are directly enforceable in U.S. federal courts. Non self-executing treaties are only enforceable through implementing legislation. The Senate has characterized every human rights treaty as non self-executing.

3.   Every human rights treaty is accompanied by reservations, declarations, and understandings, such as the Senate declarations concerning a treaty's non self-executing status.

4.   The Death Penalty arguably violates international law, and the UN General Assembly has called for a death penalty moratorium, but the U.S. has a specific reservation to the ICJ preserving it.

5.   According to the Vienna Convention on Consular Relations, the counsel of any state whose national is detained or arrested must be notified, and the person arrested must be informed of his rights.

6.   Despite growing recognition that sovereign immunity should not preclude prosecution for certain international crimes, domestic courts continue to refuse consideration of such claims.

Perspective

I. INTRODUCTION

Human rights law is a complex interrelationship of domestic and international law. International law generally defines the substance of those rights and dictates what rights must be provided domestically within each state. In the absence of treaty law or custom, however, the gaps in human rights law are often filled by general principles of international law, which are in turn a reflection of basic legal protections accorded to individuals in most legal systems. Actual enforcement of human rights on an individual basis is often dependent upon domestic enforcement in court. With a few exceptions, the United Nations-based human rights system of treaties requires only that states report on their compliance, with oversight limited to review of those reports. Other United Nations (UN) mechanisms for enforcing state obligations are only available for systematic or widespread violations. When an individual remedy is provided, as in the Optional Protocol to the International Covenant on Civil and Political Rights, the remedy is often limited to a declaration that the state is not fulfilling its obligations. The regional Inter-American and European systems of human rights are unique in creating their own court to adjudicate violations of their respective, regional human rights treaties, but again the only remedy available may be a declaration of the state's violation. More traditional remedies, monetary and injunctive, for human rights violations continue to be dependent upon the extent to which the state's courts incorporate and enforce international law, whether treaty law, custom, or general principles.

II. COURSE COVERAGE

Human rights law is taught in a variety of formats, and in depth coverage of particular areas can vary. The so-called International Bill of Rights system of the International Covenants and the UN human rights system generally are an integral part of almost every class. Coverage of at least one of the regional human rights systems—usually the Inter-American or European system—is also standard. More recently, international humanitarian law in armed conflicts is becoming a core part of most course offerings. Similarly, peacekeeping and humanitarian intervention by states and the UN is likely to be covered. From there, emphasis in coverage does vary. Also, some classes focus more on the international aspects of enforcement; others may emphasize how human rights are interpreted, implemented and enforced in U.S. courts.

III. OUTLINE COVERAGE

This outline covers the principal and more peripheral areas of course coverage. First, the outline can be used regularly for class preparation, particularly to put a specific area in the context of human rights generally. Keep in mind how interrelated seemingly unconnected areas of the law can be. The essay exam questions and answers are specifically designed to illustrate this interconnectedness. Problems in human rights law are rarely susceptible to yes or no answers, or even short answers. In this respect human rights law is more like constitutional law than property or contracts—it is often unclear if a right exists, and if it does what that right encompasses and how it is limited by other rights or limitations imposed by the law. Even if a right is identified and a violation established, remember the discussion above about the different ways in which the right might be enforced and the different *fora* in which it might be enforced.

IV. SOURCES

Beyond treaties, which may be found in the U.S. treaty series, the UN treaty series, and on the UN web site (http://www.un.org), how can it be determined how or if customary law or general principles of international law address a particular issue? An easy starting point is to look for law review articles on the topic. Remember that the writings of "publicists" are considered a subsidiary source of international law. In looking for case law, it is of course helpful if an international court or tribunal has addressed the issue. Because it takes so long for these kinds of decisions, for example those of the World Court, to be published in official reporters, the web sites for these fora are particularly helpful. The UN web page also has an icon for human rights that can lead to all kinds of sources for human rights law, including that of the Criminal Tribunals. When looking at domestic court decisions, be careful to distinguish between a court's analysis under international law and its analysis of its own domestic law. Sometimes domestic courts and other domestic sources tend to blur any differences which might arise between the two. For example, the Restatement on Foreign Relations is just that—it provides the perspective of the United States on what international law requires of it in its foreign relations with other states, which may or may not reflect the consensus of international law in the global community.

As pointed out in the section on sources of international law, the most difficult part of answering any human rights issue can be determining whether a particular provision has become binding international law as either treaty law, customary law, or a general principle of international law. One of the best ways to test your own ability to put everything covered together is to read recent news reports of human rights crises and ask yourself what rights may have been violated, what remedies or sanctions are available, and where might one go to seek enforcement.

Chapter I

Rights of Individuals

Under modern international law of human rights, *individuals are protected without regard to their status as nationals or aliens*. This approach is in sharp contrast to the traditional concept of international law as governing relations between states. The law governing a state's obligations to an alien was established within this traditional framework of international law regulating the relationship between states, but not the relationship between states and individuals. Thus an offense to an alien was considered an offense only against the alien's native state. The modern international law of human rights, however, makes nationality irrelevant.

A. Brief History

Historically, a state's treatment of individuals in its territory was considered a domestic affair, and not a matter of international law.

1. Traditional Concept

An early exception, dating as far back as Roman times, was recognition of a state's obligations to aliens. By the late 19th century there were many "minority" treaties concluded by European governments to protect ethnic minorities with which they identified in other states. The only clear early example of an internationalization of individual rights was with respect to slavery. Several major countries abolished slavery in the 19th century; the unacceptability of slavery became an international standard; and slave trade became illegal. In a related matter, the doctrines of humanitarian intervention and humanitarian rules of war have roots traceable to the 17th and 18th centuries.

2. Early Twentieth Century

A major recognition of an international law of individual human rights came with the establishment of the International Labor Organization (ILO) after World War I. The ILO set forth basic universal standards for labor and social welfare and has since promulgated over a hundred conventions. The ILO is composed of governments, businesses, and unions. A number of the peace treaties after World War I provided protection to national, religious, linguistic and ethnic minorities in Central and Eastern Europe. These treaties focused on group rights—a minority's right to his/its own schools, language, and religions—and freedom from discrimination. The Covenant of the League of Nations also created a mandate system by which the population of the colonies formerly under German and Turkish control was to be protected.

3. Post-World War II

The modern concept of international human rights law is the result of the world's reaction to the Holocaust and other Nazi atrocities during World War II. Nazi war criminals were tried for violating international law before the Nuremberg tribunal, the establishment of which demonstrated that human rights were a matter of international concern rather than a matter left solely to each state. *See* p. 116 *infra*. This modern concept of international human rights law was also key to the formation of the United Nations in 1945, having as one of its principal purposes the promotion and protection of human rights. U.N. Charter art. 1, ¶ 2; art. 3.

4. Current Status

Although the basic concept of international human rights law is now firmly established, its relatively recent emergence results in a body of law characterized by evolving ideas, institutions and procedures.

Chapter II

Human Rights & the United Nations

The UN's Charter in 1945 was a departure from earlier treaties remedying the problems of particular abuses or particular groups because it was the first attempt to provide comprehensive human rights protection for all individuals. U.N. Charter art. 1(3). In 1946, the UN established a Commission on Human Rights to draft human rights treaties, and in 1948 the UN General Assembly passed the Universal Declaration of Human Rights. In the decades since its foundation, the UN has continued to promote and protect human rights and has drafted treaties for global adoption dealing with many aspects of human rights. In addition to the Charter, the Universal Declaration of Human Rights, together with the subsequent International Covenant on Civil and Political Rights, the International Covenant on Economic, Social and Cultural Rights and the Optional Protocol to the Civil and Political Covenant form the so called "International Bill of Human Rights."

A. The UN Charter

The two main provisions of the UN Charter concerning human rights are Articles 55 and 56. These articles are the foundation of modern human rights law.

1. Article 55

Article 55 states that "the United Nations shall promote . . . universal respect for, and observance of, human rights and fundamental freedoms for all without distinction as to race, sex, language or religion."

2. Article 56

Article 56 states that "all members pledge themselves to take joint and separate action in cooperation with the Organization for the achievement of the purposes set forth in Article 55."

3. Implementation

The Commission on Human Rights was established in 1946 to draft treaties implementing Articles 55 and 56, and these two articles have been the main source of subsequent human rights treaties. The language of Article 56 may suggest that the member states are obliged to a progressive rather than present fulfillment of the goals set forth in Article 55. The imprecision of Articles 55 and 56 has led one United

States court to find that they are not self-executing treaty provisions and do not confer any rights on individuals.

In *Sei Fujii v. California*, 242 P.2d 617 (1952), the California Supreme Court held that the UN Charter lacked the mandatory quality and precision required to create enforceable rights as a matter of United States treaty law. The court failed to address enforceability as custom based in part on its determination that the challenged state law provisions restricting alien ownership of property violated the state and federal constitutions.

B. The Universal Declaration of Human Rights

In 1948, the UN General Assembly passed the Universal Declaration of Human Rights. The rights delineated fall into two general categories: *civil and political rights*, and *economic, social and cultural rights*. This declaration was intended to define the rights protected by Articles 55 and 56 of the UN Charter. As a resolution of the General Assembly, it is not *per se* legally binding. At the time of its passage, many of the forty-eight states which voted to pass the declaration regarded it as a statement of aspirations rather than a legal obligation. There is, however, an argument to be made that since 1948 it has become *binding as a rule of customary international law*. Those finding a legal obligation point to a 1968 UN resolution proclaiming the Declaration to constitute "an obligation for the members of the international community." Clearly, some of the rights listed have evolved into customary international law or general principles of international law, and the Declaration is an authoritative interpretation of the human rights provisions of the Charter. The dual purposes of the UN are to protect human rights and accomplish international peace.

1. Civil & Political Rights

The provisions dealing with civil and political rights include prohibition of slavery; torture; discrimination on grounds of race, gender, religion, language, political opinion, nationality, ethnicity, birth or other status; a right to asylum, and prohibition of arbitrary arrests or interferences with privacy. Protected rights are: the right to a fair trial, the right to marry, the right to own property, the right to political asylum, the freedoms of religion and expression, freedom of movement, freedoms of peaceful assembly and association, establishment of free elections and equal access to public positions. Political and civil rights are the *foundation of democratic political systems* and have been the focus of human rights development in those countries.

2. Economic, Social & Cultural Rights

Socialist and developing countries have pushed for greater recognition of these rights, which include the right to social security, full employment, fair work conditions, education, health care, an adequate standard of living, and participation in the community's cultural life.

3. Limitations on Human Rights

Most human rights documents contain exceptions to the protections provided as necessary to maintain public order and preserve the security of the state. Accordingly, the Universal Declaration allows limitations "for the purpose of securing due recognition and respect for the rights and freedoms of others and of meeting the just requirements of morality, public order and the general welfare in a democratic society." U.N. Decl. art. 29 & 2. Such limitations or derogations are uncertain in scope and often subject to abuse despite Article 30 which prohibits any rights to act to destroy these rights.

C. UN Human Rights Covenants

The two groups of rights set forth in the Declaration of Human Rights were the basis for the General Assembly's adoption in 1966 of two treaties: the International Covenant on Civil and Political Rights (with the subsequent Optional Protocols, to the Civil and Political Covenant) and the International Covenant on Economic, Social and Cultural Rights. Both entered into force in 1976 after ratification by thirty-five states. As of January 2009, the Statute of the International Criminal Court (ICC) had been ratified by 167 governments and would permit the prosecution of war crimes, genocide, and crimes against humanity. The ICC has jurisdiction when the government fails to prosecute individuals for crimes against humanity because the government is unable to do so. It has eighteen judges who are elected for nine-year terms by the state parties. (p. 63) *Stare decisis* does not apply in the ICC. The Peacebuilding Commission, established in 2005, consists of thirty-one government members elected for two years. The goal of the Commission is to propose an integrated strategy for rebuilding and maintaining peace.

1. The International Covenant on Civil & Political Rights

This instrument deals, in greater detail, with the same political and civil rights protected by the Declaration of Human Rights.

a. Rights Protected

In *Bwalya v. Zambia*, the UN Human Rights Committee considered a communication by Mr. Peter Bwalya, a leading figure of Zambia's main opposition party. Mr. Bwalya alleged that over the course of several decades, the government had detained him and directed threats and intimidation against him in retaliation for his political activism. The Committee held that these actions by the government violated Mr. Bwalya's rights to freely express his opinions and to disseminate the political tenets of his party under Article 19 of the ICCPR.

In addition to the many individual rights protected by the Declaration, the Covenant includes two "rights of peoples" or group rights: the *right of self-determination* and the *right of all peoples to freely dispose of their natural wealth and resources*. Article 27 also provides that ethnic, religious, and linguistic minorities "shall not be denied the right, in community with the other members of their own group, to enjoy their own culture, to profess and practice their own religion, or to use their own language." Interestingly, neither Covenant includes the right to property included in the Universal Declaration.

b. Limitations

Several of the rights may be limited as "necessary to protect public safety, order, health, or morals or the fundamental rights and freedoms of others." There are also rights of derogation in times of war or other public emergency. *See* pp. 55–56 *infra*.

c. Review of Compliance

The Covenant requires immediate, not progressive, implementation. The Covenant itself provides for periodic submission of state reports on compliance to the Human Rights Committee, a UN body of human rights experts established by the Covenant to oversee compliance. In addition, the Covenant authorized submission of interstate petitions to the Committee for its review against states that have agreed to be subject to such petitions. No interstate petition has ever been filed. In 1976 the First Optional Protocol went into effect, allowing for individual complaints to the Committee against any state that has ratified the Protocol. In both instances, the Committee issues its views on the complaint, with a follow up on the actions taken by states in response to be included in their state reports and ultimately in the Committee's annual report to the General Assembly. The Committee also issues influential General Comments expressing its interpretations of the Covenant requirements. A Second Optional Protocol seeks to abolish the death penalty (*see* p. 75 *infra*).

2. International Covenant on Economic, Social & Cultural Rights (ECOSOC)

This Covenant, like the one on civil and political rights, amplifies the rights set forth in the Universal Declaration. The ECOSOC operates under the authority of the General Assembly and consists of fifty-four members, each elected for three year terms by the General Assembly. It receives recommendations from the Commission on Crime Prevention and Criminal Justice and the Commission on Women. It is also responsible for reviewing compliance with the Covenant on Economic, Social and Cultural Rights. It has interpreted covenants to bind businesses regarding rights of privacy, adequate food and the highest reachable standard of health.

a. Rights Protected

In addition to elaboration on the economic, social, and cultural rights in the Universal Declaration, the Covenant also guarantees two collective rights: the *right of self-determination* and the *right of all peoples to freely dispose of their natural wealth and resources*.

b. Limitations

The legal obligations of the Covenant are much less precise and demanding than those in the Covenant on Civil and Political Rights. Article 2 only requires states to "take steps . . . to the maximum of its available resources . . . with a view to achieving progressively" the rights in the Covenant. Moreover, the state may limit rights "for the purpose of promoting the general welfare in a democratic society." ICESC Art. 4.

c. Review of Compliance

Review of compliance is also more limited than in the other Covenant. Implementation is limited to review of periodic state reports by the Economic and Social Council, which has established an expert Committee on Economic, Social and Cultural Rights to review reports, which also issues General Comments.

D. UN Human Rights Institutions

The UN Charter itself authorizes the establishment of several important human rights bodies. These include the Human Rights Council (successor to the Commission on Human Rights), the UN High Commissioner for Human Rights, the Commission on the Status of

Women, and the Sub-Commission on the Promotion and Protection of Human Rights. The Peacebuilding Commission, established in 2005, consists of thirty-one government members elected for two years. The goal of the Commission is to propose an integrated strategy for rebuilding and maintaining peace.

Other UN commissions that help to protect human rights include the International Labour Organization, the UN Educational Scientific and Cultural Organization, the UN High Commissioner for Refugees, the Food and Agriculture Organization, the UN Children's Fund and the World Health Organization. Individuals may bring complaints against their governments to these human rights committees.

1. Human Rights Council

The UN general assembly established the Human Rights Council as the successor to the Commission on Human Rights in 2006. There were three major structural changes. First, the Council was authorized to establish a universal periodic review (assesses the fulfillment of each UN member state's human rights obligation). Second, a membership requirement was imposed that prevented a state from serving a third consecutive three-year term. The last major structural change allowed the general assembly (with a two thirds vote), to suspend a state's membership on the Council if they were found to be in 'gross and systematic' violation of human rights.

The Commission on Human Rights was replaced with the Human Rights Council in 2006. It is designed to meet more regularly and the members are elected on the basis of their human rights performances.

2. UN High Commissioner for Human Rights

In 1993 the General Assembly created this post, which has the principal responsibility, along with the Secretary General, of overseeing all UN human rights activities.

3. Commission on the Status of Women

Established by ECOSOC in 1946, this Commission (like the Human Rights Commission) is a political body responsible for overseeing women's issues. It has a procedure for reviewing confidential communications that is rarely utilized. The function is to prepare recommendations and reports for the ECOSOC on promoting women's rights and equality. Their objectives are to ensure that men and women have equal rights, develop proposals to give weight to their recommendations, and adopt their own resolutions and decisions. It is located in New York.

4. The Sub-Commission on the Promotion & Protection of Human Rights (Formerly the Sub-Commission on the Prevention of Discrimination & Protection of Minorities)

Unlike the other commissions, the Sub-Commission representatives were elected by the Human Rights Commission to act in their individual capacities. It studied human rights issues and reported to the Human Rights Commission. Both entities were responsible for addressing large scale, gross violations of human rights under ECOSOC Resolutions 1235 and 1503.

Under the First Optional Protocol, the Committee was permitted to hear complaints from individuals who claimed that their rights under the covenant had been violated. In order to file a complaint, however, the victim must have been subject to the jurisdiction of a state party to the protocol. The participating governments were required to file reports (generally every five years). The goal was to help governments bring laws into conformity with the committee's obligations. The committee could also request emergency reports when the committee believed that the human rights in a state were being violated. Unfortunately, many of these states were delinquent in their reporting and more than forty-nine states had reports that were over five years overdue. More than sixty percent of UN reports were overdue. The Sub-Commission concluded its work in 2006.

a. Resolution 1235

This resolution authorized both Commissions to address any "consistent pattern of violations of human rights" such as apartheid. Either was permitted to undertake a "thorough study" to be provided to ECOSOC.

b. Resolution 1503

This resolution authorized individuals and groups to bring to the attention of the Sub-Commission "a consistent pattern of gross and reliably attested violations of human rights and fundamental freedoms." The Sub-Commission was able to bring the matter to the Commission, which could conduct a "thorough study" or investigate with the consent of the state concerned. The process was confidential (unlike the 1235 procedure) with only the names of states under consideration being made public, unless the Commission referred the matter to ECOSOC for its recommendations.

E. The Role of Specialized Agencies of the UN

A number of specialized agencies, particularly UN commissions, the International Labor Organization (ILO), the United Nations Economic and Social Council (ECOSOC), and the Commission on Human Rights, have been active in the area of developing human rights law. The Commission on Human Rights should not be confused with the Committee on Human Rights which oversees compliance with the International Covenants.

UN development agencies do not have a mandate to report or monitor human rights. Darrow & Arbour, *The Pillar of Glass: Human Rights in the Development Operations of the United Nations*, 103 AM. J. INT'L L. 446, 447 (2009). These development agencies usually turn away from human rights violations in order to maintain government relations and development projects despite negative effects on human rights. Darrow & Arbour, *The Pillar of Glass: Human Rights in the Development Operations of the United Nations*, 103 AM. J. INT'L L. 446, 454 (2009).

It will remain a challenge for the UN to pursue human rights while coordinating country teams for development. Darrow & Arbour, *The Pillar of Glass: Human Rights in the Development Operations of the United Nations*, 103 AM. J. INT'L L. 446, 499 (2009).

In 2008 the UN recognized that climate change affected human rights. The UN Deputy High Commissioner for Human Rights spoke about the disastrous effects climate change could have on people: hunger, malnutrition, lack of access to water, displacement, and disease. The Bali Action Plan is designed to propose new negotiation processes to examine the human rights problems posed by global climate change.

In November of 2010, the United States participated in the first U.S. report under the authority of the UN Human Rights Council's Universal Periodic Review. The review included fifty-six statements from a variety of delegations. Several were political criticisms of the United States as a whole, coming from such countries as North Korea,

Venezuela, and Nicaragua, while nations friendlier with the United States called for the country to end capital punishment and implement more treaties relating to human rights.

The UN Human Rights Council has been criticized by some observers, including representatives at the January 2011 Congressional Hearings. Representative Ileane Ros-Lehiten was critical of the Council for various reasons, including its inclusion of countries such as China and Cuba, which have abused human rights. However, the Council did have its supporters. Assistant Secretary of State Esther Brimmer praised the Council as a valuable setting through which respect for universal values can be spread, though she did acknowledge that the Council has substantial shortcomings as well. The Council, according to Brimmer, has substantially improved through U.S. involvement in the organization.

Since the U.S. joined in 2009, the Council has developed new UN procedures on countries with serious human rights situations, a strong statement has been made on human rights in Iran, and they have defeated attempts by Cuba to politicize the High Commissioner for Human rights, as well as a proposal by Pakistan that would have resulted in restriction of free speech. John R. Crook, ed., *Contemporary Practice of the United States: Department of State Official Defends U.S. Participation in UN Human Rights Council*, 105 AM. J. OF. INT'L LAW 354, 354–356.

Chapter III

Fundamental Human Rights

Many of the rights discussed below are addressed by specific UN treaties and resolutions. Although those instruments are emphasized here, support for these fundamental rights can often be found in other international agreements, as well as regional human rights conventions.

A. Right of People to Self-Determination

The principle of self-determination is the *right of people in a territory to decide the political and legal status of that territory*. The concept has its political origins in the American Declaration of Independence (1776) and has been invoked throughout the 19th and 20th centuries by nationalist movements as the basis for their right to establish independent states. In 1945, the concept of self-determination was incorporated into the UN Charter.

1. The UN Charter

Although the UN Charter incorporates the concept of self-determination, the general principles of "self determination of peoples" referred to in the Charter lack concrete definition. The main provisions referring to self-determination are in Articles 1(2), 55, 73, and 76(b). Article 1(2) states one purpose of the Charter is the promotion of "equal rights" and "self determination of peoples." Article 55 states that the UN promotes solutions to international economic, social, health and related problems with a view to creating stability and friendly relations amongst nations "based on the respect for the principle of equal rights and self-determination of peoples." Article 73 is aimed at UN members assuming responsibility for the administration of non-self-governing territories. Such members are to assist in the development of self-government through the establishment of free political institutions. Chapter XII states that a basic objective of the international trusteeship system established for the trust territories after World War II is to promote "progressive development towards self-government or independence as may be appropriate to the particular circumstances of each territory and its peoples and the freely expressed wishes of the peoples concerned." U.N. Charter art. 76, § b.

2. Other UN Documents

The UN General Assembly has contributed to the development of the principle of self-determination. In 1960, the UN General Assembly adopted the Declaration on the

Granting of Independence to Colonial Countries and Peoples, viewed as the basis for the UN policy of decolonization.

As discussed above, *see* p. 20 *supra* and p. 27 *infra*, the International Covenants on Civil and Political Rights (ICCPR) and on Economic, Social and Cultural Rights also provided for the right of all peoples to self-determination. The most comprehensive and authoritative treatment of the principle of self-determination is the UN Declaration on Principles of International Law concerning Friendly Relations and Cooperation among States.

B. Defining a "People"

For a group to be characterized as a "people" there must exist the proper objective and subjective elements. The objective element is the existence of an *ethnic group* linked by some *common history*. The common history is often, but not always, expressed by a common language, religion, or territory. The subjective element is the group's *own identification of itself as a "people."* The group maintains the desire to live together and uphold common traditions.

U.S. law governing Native Americans stems from *Santa Clara Pueblo v. Martinez*, 436 U.S. 49 (1978). In that case, the U.S. Supreme Court recognized that tribes have certain self-determinative rights concerning cases that the legislative branch wanted to be heard in tribal courts instead of other federal courts.

The Organization of American States, as of 2007, had a Draft American Declaration on the Rights of Indigenous Peoples under consideration. It includes indigenous rights to collective action, administration of land and natural resources, cultural expression, as well as fundamental rights for indigenous women.

The United Nations in 2007 passed the UN Declaration on the Rights of Indigenous Peoples, which among other things calls for indigenous rights to autonomy with regard to internal affairs, freedom from discrimination based on their indigenous status, an equal guarantee of rights among indigenous men and women, and special examinations of the needs of the indigenous elderly, children, and other certain groups. In December 2010, President Obama announced that the U.S. was "lending its support" to the UN Declaration on the Rights of Indigenous People. This change in position resulted from a comprehensive interagency policy review, which included extensive consultation with tribes. The Declaration carries considerable moral and political force, although it is not legally binding. Similarly, Australia, Canada, and New Zealand have also changed their position on the Declaration and endorsed it since their original opposition in 2007.

Countries and regional or international organizations often conflict over the proper definition of some key terms relating to indigenous peoples. Principles like sovereignty and self-determination can be interpreted in different ways, and there are disagreements as to whether indigenous peoples also control the resources that exist on and under their lands.

C. Legal Status of Principle of Self-Determination

Despite its inclusion in several UN documents, the uncertainty of its legal status results from the lack of concrete definition, as well as its conflict with the well-established principle of sovereignty. The law of decolonization and the right of the inhabitants of an *established* state to determine their own government are well accepted, but there is little or no agreement on: the right of groups to secede from states of which they form a part, reunification of peoples in divided states, or the right of minorities to preserve their own separate identities within a state.

D. Rights of Indigenous Peoples

1. Indigenous peoples have asserted a right to self-determination to prevent their complete absorption into states dominated by non-aboriginal populations. Indigenous peoples may be seeking to secede to form their own states, or to retain control over their own communities and land. Recognition of such a right of self-determination for indigenous peoples presents conflicts with respect to territorial claims and competition between the sovereignty of the state and the traditional institutions of the indigenous people. The UN has appointed a Special Rapporteur on Human Rights of Indigenous Peoples to analyze the concerns of indigenous peoples on an international level. The emphasis on integration and assimilation in the Convention Concerning the Protection and Integration of Indigenous and Other Tribal and Semi-Tribal Populations in Independent Countries is disfavored by many indigenous leaders.

2. In *Apirana Mahuika et al. v. New Zealand*, the UN Human Rights Committee heard the petition of members of the Maori people who claimed that an agreement to regulate fishing quotas violated their rights as a minority group under Article 27 of the ICCPR. They claimed that there was not adequate consultation between the government and the Maori people outside of the representatives of a few *iwi* (sub-tribes). The Committee found in favor of the government. The consultations undertaken by the government complied with the applicable legal requirements because the government paid special attention to the cultural and religious significance of fishing for the Maori. Thus, the Committee evaluated both the process and the substantive balance between majority and minority interests.

E. Civil & Political Rights

See p. 35 *infra.*

F. Economic, Social & Cultural Rights

See p. 20 *supra.*

G. Prohibition of Slavery

An early development in the internationalization of human rights was the widespread prohibition against slavery. During the 19th century, major countries abolished slavery resulting in the development of an international standard prohibiting slavery and outlawing the slave trade. This antislavery movement eventually led to the adoption of the Slavery Convention of 1926 and the 1957 Convention supplementing that Convention by prohibiting slavery, debt bondage, and forced marriages. The prohibition against slavery is a *fundamental norm as a matter of customary international law* and the norm is recognized as *jus cogens* from which no derogation is permitted.

H. Genocide

The 1948 Convention on the Prevention & Punishment of the Crime of Genocide was adopted by the General Assembly in response to the atrocities of the Holocaust in World War II. Genocide is a crime for which individuals are punishable under international law.

Convention on the Prevention & Punishment of the Crime of Genocide, Dec. 9, 1948, 78 U.N.T.S. 277. As of May 2021, 152 countries, including the U.S., were parties to the Convention.

1. Definition

Article 2 defines genocide as acts "committed with the intent to destroy, in whole or in part, a national, ethnic, racial or religious group, as such." Prohibited acts include killing members of the group, inflicting serious mental or bodily harm, inflicting living conditions calculated to destroy the group, imposing birth control measures to prevent births within the group, and forcibly transferring children of the group to another group. Under both the Convention and customary international law, genocide is a crime which states *must* undertake to prevent and to punish. The standard of proof for a finding of genocide for an initial arrest warrant is "reasonable grounds to believe", followed by "substantial grounds to believe" at the confirmation of charges and finally "beyond reasonable doubt" at conviction. This has proven problematic because short of an admission showing *mens rea* for genocidal intent, proof of mindset is near impossible and must therefore be inferred from the surrounding facts/events. The ICJ has held that proof may be inferred from proven circumstances such as policies upon which acts of violence were based, the frequency of such violent acts, and discriminatory biases that prompted acts of violence against members of a specific group. Johan D. Van Der Vyver, *Prosecutor v. Omar Hassan Ahmed Al Bashir*, 104 AM. J. INT'L L. 461, 461–467 (2010).

2. Punishable Acts

Article 3 makes punishable: genocide, conspiracy to commit genocide, direct and public incitement to commit genocide, complicity in genocide, and attempt to commit genocide.

3. Jurisdiction

Given the absence of an established international criminal court until 2002, punishment was left to the domestic courts of states and, more recently, to the tribunals for Yugoslavia and Rwanda established by the UN Security Council. *See* p. 102 *infra*. Genocide is generally acknowledged as a *universal crime punishable in any state*.

4. "Effective Control" Test

In *Case Concerning the Application of the Convention on the Prevention and Punishment of the Crime of Genocide (Bosnia and Herzegovina v. Serbia and Montenegro)* 2007 I.C.J. 91 (Feb. 26), the International Court of Justice determined that there was insufficient evidence to find Serbia legally responsible for genocide committed in Bosnia and Herzegovina by those military forces it supported.

Applying the "effective control" test, the ICJ found that Bosnia failed to demonstrate that Serbian leaders knew of the genocidal acts or knowingly aided in their commission. Evidence that Serbia merely supported the armed forces that committed genocide was insufficient to establish their complicity under the Genocide Convention.

In 2009 however, an arrest warrant was issued for Sudanese President Omar Hassan Ahmed Al Bashir by a pretrial chamber of the ICC for the crime of genocide. Under the "effective control test," the ICC found that Bashir "knew or consciously disregarded information which clearly indicated, that his subordinates were committing or about to commit such crimes" (Article 28(b)(i)) and/or that the "crimes concerned activities that were within the effective responsibility and control of . . . [Bashir,] who failed to take all necessary and reasonable measures within his . . . power to prevent or repress their commission or to admit the matter to the competent authorities for investigation and prosecution (Article 28(b)(iii))". Johan D. Van Der Vyver, *Prosecutor v. Omar Hassan Ahmed Al Bashir*, 104 AM. J. INT'L L. 461, 461–467 (2010).

5. Successor States

On November 18, 2008, the ICJ determined that the Republic of Serbia was the successor state to the Federal Republic of Yugoslavia. In 1999 Croatia had filed a claim concerning genocide against Yugoslavia in the ICJ. However, Yugoslavia ceased to exist shortly thereafter. Serbia claimed that Croatia could not continue its claim against Serbia because that country had not acceded to the genocide convention until June 2001. The court determined that Serbia was bound by the convention because Yugoslavia had acceded to it. Yulia Andreeva *et al., International Courts*, 43 INT'L L. 425, 432–33 (2009).

<u>Examples:</u>   **Burma:** In 1997, President Clinton imposed sanctions on Burma due in part to repression of democratic opposition. Sanctions were further developed by President Bush and eased by President Obama. In August 2017, Rohingya militants attacked security forces in the Rakhine State, a region in western Burma. Rather than working toward peace, as the U.S. State Department encouraged in a statement, the Burmese military and police forces responded with attacked against the Rohingya. It is alleged that these forces have killed thousands and forced hundreds of thousands more to flee to Bangladesh. In November 2017, Secretary of State Tillerson released a statement concluding that the situation in northern Rakhine state in Burma constitutes ethnic cleansing against the Rohingya. In January 2018, the State Department re-designated Burma as a Country of Particular Concern under the International Religious Freedom Act of 1998, a designation for countries whose governments have engaged in or tolerated systematic, ongoing, and egregious violations of religious freedom.

Islamic State of Iraq and the Levant (ISIL): In March 2016, Secretary of State John Kerry made a formal determination that ISIL is responsible for genocide. This is only the second time that the US has attached that label to an ongoing crisis, the first being in Darfur in 2004. The State Department considers the definition from the 1948 Convention to be the internationally accepted definition of genocide under customary international law. Kerry's announcement noted that ISIL is genocidal "by self-proclamation, by ideology, and by actions." U.S. Dep't of State Press Release, Sec'y of State John Kerry, Remarks on Daesh and Genocide (Mar. 17, 2016), https://2009-2017.state. gov/secretary/remarks/2016/03/254782.htm. His remarks place responsibility for genocide against groups in areas under ISIL's control, including Yezidis, Christians, and Shia Muslims. Kerry noted that ISIL was also responsible for crimes against humanity and ethnic cleansing directed at the same groups and also against Sunni Muslims, Kurds, and other minorities in some cases.

I. Crimes Against Humanity

The Nuremberg Tribunal was established after World War II to punish Nazi leaders in accordance with international law. *See* p. 116 *infra*. The Nuremberg Charter, charging Nazi leaders with "crimes against humanity" invoked the customary law of human rights and was an important step in the development of international human rights law. "Crimes against humanity" were defined as "murder, extermination, enslavement, deportation, and other inhumane acts committed against any civilian population, before or during the war, or persecutions on political, racial or religious ground . . . whether or not in violation of the domestic law of the country where perpetrated." *Agreement for the Prosecution and Punishment of the Major War Criminals of the European Axis*, Art. 6, 59 Stat. 1544, 1547–1548. Crimes against humanity can be committed in peacetime as well as war and by a government against its own population. *See* p. 115 *infra*.

Recently, an ICC pretrial chamber decision on the standard for the prosecutor to initiate investigations under the Rome Statute lowered the threshold for "organizational policy" of crimes against humanity as much as possible by glossing over what type of organizations and persons could develop such a policy. This was done in response to the turmoil following a disputed election in Kenya in 2007.

There was a fierce dissent because no linkage is any longer necessary between the state and offending policy. A link between certain officials and/or extra-governmental organizations is all that is now needed. Charles Chernor Jalloh, *Situation in the Republic of Kenya*, 105 AM. J. INT'L L. 540, 540–543 (2011).

J. Prohibitions of Discrimination

Racial, sexual, and religious discrimination have been prohibited in certain international treaties.

1. Racial Discrimination

The principal treaties are the Convention on the Elimination of All Forms of Racial Discrimination, and the International Convention on the Suppression and Punishment of the Crime of Apartheid. The first convention entered into force in 1969, and the Apartheid Convention entered into force in 1976.

a. International Convention on the Elimination of All Forms of Racial Discrimination

This convention defines "racial discrimination" as "any distinction, exclusion, restriction or preference based on race, colour, descent of national or ethnic origin which has the purpose or effect of nullifying or impairing the recognition, enjoyment or exercise, on an equal footing, of human rights and fundamental freedoms in the political, social, cultural or any other field of public life." *International Convention on the Elimination of All Forms of Racial Discrimination, opened for signature* Mar. 7, 1966, Art. 1, 660 U.N.T.S. 195 [hereinafter Race Convention].

State parties must eliminate racial discrimination, (Art. 2), and are permitted in some circumstances to take special measures to secure advancement of racial or ethnic groups. Art. 1. States are also obligated to prevent, prohibit and eradicate the practice of apartheid in their territories. Art. 3. The enforcement machinery of this Convention goes beyond the usual reporting mechanisms for implementation. A Committee on the Elimination of Racial Discrimination has jurisdiction to hear complaints by one state against another, as well as individual petitions if the state has agreed to be subject to such petitions. Arts. 11, 14. The action it can take, however, is limited to reports and recommendations. The United States ratified the Convention in 1994, with reservations. The Race Convention had been ratified by 174 countries as of September 2011.

In Feb. 2008, the UN Committee on the Elimination of Racial Discrimination (CERD) praised some U.S. policies but also called on the United States to alter its reservations to the Convention. Criticisms stemmed from continued racial profiling, U.S. Supreme Court limitations on the use of race-based affirmative action, racial segregation in housing and education, and other matters involving insufficient measures to combat racial disparities. John R. Crook, ed., *Contemporary Practice of the United States Relating to International Law,* 103 AM. J. INT'L L. 575, 596 (2009).

In the fall of 2008, Georgia applied to the International Court of Justice (ICJ) for provisional measures against Russia over the latter country's invasion of South Ossetia. Georgia claimed that the CERD gave the ICJ jurisdiction. The ICJ determined that CERD did appear to give the court jurisdiction, but at the time it was appropriate for the court to address measures to both parties. The ICJ has not determined if CERD gives the court jurisdiction over the merits of the case. Yulia Andreeva, *et al.,* *International Courts,* 43 INT'L L. 425, 432 (2009).

b. The International Convention on the Suppression & Punishment of the Crime of Apartheid

This convention defines apartheid as a *crime against humanity,* involving "inhuman acts committed for the purpose of establishing and maintaining domination by one racial group of persons over any other racial group of persons and systematically oppressing them." "Inhuman acts" include denial of life and liberty through murders, infliction of serious bodily or mental harm, and arbitrary arrests and imprisonment; certain suppressive or divisive legislative measures; and forced labour. *International Convention on the Suppression and Punishment of the Crime of Apartheid,* Nov. 30, 1973, Art. II, 13 I.L.M. 50 (1974).

Liability extends to conspiracy to commit, aiding and abetting, and direct incitement of the inhumane acts listed in Article II. A person charged with the offense may be tried by any state party or before an international penal tribunal, and implementation consists of periodic reports to a group of experts. This treaty was adopted by the United States in 1994.

2. Sexual Discrimination

The first international document to recognize equal rights without regard to sex was the UN Charter. The Convention on the Elimination of All Forms of Discrimination Against Women (CEDAW), which was adopted by the General Assembly in 1979 and entered into force in 1981, focuses on the status of women and provides an extensive bill of rights for women including the right to equal education, health care, and equality before the law. Other organizations also have provisions granting women certain equal rights and protections, including the Inter-American Convention on Violence Against Women in the Organization of American States framework. By June 2011, 187 countries were parties to CEDAW, not yet including the United States.

In November of 2010, the U.S. Senate Judiciary Committee's Subcommittee on Human Rights and the Law held hearings regarding whether the United States should ratify CEDAW. The hearings mostly portrayed a ratification of CEDAW as a positive step; however, the Senate Judiciary Committee as a whole has not yet considered the issue.

a. General Protections

"Discrimination against women" is defined as "any distinction, exclusion or restriction made on the basis of sex which has the effect or purpose of impairing or nullifying the recognition, enjoyment or exercise by women, irrespective of their marital status, on a basis of equality of men and women, of human rights and fundamental freedoms in the political, economic, social, cultural, civil or any other field." *Convention on the Elimination of All Forms of Discrimination Against Women*, Dec. 18, 1979, Art. 1, U.N.G.A. Res. 34/180 (xxxiv) [hereinafter Sex Discrimination Convention]. Under Article 3 of the Convention on the Elimination of All Forms of Discrimination Against Women, "[s]tate Parties shall take in all fields, in particular in the political, social, economic and cultural fields, all appropriate measures, including legislation to ensure the full development and advancement of women, for the purpose of guaranteeing them the exercise and enjoyment of human rights and fundamental freedoms on a basis of equality with men."

Special measures designed to achieve equality between men and women shall not be considered discrimination, but shall be discontinued when the objective of equality has been achieved. *Sex Discrimination Convention*, Art. 4, U.N.G.A. Res. 34/180 (xxxiv). State parties must take all "appropriate measures" "(a) To modify the social and cultural patterns of conduct of men and women, with a view to achieving the elimination of prejudices and customs and all other practices which are based on the idea of the inferiority or the superiority of either of the sexes or on stereotyped roles for men and women. (b) To ensure that family education includes a proper understanding of maternity as a social function and the recognition of the common responsibility of men and women in the upbringing and development of their children." *Sex Discrimination Convention*, Art. 5, U.N.G.A. Res. 34/180 (xxiv).

It is recognized that an achievement of substantive equality may, in certain circumstances, require differing treatment of men and women because of biological and social and cultural differences between the sexes. The Convention on the Elimination of All forms of Discrimination Against Women Committee, General Recommendation No. 25, on article 4, paragraph 1, of the Convention on the Elimination of All forms of Discrimination against Women, on Temporary Special Measures. 78 U.N. Doc. A/59/38 (Supp.) (2004).

b. Optional Protocol to the Convention on the Elimination of All Forms of Discrimination Against Women (CEDAW) (the "Convention") (1999)

The Protocol authorizes the treaty enforcement body, the Committee on the Elimination of Discrimination Against Women (the "Committee"), to receive communications submitted by or on behalf of groups or individuals who allege having been victims of violations of the rights protected by the Convention. The Committee will have jurisdiction only over communications regarding violations by states that are parties to both the Convention and the Protocol. The Protocol went into effect on December 22, 2000.

During 2009, The Responsibility for the CEDAW Committee was transferred from the Division for the Advancement of Women to the office of the UN High Commissioner for Human Rights.

c. Review of Compliance

Implementation is reviewed through submission of periodic reports by state parties to the Committee on the Elimination of Discrimination Against Women. *Sex Discrimination Convention, supra,* Art. 17, U.N.G.A. Res. 34/180 (xxxiv).

In *Vertido v. The Philippines* (2010), the Executive Director of the Chamber of Commerce and Industry brought a case against a former president of the Chamber of Commerce, for alleged rape. The case took eight years to be prosecuted, the man was acquitted, and the judge made disparaging comments about women and rape. The Executive Director then brought the case under CEDAW, using the individual complaint process.

In 2009 The High Court in Bangladesh issued a decision that prohibits sexual harassment.

On March 2, 2009 judgment was issued in *Prosecutor v. Issa Hassan Sesay, Morris Kallon & Augustine Gbao*, also known as the *Revolutionary United Front* case. This judgment was the first to enter a conviction in an international criminal tribunal for the war crime of sexual slavery and forced marriage. The court held that absence of consent, on the part of the accused, was not an element of sexual slavery or forced marriage. In addition, the court identified forced marriage as a gender based crime with sexual and nonsexual characteristics. As a result of the forced marriage the "wives" sustain physical injuries as well as a social stigma, which keeps them from reintegrating themselves into society. Valerie Oosterveld ed., *Prosecutor v. Issa Hassan Sesay, Morris Kallon & Augustine Gbao*, 104 AM. J. INT'L L. 73, 80–81 (2010).

The U.S. has recently undertaken to support UN Consultative Status for ILGHRC (The International Lesbian and Gay Humans Rights Commission). ILGHRC petitioned to be awarded the consultative status that 3200 other NGOs have been granted. This petition was blocked by Egypt but garnered the support of the U.S. in July 2010. The U.S. found the "no action" vote used by Egypt to remove ILGHRC's status vote from discussion to be of questionable legality, and basically a delaying tactic. In 2011, ILGA (The International Lesbian and Gay Association, also known as ILGBTIA) was granted special consultative status.

The UN Human Rights Council was the first UN body to acknowledge human rights violations based on sexual orientation and gender identity in 2011, adopting the first UN resolution on the human rights of LGBT people. The HRC expressed concern over acts of violence and discrimination, and it called for a study to document discriminatory laws, practices, and acts of violence based on sexual orientation and gender identity around the world. In 2016, the UN Security Council condemned the Pulse nightclub shooting in Orlando, the first time the Security Council recognized violence targeting the LGBTQ+ community.

While the UN is progressing toward LGBTQ+ protections, individual states have not necessarily done the same. In 2014, Uganda passed the Anti-Homosexuality

Act, 2014. This Act criminalized any acts of "homosexuality" and any "attempt to commit homosexuality," and same-sex marriage was made punishable by life imprisonment. President Obama condemned this legislation. The US and other Western countries and organizations responded to this law by cutting funding to Uganda. Later that same year, the Constitutional Court of Uganda struck down the Act, holding that Parliament had passed the Act without a proper quorum.

3. Religious Discrimination

Of more recent origin than the other discrimination prohibitions, the prohibition against discrimination on religious grounds is embodied in the 1981 UN General Assembly resolution entitled Declaration on the Elimination of All Forms of Intolerance and of Discrimination Based on Religion or Belief. It affirms the fundamental freedom of all thought, conscience, and religion; the elimination of discrimination; and the right of children to have religious education. Freedom of religion is subject only to "such limitations as are prescribed by law and are necessary to protect public safety, order, health or morals or the fundamental rights and freedoms of others." Art. 1 & 3. States have an affirmative duty to enact or rescind legislation in order to prevent or eliminate discrimination based on religious beliefs. Art. 4. Among other specific rights, the Declaration acknowledges the right of parents to have access to religious education and the right to teach a religion or belief in suitable places. Arts. 5, 6. Nothing in the Declaration, however, is to restrict or derogate from any right in the Universal Declaration on Human Rights or the International Covenants on Human Rights. Art. 8.

Note: Many human rights treaties contain general nondiscrimination clauses. They often differ, however, in what types of discrimination they prohibit.

K. Freedom from Torture

There are *no legal justifications for torture* or exceptions to its prohibition. *Convention Against Torture and Other Cruel Inhuman or Degrading Treatment or Punishment*, *entered into force* June 26, 1987, Art. 2, §§ 2, 3, U.N. Doc. E/CN. 4/1984/72, 23 I.L.M. 1027 [hereinafter Torture Convention or UNCAT]. States must adopt measures to prevent torture in their jurisdiction, and ensure that torture, complicity, and attempts to commit torture are criminal offenses. Art. 2 § 1; Art. 4. UNCAT requires that states take effective legislative, administrative, judicial or other measures to prevent acts of torture in any territory under its jurisdiction.' Art. 2. Torture is an extraditable offense, and no one may be extradited if there is "danger of being subjected to torture." Articles 8 § 3.

1. Definition of Torture

The Convention Against Torture and other Cruel, Inhuman or Degrading Treatment or Punishment, which entered into force in 1987, defines torture as

> ". . . any act by which severe pain or suffering, whether physical or mental, is intentionally inflicted on a person for such purposes as obtaining from him or a third person information or a confession, punishing him for an act he or a third person has committed or is suspected of having committed, or intimidating or coercing him or a third person, or for any reason based on discrimination of any kind, when such pain or suffering is inflicted by or at the instigation of or with the consent or acquiescence of a public official or other person acting in an official capacity. It does not include pain or

suffering arising only from, inherent in or incidental to lawful sanctions." Torture Convention, *supra*, Art. 1.

This treaty was adopted by the United States in 1994.

2. Committee Against Torture (CAT)

Implementation of Article 2(1), 4 is monitored through periodic state reports to a Committee Against Torture. If a state consents, the Committee can hear interstate complaints and individual complaints. Torture Convention, p. 34 *supra*, Arts. 21, 22. If no solution is reached, the Committee issues a report to the parties involved. The Committee also has the unusual power to initiate inquiries, unless a state has declined to recognize this Committee function at the time of its signature on ratification. Arts. 20, 28. The Committee also publishes "general comments" that address common human rights violations, articulating the Committee's understanding of obligations under the treaty. None of the Committee's pronouncements are legally binding.

3. UNCAT

The prohibition of torture in the UNCAT is absolute. The UNCAT explicitly states that, "No exceptional circumstances whatsoever, whether a state of war or a threat of war, internal political instability or any other public emergency, may be invoked as a justification of torture." Art. 2.2.

The UNCAT (CID) does not define cruel, inhuman, or degrading treatment or punishment. It does prohibit, however, treatment or punishment "which does not amount to torture as defined in Article 1, when such acts are committed by or at the instigation of or with the consent or acquiescence of a public official or other person acting in an official capacity." Art. 16. The UNCAT does not make it clear whether exceptional circumstances may justify CID treatment or punishment.

4. ICCPR & HRC

Another major multilateral treaty that has shaped international human rights is the International Covenant on Civil and Political Rights (ICCPR). The ICCPR was adopted in 1966, establishing a treaty body, the UN Human Rights Committee (HRC), similar to the UNCAT. The HRC reviews reports from state parties, writes general comments, and receives individual complaints against consenting state parties. None of its pronouncements are legally binding. The ICCPR is an absolute prohibition of torture, stating that "no one shall be subjected to torture or to cruel, inhuman or degrading treatment or punishment." Art. 7. The United States ratified the ICCPR in 1992.

5. The Distinction Between Torture & CID Treatment or Punishment

Neither the UNCAT or the ICCPR define cruel, inhuman or degrading treatment or punishment. Case law from the European Court of Human Rights (ECHR) provides the best distinction between torture and CID treatment or punishment. The ECHR has argued that, "[i]n order for a punishment or treatment associated with it to be 'inhuman' or 'degrading', the suffering or humiliation involved must in any event go beyond that inevitable element of suffering or humiliation connected with a given form of legitimate treatment or punishment." *Jalloh v. Germany*, App. No. 54810/00, 2006–IX Eur. Ct. H.R. (Grand Chamber).

6. Geographic Reach

The extent to which the UNCAT applies extraterritorially is a major issue of contention in human rights law. The ICCPR requires that each state party must make efforts "to respect and to ensure to all individuals within its territory and subject to its jurisdiction the rights recognized in the present Covenant." Art. 2.1. The HRC has interpreted this mandate broadly. It held in *Lopez Burgos v. Uruguay* that state parties cannot get around the requirement to abstain from torture by doing it on another country's territory. Comm. No. 52/1979, U.N. Doc. A/36/40, at 176. In 2004, the HRC further clarified this point in General Comment No. 31. The Committee interpreted the mandate to respect and ensure Covenant rights within State Party's jurisdiction as extending to "anyone within the power or effective control of the State Party." The Committee further asserted, controversially, that this principle should apply "regardless of the circumstances in which such power or effect control was obtained, such as forces constitutional a national contingent of a State Party assigned to an international peace-keeping or peace enforcement operation." U.N. Doc. CCPR/C/21/Rev.1/Add.13 (2004). The International Court of Justice found the HRC's interpretation persuasive and incorporated it into its 2004 decision, *Legal Consequences of the Construction of a Wall in the Occupied Palestinian Territory*, where it argued that the ICCPR is "applicable in respect of acts done by a State in the exercise of its jurisdiction outside its own territory." 2004 I.C.J. 136 (July 9).

The United States has continually contested that the ICCPR applies extraterritorially. In response, the HRC argued that based on a plain meaning interpretation of the Covenant, it applied to both individuals "*within* the territory of a State Party *and* subject to that State Party's sovereign authority." Consideration of Reports Submitted By States Parties Under Article 40 of the Covenant: Third Periodic Report of the United States of America, Annex I, U.N. Doc. CCPR/C/USA/Q/3/Annex (2005). The HRC expressed concern over the United States' "restrictive" interpretation in regards to extraterritoriality in a 2006 report. Concluding Observations of the Human Rights Committee: United States of America, U.N. Doc. CCPR/C/USA/CO/3/Rev.1 (2006).

In response, the United States has argued that the Covenant does not apply extraterritorially, only that it applies to individuals both within a State Party's territory and simultaneously subject to its jurisdiction. United States Responses to Selected Recommendations of the Human Rights Committee, U.N. Doc. CCPR/C/USA/CO/3/Rev.1/Add.1 (2007).

In 2006, the CAT also affirmed this "effective control" interpretation in response to the United States second periodic report. The Committee reiterated "its previously expressed view that this includes all areas under the *de facto* effective control of the State party, by whichever military or civil authorities such control is exercised." The CAT went on to comment on the United States' limited interpretation of its obligations, characterizing it as regrettable. U.N. Comm. Against Torture, Conclusions and Recommendations, United States of America, CAT/C/USA/CO/2 (July 25, 2006), para. 15.

The Supreme Court decided in *Mohamad v. Rajoub*, 634 F.3d 604 (D.C. Cir. 2010) on the question of whether the Torture Victim Protection Act allows suits against defendants who are not natural persons. *See* § XV.B.2.b *infra*.

7. Non-Refoulement Provisions

The UNCAT provides that no state party "shall expel, return ('refouler') or extradite a person to another State where there are substantial grounds for believing that he would be in danger of being subjected to torture." Art. 3. While the ICCPR does not specifically prohibit refoulement, it has a general provision requiring state parties to "respect and to ensure" all of the rights outlined in territories subject to their jurisdiction. Art. 2. In 1992, the HRC issued a general comment on torture and CID treatment or punishment, stating that "State parties must not expose individuals to the danger of torture or cruel, inhuman or degrading treatment or punishment upon return to another country by way of their extradition, expulsion or refoulement." U.N. Human Rights Comm., General Comment No. 20, Concerning the Prohibition of Torture and Cruel, Inhuman or Degrading Treatment or Punishment (Article 7), U.N. Doc. A/47/40 (1992). The HRC clarified this requirement further in 2004, stating that the "article 2 obligation requiring that States Parties respect and ensure the Covenant rights for all persons in their territory and all person under their control entails an obligation not to extradite, deport, expel or otherwise remove a person from their territory, where there are substantial grounds for believing that there is a real risk of irreparable harm." U.N. Human Rights Comm., General Comment No. 31, Nature of the General Legal Obligation Imposed on States Parties to the Covenant (Article 2), U.N. Doc. CCPR/C/21/Rev.1/Add.13 (2004).

The United States has adopted the position that the non-refoulement provision in the UNCAT is simply territorial. It argues that it does not "impose obligations on the United States with respect to an individual who is outside the territory of the United States." List of Issues to be Considered During the Examination of the Second Periodic Report of the United States of America: Response of the United States of America 36 (Apr. 28, 2006). The United States did emphasize, however, that it does not transfer individuals to countries where it believes that they will be tortured as a matter of policy. *Id.*

The United States ratified the UNCAT subject to its "understanding" that the treaty's mandate not to extradite in Article 3 meant that they could not extradite individuals to states if it is more likely than not that he would be tortured. The United States argues that there is no legal difference between its obligations under the language of the treaty and the language of its "understanding."

The United States has also rejected the HRC's finding that the ICCPR has an implicit obligation not to extradite people to countries that torture. The United States has argued that a non-refoulement obligation in the ICCPR "not only poses a new obligation not contained in the plain language of Article 7 . . .but also poses an obligation beyond the non-refoulement protection contained in Article 3 of the Convention Against Torture." The United States argued that it expanded the scope of other treaties by requiring states not to extradite for CID treatment or punishment as well. U.S. Dept. of State, List of Issues to Be Taken up in Connection with the Consideration of the Second and Third Periodic Reports of the United States of America (July 16, 2006), *available at* https://2009-2017.state.gov/j/drl/rls/70385.htm. It is worth note that the CAT's non-refoulement provision only applies to torture and not the CID treatment or punishment. U.N. Comm. Against Torture, General Comment No. 2, Implementation of Article 2 by State Parties, CAT/C/GC/2/CRP.1/Rev.4 (Nov. 23, 2007), para. 6.

When Obama took office he said he shut down the Bush Administration's "extraordinary rendition program." *Mohamed v. Jeppesen Dataplan* Inc., 614 F.3d

1070 (9th Cir. 2010); *Mohamed v. Jeppesen Dataplan Inc.*, 539 F. Supp. 2d 1128 (N.D. Cal. 2008). In 2008, however, in *Mohamed v. Jeppesen Dataplan, Inc.*, a case where five men sued the CIA for detaining and torturing them, the Obama administration had the case dismissed based on the "State secrets" privilege. *Mohamed v. Jeppesen Dataplan Inc.*, 539 F. Supp. 2d 1128 (N.D. Cal. 2008).

The Senate Select Committee on Intelligence declassified, in late 2014, an executive summary of its investigation in the CIA's Detention and Interrogation Program, detailing detention conditions and interrogation techniques used by the U.S. on 119 detainees between 2001 and 2009. S. Select Comm. On Intelligence, 114th Cong., Committee Study of the Central Intelligence Agency's Detention and Interrogation Program, Executive Summary (2014), https://www.intelligence.senate.gov/sites/default/files/press/executive-summary_0.pdf. The summary concludes that the CIA had ignored its pre-September 11 view that coercive techniques were ineffective and instead developed a new program that used harsher techniques, which were less effective than the CIA represented. S. Select Comm. On Intelligence, 114th Cong., Committee Study of the Central Intelligence Agency's Detention and Interrogation Program, Findings and Conclusions (2014), https://www.intelligence.senate.gov/sites/default/files/press/findings-and-conclusions.pdf. The program was riddled with problems, from undisciplined development and paying off foreign officials to host detention sites to inexperienced program personnel, highlighting the role of two contract psychologists who developed the "enhanced interrogation techniques" based on ideas of "learned helplessness." The summary noted that under any common meaning of "torture," CIA detainees were tortured.

In response, the Obama administration reaffirmed its commitment to the ban on torture moving forward. In January 2009, President Obama issued Executive Order 13, 491, prohibiting long-term detention by the CIA and limiting interrogation techniques to those included in the Army Field Manual. Exec. Ord. No. 13, 491, 74 C.F.R. 4893 (Jan. 22, 2009). There have been international calls for criminal investigations as a result of the summary, including from UN representatives, noting that under international law (The UN Convention Against Torture and the UN Convention on Enforced Disappearances), the U.S. is legally obligated to prosecute. The U.S., however, seems unlikely to prosecute anyone for this program.

L. Rights of Refugees

The principal international instruments concerning refugees are the 1951 Geneva Convention Relating to the Status of Refugees, the 1957 Hague amendments to that convention, and the 1967 Protocol Relating to the Status of Refugees. At present, customary international law *does not appear to recognize a right to asylum*, although this rule has been the subject of much criticism. In 1950, the UN established a High Commissioner for Refugees to oversee refugee issues.

1. Definition of a Refugee

The 1951 Geneva Convention defines a refugee as a person who "owing to well-founded fear of being persecuted for reasons of race, religion, nationality, membership of a particular social group or political opinion, is outside the country of his nationality and is unable or, owing to such fear, is unwilling to avail himself of the protection of that country; or who, not having a nationality and being outside the country of his former habitual residence as a result of such events, is unable, or owing to such fear, is unwilling to return to it." Convention Relating to the Status of Refugees, July 28, 1951, Art. 1, § A, & 2, 189 U.N.T.S. 137. In *INS v. Elias-Zacarias*,

502 U.S. 478 (1992) the Supreme Court held that a Guatemalan native had failed to show persecution on account of political opinion based on his resistance to recruitment by a guerilla movement because he was afraid the government would retaliate against him or his family.

2. State's Obligation to Refugees

The Convention aims to secure the best possible treatment of refugees lawfully within a state, and its provisions address many topics, including access to courts, employment, housing and education. Refugees illegally within a state must be given a reasonable time to resettle. The Convention and subsequent instruments do not, however, guarantee any right of entry into a country, or impose any duty on the state to admit refugees. The state has a *right to grant asylum*, but the individual has *no right to be granted asylum*. Articles 13 and 14 of the Universal Declaration of Human Rights and the General Assembly's 1967 Declaration on Territorial Asylum recognize the "right to leave any country, including [one's] own" and the "right to seek and to enjoy in other countries asylum from persecution." Those rights, however, are not coupled with a corresponding state obligation to grant asylum. In the United States, for example, an amendment to the Refugee Act of 1980 was passed as part of the REAL ID Act of 2005. Before granting asylum, this amendment requires proof that "at least one central reason" for the asylum applicant's persecution is race, religion, nationality, political opinion or membership in a particular social group. The principle of non-refoulement prohibits return of the refugee to the state of persecution, and an admitted refugee may only be deported for reasons of state security.

3. The Haitian Refugees Case

In the controversial decision of *Sale v. Haitian Centers Council, Inc.*, 509 U.S. 918 (1993), the U.S. Supreme Court held that neither domestic immigration law or Article 33 of the Refugee Convention, prohibiting return of a refugee to the state of persecution, applied extraterritorially to interception upon the high seas.

4. Diplomatic Asylum

Diplomatic asylum is the *granting of refuge by a state in its embassies*, ships, or aircraft in the territory of another state. Once diplomatic asylum is granted, there is a right of safe conduct from the foreign state. Beyond that, the rules of asylum are generally based on treaty rather than customary international law.

In late December 2009, Thailand returned about 4000 ethnic Hmong asylum seekers to Laos. John R. Crook, ed., *Contemporary Practice of the United States Relating to International Law,* 104 AM. J. INT'L L. 100, 121 (2010). During the Vietnam War many Hmong served in the CIA's "secret war" against the Viet Cong and North Vietnamese Army. *Id.* After the Pathet Lao took control of Laos in 1975 the Hmong were repressed and many fled to Thailand. *Id.* Thailand is not party to the 1951 Refugee Convention. *Id.* The U.S. has protested these actions and has accepted 150,000 Hmong for resettlement. *Id.* Furthermore, the senior Department of State official in charge of refugee affairs delivered a letter to the Thais in which the U.S., in conjunction with other Western Countries, undertook to resettle any Hmong refugees. *Id.* In a similar situation, also in December 2009, the Royal Government of Cambodia returned twenty Uighur refugees to China. *Id.* All of the refugees that were returned had been issued "Persons of Concern" letters by the UN High

Commissioner for Refugees in Cambodia. The U.S. strongly opposed Cambodia's involuntary return of these asylum seekers. *Id.*

5. Gender-Based Asylum Claims

a. FGM as Grounds for Asylum

Decisions have defined when gender based violence and discrimination amount to persecution entitling the applicant to asylum. One landmark decision in that regard is the decision of the U.S. Board of Immigration Appeals (BIA) in *In Re Kasinga,* Board of Immigration Appeals Interim Decision 3278, June 13, 1996. Kasinga, a nineteen year old native of Togo, would normally have been subjected to female genital mutilation (FGM) at the age of fifteen in her tribe. She sought asylum in the United States. The BIA confirmed its prior decisions that "persecution can consist of the infliction of harm or suffering by a government, or persons a government is unwilling or unable to control, to overcome a characteristic of the victim." Finding that FGM is persecution, the Board narrowly defined the social group persecuted as the young women of Kasinga's tribe who have not had FGM and who oppose the practice. Relying upon widespread condemnation of FGM, the majority concluded that her well-founded fear of persecution was "on account of" her membership in the social group as the practice was designed "at least in some significant part, to overcome sexual characteristics of young women of the tribe who have not been, and do not wish to be, subjected to FGM." *Id.* Since *In Re Kasinga*, U.S. law has established that FGM or risk of FGM is "persecution" with regard to asylum applications.

In *K. v. Secretary of State for the Home Department*, [2006] U.K. HL 46, the British House of Lords heard an appeal from F, a citizen of Sierra Leone who claimed asylum in the United Kingdom on the basis that if returned to Sierra Leone, she would be at risk of subjection to female genital mutilation (FGM). The House of Lords held that in the context of Sierra Leonean society, it was clear that women in Sierra Leone were a group of persons sharing a common characteristic which, without a fundamental change in social mores was unchangeable, namely a position of social inferiority as compared with men. To define the group in that way was not to define it by reference to the persecution complained of: it was a characteristic which would exist even if FGM were not practiced, although FGM was an extreme and very cruel expression of male dominance. Accordingly, because F faced persecution by reason of her membership in a particular social group, she was granted asylum in the United Kingdom.

b. Spousal Violence as Grounds for Asylum

Courts and immigration authorities have had difficulty deciding whether persons who have been victimized by spousal violence qualify for asylum relief, and there is no controlling precedent on this issue in U.S. immigration law. In the decision *Matter of R-A-*, 22 I & N Dec. 906 (BIA 1999), the U.S. Board of Immigration Appeals denied asylum for a woman who claimed that her abuse by her husband constituted persecution on account of her inclusion in a particular social group. That decision was later vacated by the Attorney General and remanded for further proceedings and reconsideration by the BIA.

6. Bars to Asylum

In the United States, to establish an asylum claim the applicant has the burden of proving that the threat of persecution is country-wide and that internal relocation is not a reasonable solution. Additionally, the persecution at issue in the asylum claim must normally be related to actions by the authorities of a country. Serious acts of persecution committed by a local populace can be considered persecution if they are knowingly tolerated by the authorities, or if the authorities prove unwilling or unable to provide effective protection.

7. Temporary Protection

Temporary protected status is a form of protection extended in situations of mass influx, in which a flow of forced migrants is likely to include both refugees that meet the Convention's definition as well as persons fleeing generalized violence and danger. At the national level, temporary protection programs vary widely. In some countries, temporary protection measures function as a means of admission into the country under a standard of treatment less favorable than that enjoyed by recognized refugees. In the United States, Temporary Protected Status is a form of "leave to remain" for persons who are present in the United States when the Attorney General designates their country for receipt of the status. *See* 8 U.S.C. § 1254(a).

a. Representative Cases

Agiza v. Sweden, Comm. No. 233/2003, U.N. Doc. AT/C/34/D/233/2003. The CAT considered an individual complaint in 2003 when Sweden extradited a terrorist suspect to Egypt after getting an assurance from the Egyptian government that he would not be tortured. After considering whether there were substantial grounds for believing that Agiza was in danger of being subjected to torture when sent to Egypt, the Committee found that Sweden had breached its obligation under Article 3. It held that states must consider the potential for torture on an individual basis.

Alzery v. Sweden, Comm. No. 1416/2005, U.N. Doc. CCPR/C/88/D/1416/2005. The CAT held Sweden liable once again for extraditing a terrorist suspect to Egypt after assurances from the Egyptian government that they would not torture him. The CAT determined that the assurances were insufficient because they contained no "mechanism for monitoring their enforcement." It concluded that the diplomatic assurances were not "sufficient in the present case to eliminate the risk of ill-treatment to a level consistent with the requirements of article 7."

Example: | **Hong Kong:** In November 2019, the U.S. Congress passed and President Trump signed the Hong Kong Human Rights and Democracy Act of 2019 (HKHRDA), sending a strong indication of congressional support for protestors in Hong Kong. The Act dictates that it is U.S. policy to support the fundamental rights and freedoms of the people of Hong Kong as enumerated by three different treaties (the joint Declaration of the Government of the United Kingdom of Great Britain and Northern Ireland and the Government of the People's Republic of China on the Question of Hong Kong, done at Beijing December 19, 1984; The International Covenant on Civil and Political Rights, done at New York December 19, 1966; and The Universal Declaration of Human

Rights, done at Paris December 10, 1948). Most importantly, the Act requires annual recertification of Hong Kong's special status under the United States-Hong Kong Policy Act of 1992. The secretary of state is to consider the extent to which the government of Hong Kong upholds human rights and the rule of law.

In September 2020, The U.S. Department of State submitted the President's Report to Congress on the Proposed Refugee Admissions for the Fiscal Year 2021, including Hong Kong refugees as a group that will receive priority. This is the first time that Hong Kong has been included in the annual refugee admissions proposal. On October 27, 2020, President Trump approved this refugee admissions determination. The U.S. Congress is also considering three bills that would increase protections for refugees from Hong Kong in the U.S.

8.   Asylum in the Trump Era

The Trump administration made many efforts to limit the availability of asylum in the U.S. In November 2018, the administration announced its intent to limit access to asylum to those who had entered the U.S. at an official port of entry. Swift litigation contesting the rule followed.

In July 2019, the Department of Homeland Security and Department of Justice implemented an interim final rule disqualifying asylum applicants who passed through third countries without seeking protection in those countries. The 1951 Geneva Convention does not require an asylum seeker to apply for protection in the first country transited, so long as that person has not "acquired a new nationality, and enjoys the protection of the country of his new nationality" or been "recognized by the competent authorities of the country in which he has taken residence as having the rights and obligations which are attached to the possession of the nationality of that country." UN Convention Relating to the Status of Refugees, Art. I, July 28, 1951, 189 UNTS 150. (The United States is not a party to the Refugee Convention but has accepted its obligations by acceding to the 1967 Protocol Relating to the Status of Refugees, January 31, 1967, 606 UNTS 267.) The 2019 U.S. agreement with Guatemala would allow asylum applicants who transited through Guatemala on their way to the U.S. to be returned to Guatemala to pursue their asylum claims. El Salvador and Honduras reached similar signed similar agreements with the U.S. that same year.

The Office of the United Nations High Commissioner for Refugees expressed deep concern about the DHS and DOJ interim final rule and its compliance with international law. UNHCR noted that the rule "excessively curtails the right to apply for asylum, jeopardizes the right to protection from refoulement, significantly raises the burden of proof on asylum seekers beyond the international legal standard, sharply curtails basic rights and freedoms of those who manage to meet it, and is not in line with international obligations. UN High Commissioner for Refugees (UNHCR) Press Release, UNHCR Deeply Concerned about New U.S. Asylum Restrictions (July 15, 2019), https://www.unhcr.org/news/press/2019/7/5d2cdf114/unhcr-deeply-concerned-new-asylum-restrictions.html.

Similarly, the Migrant Protection Protocols are a Trump administration policy under which asylum seekers arriving from Mexico await their U.S. immigration proceedings in Mexico rather than in the U.S. Further, in 2019, Attorney General Barr issued binding immigration decisions designed to deter asylum seekers from coming to the U.S.: all asylum seekers in DHS custody are subject to mandatory detention pending the adjudication of their claims unless the government allows release on parole for an individual applicant, and Barr narrowed the standard of a "particular social group" in relation to claims involving family groups. *Matter of M.S.*, 27 I&N Dec. 509 (A.G. 2019); *Matter of L.E.A.*, 27 I&N Dec. 581 (A.G. 2019).

9. Other Immigration Concerns in the Trump Era

Throughout 2017, President Trump issued three versions of a travel ban, blocking entry of citizens largely from Muslim-majority countries. The final version, issued on September 24, 2017, restricted immigrant and nonimmigrant entry into the U.S. indefinitely. Proclamation No. 9645, 82 Fed. Reg. 45,161 (Sept. 24, 2017) [hereinafter Proclamation 9645]. This final iteration restricted entry of nationals from Iran, Libya, Somalia, Syria, Yemen, North Korea, Venezuela, and Chad. It was fully implemented by December 8, 2017. Proclamation 9645 did identify several categorical exceptions to the travel restrictions, including lawful permanent residents, foreign nationals previously granted asylum in the U.S. or traveling on a diplomatic visa, dual citizens traveling using a passport from an unrestricted country, and anyone granted advance parole or protection under the Convention Against Torture. For a waiver to be granted to a foreign national, they must demonstrate a minimum of three requirements: (1) undue hardship; (2) that entry would not pose a threat to national security; and (3) that entry would be in the national interest.

Shortly after Proclamation 9645, Trump announced the American First Refugee Program, capping refugee admission to 45,000 for the 2018 fiscal year, significantly cutting the 110,000 cap that President Obama had set for 2017.

Given his past remarks as both candidate and president, many argued that these orders were motivated by religious animus. Scholars have also argued that Proclamation 9645 and its predecessors violate international law as well as U.S. law: specifically the International Covenant on Civil and Political Rights, prohibiting discrimination based on religion or national origin; the United Nations Convention Against Torture, which prohibits states parties from involuntarily returning someone to another State where there are "substantial grounds for believing that he would be in danger of being subject to torture; and the International Convention on the Elimination of All Forms of Racial Discrimination, barring discrimination based on national origin unless necessary and narrowly tailored to achieve a legitimate government aim.

In two of many suits filed following the second iteration, Executive Order No. 13,780, upon which Proclamation 9645 expanded, district courts in Hawaii and Maryland granted temporary restraining orders enjoining enforcement of this order. 82 Fed. Reg. 13,209 (Mar. 6, 2017); *Hawai'i v. Trump*, 245 F. Supp. 3d 1227 (2017); *Int'l Refugee Assistance Project v. Trump*, 265 F. Supp. 3d 570 (2017). While the Ninth and Fourth Circuits, respectively, upheld these TROs, the Supreme Court permitted Proclamation 9645 to take effect, staying the Hawaii and Maryland orders. Litigation continued in both circuits. In January 2021, President Biden signed Presidential Proclamation 10,141, ending these travel restrictions and directing the State Department to pursue the processing of visa applications for individuals from affected nations consistent with applicable law and visa processing procedures.

M. Convention on the Rights of the Child

Fundamental Right to Education

Unni Krishnan, J/P. and Others v. State of Andhra Pradesh and Others: The Indian Supreme Court held that there was a fundamental right to education. A child under the age of fourteen has a fundamental right to education. The Court held that the right to education is one of transcendental importance in the life of an individual. It does not mean that the obligation can be performed only through the State Schools. It can also be done by permitting, recognizing, and aiding voluntary non-governmental organizations, who are prepared to impart free education to children. Private schools are also important and they may charge fees if they wish.

The Children's Convention, adopted by 191 states, is the most widely adopted human rights treaty (with the notable exceptions of the U.S. and Somalia). Adopted by the UN General Assembly in 1989, it went into effect in 1990, less than a year later. It is also the only gender neutral human rights treaty with respect to its references to "the child" or "children". This convention was the quickest and the most universally signed in international human rights history.

1. Child Defined

A child is any human being below the age of eighteen, "unless under the law applicable to the child, majority is attained earlier."

2. Rights Protected

In addition to a full range of civil, political, economic, social and cultural rights, the treaty also seeks to protect children from sexual exploitation, abuse, and trafficking.

3. Enforcement

The Convention is overseen by a Committee on the Rights of the Child. The only enforcement mechanism is Committee review of states' reports on their implementation of the Convention.

4. The Optional Protocols

The First Protocol, which only entered into force in February 2002 raises the minimum age for participation in armed conflicts from fifteen to eighteen in the Convention. Voluntary recruitment of those under eighteen is also regulated. The Second Protocol, which entered into force in January of 2002, seeks to criminalize specified acts including the sale of children, child pornography, and child prostitution.

5. The U.S. Position

The U.S. has not ratified the Convention. Frequently articulated concerns include the preservation of parental rights and corporal punishment. The U.S. has evaluated children's issues through domestic policy, like the U.S. Child Soldier Accountability Act passed in 2008, which forbids recruiting or enlisting a child under the age of 15.

N. Fundamental Human Right to Health

The Committee on Economic, Social and Cultural Rights, General Comment 14, The Right to the Highest Attainable Standard of Health:

Health is a fundamental human right indispensable for the exercise of other human rights. Every human being is entitled to the enjoyment of the highest attainable standard of health conductive to living a life in dignity. The realization of the right to health may be pursued through numerous, complementary approaches. The right to health is not be understood a right to be healthy. The right to health contains both freedoms and entitlements. The freedoms include the right to control one's health and body, including sexual and reproductive freedom, and the right to be free from interference, such as the right to be free from torture, non-consensual medical treatment and experimentation. By contrast, the entitlements include the right to a system of health protection which provides equality of opportunity for people to enjoy the highest attainable level of health.

The right to health must be understood as a right to the enjoyment of a variety of facilities, goods, services, and conditions necessary for the realization of the highest attainable standard of health.

On July 28, 2010, the General Assembly voted 122–0 to adopt a resolution that recognizes a human right to water. Forty-one states, including most industrialized nations, abstained from voting. Most of the abstaining countries are those for which a recognized right to water would not make much of a difference; other international legal agreements provide indirect support for the recognition of the right. The U.S. was one of the nations that abstained from voting due to drafting issues and dispute over whether there is an actual "right to water and sanitation" in international law.

In *Mandal v. Deen Dayal Harinagar Hosp. & Ors.*, (2010) W.P.(C) 8853/2008 (Delhi) (India), the Indian Supreme Court held that women's reproductive health is part of a woman's right to life.

Availability: Functioning public health and health-care facilities, goods and services, as well as programs, have to be available in sufficient quantity within the State Party. The precise nature of the facilities, goods and services will vary depending on numerous factors, including the State Party's developmental level. They will include, however, the underlying determinants of health, such as safe and potable drinking water and adequate sanitation facilities, hospitals, clinics and other health-related buildings, trained medical and professional personnel receiving domestically competitive salaries, and essential drugs, as defined by the WHO Action Program on Essential Drugs.

Accessibility: Health Facilities, goods and services have to be accessible to everyone without discrimination, within the jurisdiction of the State Party. Accessibility has four overlapping dimensions: non-discrimination, physical accessibility, economic accessibility (affordability) and information accessibility (accessibility includes the right to seek, receive, and impart information and ideas regarding health issues).

Acceptability: All health facilities, goods and services must be respectful of medical ethics and culturally appropriate

Quality: Health facilities, goods and services must also be scientifically and medically appropriate and of good quality.

The right to health, like all human rights, imposes three types or levels of obligations on States Parties: the obligations to respect, protect, and fulfill. In turn, the obligation to fulfill contains obligations to facilitate, provide and promote. The obligation to respect requires States to refrain from interfering directly or indirectly with the enjoyment of the right to health. The obligation to protect requires States to take measure that prevent third parties from interfering with Article 12 guarantees. Finally, the obligation to fulfill requires States to adopt appropriate legislative, administrative, budgetary, judicial, promotional, and other measures towards the full realization of the right to health.

The State Parties have a core obligation to ensure the satisfaction of, at the very least, minimum essential levels of each of the rights enunciated in the Covenant, including essential primary health care.

Soobramoney v. Minister of Health (KwaZulu-Natal): The plaintiff was a forty-one year-old unemployed man with diabetes and heart disease who was in the final stages of irreversible chronic renal failure, as a result of a stroke and kidney failure in 1996. He had sought treatment (regular renal dialysis) in the state hospital but the hospital could, however, only provide dialysis treatment to a limited number of patients. Because of the limited facilities that are available for kidney dialysis the hospital had been unable to provide the plaintiff with the treatment he has requested. The plaintiff bases his claim on the South African Constitution, which provides that "no one may be refused emergency medical treatment" and another statutes that stipulate "everyone has the right to life".

The Court found for the defendant, holding that the plaintiff does not have free access to this treatment because the access to health care services provided by the state must be done "within its available resources". Since the plaintiff would require treatment two to three times a week and it is an incurable deterioration, the above statute does not apply. This is not the meaning of 'emergency medical treatment' meant in the statute.

Minister of Health v. Treatment Action Campaign

The Treatment Action Campaign brought suit under the South African Constitution, asserting the unreasonableness of the South African government's decision to limit the availability in the public health sector of the anti-retroviral drug nevirapine, which diminishes the likelihood of HIV transmission from mother to child during childbirth. The Campaign also challenged the government's failure to plan and implement an effective, comprehensive and progressive program for the prevention of mother-to-child transmission of HIV throughout the country. The Minister of Health, in his defense, stated that the drug was available at pilot test sites, so that they could monitor and research the drug. The Court determined that the drug (which is labeled as an essential drug under WHO) should be available to every health care provider, so that mothers who cannot afford private health care and who do not live near the pilot sites can still have access to the medicine. The Court ordered the government to remove restrictions to the drug at the non-pilot sites, to permit and facilitate the drug, and to extend testing and counseling at hospitals around the country.

O. Freedom of Expression

1. Domestic Law

In *Dennis v. United States*, 341 U.S. 494 (1951), the Court used a "clear and present danger" test for determining when the government may limit speech. The Court held the "gravity of the 'evil,' discounted by its improbability, justifies such invasion of free speech as is necessary to avoid the danger." Under this test, the Court upheld convictions of Communist Party officials that organized and advocated overthrowing the United States government.

The Court later abandoned the clear and present danger test in *Brandenburg v. Ohio*, 395 U.S. 444 (1969) The Court held that States may not forbid or proscribe advocacy unless "such advocacy is directed to inciting or producing imminent lawless action and is likely to incite or produce such action." Using this test, the Court struck down an overbroad Ohio law under which members of the Ku Klux Klan were incriminated for advocating violence.

In *R.A.V. v. City of St. Paul*, 505 U.S. 377 (1992), a Minnesota ordinance was held unconstitutional under the First Amendment because it prohibited otherwise permissible speech on the basis of its content. The ordinance forbade the use of symbols, including burning crosses, known to cause anger, alarm, or resentment on the basis of race, color, creed, religion or gender. The ordinance was unconstitutional because it did not just target "fighting words," it targeted particular messages.

2. International Law

In *Sürek v. Turkey*, a publication owner was penalized for disseminating propaganda after printing incendiary letters protesting the Turkish government. The European Court of Human Rights determined that no Article 10 violation occurred. Despite the importance of a free press, the unstable security situation in Turkey and the appeal to violence in the letters demonstrated the necessity of government interference under Article 10 § 2.

The European Court of Human Rights held in *Jersild v. Denmark* that an Article 10 violation occurred when a Danish journalist was convicted for creating a film documenting the racist views of a group called the "Greenjackets." Particularly due to the journalist's disclaimer at the beginning of the film, the Court found that the journalist sought to address the problem of racism. Given the objective of the film, the government's interference was not "necessary in a democratic society."

In *Faurrison v. France*, the Human Rights Committee upheld the conviction of a French man who publicly questioned whether the Nazi regime used gas extermination chambers. The remarks violated France's Gayssot Act, which made it an offence to question the existence of crimes for which Nazi leaders were convicted at Nuremberg. The conviction served the purpose of allowing the Jewish community to live free from fear and without anti-Semitism, a permissible purpose under Article 19, paragraph 3(a). The Committee noted that the law merely outlawed expression of these ideas, not the ideas themselves.

In *Granier v. Venezuela*, the Inter-American Court of Human Rights held that Venezuela's refusal to renew the broadcasting license of Radio Caracas Televisión (RCTV) in May 2007 was an indirect violation of the right to freedom of expression protected by the American Convention on Human Rights. Granier v. Venezuela, Preliminary Objections, Merits, Reparations and Costs, Inter-Am. Ct. H.R. 9 (ser. C) No. 293 (June 22, 2015) https://www.corteidh.or.cr/docs/casos/articulos/resumen_293_esp.pdf; American Convention on Human Rights, Nov. 22, 1969, OASTS, No. B-32, 1144 UNTS 123. The Court found that the government's undeclared purpose in refusing to renew RCTV's license was to shut down a network that had taken a critical editorial stance toward the Venezuelan government. The Court reaffirmed that the right to freedom of expression formed the "cornerstone for the existence of a democratic society." Granier, para. 140. While the Court did not find a direct violation, as neither the Convention nor international law generally require a state to renew a broadcasting license, it did find that Venezuela indirectly violated the right to freedom of expression of RCTV's shareholders and employees, as well as the general population. *Id.* para. 198. Despite this ruling, the Venezuelan Supreme Court has rejected the decision as unenforceable, so RCTV is unlikely to see Venezuela comply. TSJ, CC, 10 de septiembre de 2015, Decisión No. 1175.

According to Judge Ventura Robles, *Granier* should be read as overruling *Mémoli v. Argentina,* which had upheld a criminal conviction for defamation, viewed as a step backward in protecting freedom of expression. *Mémoli v. Argentina*, Preliminary Objections, Merits, Reparations and Costs, Inter-Am. Ct. H.R. (ser. C) No. 265 (Aug. 22, 2013).

In *Konaté v. Burkina Faso*, the African Court on Human and Peoples' Rights imposed strict limits on penalties for expression, particularly for journalists, in states party to the African Charter on Human and People's Rights. *Konaté v. Burkina Faso*, App. No. 004/2013 (Afr. Ct. Hum. & Peoples' Rts. Dec. 5, 2014); African Charter on Human and Peoples' Rights, June 27, 1981, 1520 UNTS 217, 21 ILM 58 (1982) (entered into force Oct. 21, 2001). The editor-in-chief of an independent weekly newspaper dedicated to politics and public policy was prosecuted for and convicted of criminal defamation, public insults, and contempt of court. He was sentenced to twelve months imprisonment, a fine, and civil damages. The Court found that the law under which Konaté was charged violated his right to freedom of expression, as well as the application of the law in domestic courts. The Court's holding limits the scope of criminal defamation statutes, while leaving open the possibility of sanctions other than incarceration. In this case, the fines were deemed excessive and unnecessary to protect the rights and reputation of the prosecutor about whom Konaté had written.

3. Internet Freedom

In July 2012, the U.S. co-sponsored a resolution with the Human Rights Council underscoring that all individuals are entitled to the same human rights and fundamental freedoms online as they are offline. This includes the freedom of expression. All governments should protect those rights regardless of the medium.

P. Religious Freedom

1. Domestic Law

The Supreme Court held in *Employment Division, Department of Human Resources of Oregon v. Smith*, 494 U.S. 872 (1990), an individual's religious beliefs do not allow the individual to violate otherwise valid laws prohibiting conduct that the State may regulate. The Court held that an employer did not violate the Free Exercise Clause when it fired employees after they illegally ingested peyote in conjunction with a religious ceremony.

2. International Law

In *Wingrove v. United Kingdom*, the United Kingdom determined that an erotic film featuring religious figures violated the criminal provision against blasphemy and refused to allow film distribution. The European Court of Human Rights agreed, deferring to the national authorities. Prohibiting this freedom of expression fell within one of the Convention's exceptions for protecting the "rights of others." The prohibition protected Christians that would be offended by the imagery.

In *Leyla Sahin v. Turkey*, the European Court of Human Rights held that a university policy prohibiting religious or political clothing did not violate the rights of a student who wished to wear a religious headscarf.

In *Singh Binder v. Canada*, the Human Rights Committee found no violation occurred when the Canadian National Railway Company terminated an employee who refused to abide by company requirements to wear a hard hat. The terminated employee claimed a violation of Article 18 because, as a Sikh, he was required to wear only a turban and could not wear a hard hat. The safety limitation was justified by Article 18, paragraph 3. No violation of Article 16 occurred because requiring hard hats was reasonable and directed towards objective purposes compatible with the Covenant.

In *Sister Immaculate Joseph v. Sri Lanka*, the Human Rights Committee held that Article 26 and Article 18 violations arose when Sri Lanka did not allow an order of Roman Catholic nuns to incorporate. The Order stated that incorporation would allow them to propagate their beliefs and assist others, a religious manifestation protected by Article 18. Sri Lanka did not demonstrate that the restriction was necessary within one of the enumerated exceptions through its argument that incorporation could harm the practice of Buddhism. No reasonable and objective reason for these distinguishing between Catholicism and other religions existed, also establishing an Article 26 violation.

In *Yoon and Choi v. Republic of Korea*, Korea's prosecution of conscientious objectors who refused to be drafted into military service violated Article 18. The Human Rights Committee noted that compelling an individual to use lethal force if doing so would conflict with the individual's conscience or religious beliefs falls within Article 18. The State was unable to demonstrate that alternative national services could not be substituted for military service.

On April 29, 2010, European Union Commission Regulation No. 185/2010, a regulation regarding airport screening, came into effect and binding on all EU member states. Some of the regulations could be interpreted as forcing the physical pat-down or total removal of turbans. The Sikh community in many EU states felt that these regulations were undignified and discriminatory in the way they treated an article of the Sikh faith. There are also arguments that the law unreasonably restricts the free movement of Sikh people in and around the EU, possibly in violation of the International Covenant on Civil and Political Rights or the Charter of Fundamental Rights for the European Union.

In an effort to mitigate the regulation, the Secretary of State for the United Kingdom ordered all UK airports to revert to the screening methods in place before April 29, 2010, under an EU provision that states that "[t]he appropriate authority may create categories of passengers that, for objective reasons, shall be subject to special screening procedures or may be exempted from screening," *Commission Regulation 185/2010*, at 4.1.1.7. The United Kingdom plans to keep them in place until a permanent solution can be reached with the Sikh community.

Q. Rights of Persons with Disabilities

The UN Convention on the Protection of the Rights of Persons with Disabilities went into force on May 3, 2008. This Convention is designed to provide persons with disabilities the same rights and access to information as those without disabilities. Some of the rights specifically protected in the Convention include the right to live independently; the right to personal mobility; and the right to access roads, buildings, and information.

R. Protection of All Persons from Enforced Disappearances

The UN Convention for the Protection of all Persons from Enforced Disappearances went into effect on December 23, 2010. The Convention calls for states parties to investigate claims of enforced disappearance and bring the perpetrators to justice, to cooperate with other states parties to bring people involved in the enforced disappearance to justice, and to ensure that victims of enforced disappearance receive adequate compensation.

S. Human Trafficking

The Council of Europe Convention on Action Against Trafficking in Humans entered into force on February 1, 2008. As of September 13, 2011, thirty-four states had ratified this treaty. *Council of Europe Convention on Action Against Trafficking in Human Beings*, Council of Europe, Sept. 13, 2011, http://conventions.coe.int/treaty/Commun/ChercheSig.asp?NT=197&CM=0&DF=&CL=ENG. This convention focuses on victim protection measures.

Other regions and countries have been taking action against human trafficking, as well, including Mozambique, Southeast Asia, and the United States. The UN has created a position, Special Rapporteur on Trafficking in Persons, Especially Women and Children, to report to the UN High Commissioner for Human Rights. This person may visit countries and make recommendations on combating this global problem. Robert Gaudet, Jr., *Human Rights*, 43 INT'L I. 861, 866 (2009).

At the 2010 Kampala Review Conference of the parties to the Statute of the ICC, the U.S. delegation helped in amending the Rome Statute to include a newly-defined crime of aggression. Aggression is now defined as a "crime committed by a political or military leader, which, by its character, gravity, and scale constituted a manifest violation of the [UN] Charter." A UN prosecutor initiates actions for the charge of aggression, but must first procure approval of the Pre-Trial Division of the ICC. A significant weakness of the current language states that the ICC does not have jurisdiction over non-state parties, or parties that declared the court had no jurisdiction under the aggression charge. State Parties will have to activate the ICC's jurisdiction by mustering at least thirty ratifications of the amendment and taking a separate decision on this issue in 2017 at the earliest. This will allow for criminal prosecution of aggression on the international level for the first time since the Tokyo and Nuremberg tribunals in the late 1940s. John R. Crook, *U.S. Delegation Active in ICC Negotiations to Define Crime of Aggression*, 104 AM. J. INT'L L. 511, 511–513 (2010).

Freedom to Connect

In January 2010, Secretary of State Hillary Clinton delivered a speech about the relationship between the Internet and human rights, and what she considered to be a new freedom: the freedom to connect. Her speech was given in response to alleged attacks on computers belonging to Google and other U.S. companies, as well as Google's decision to limit operations in China instead of complying with their censorship requirements. In her opinion, actions such as these violate the Universal Declaration on Human Rights, which says that all people should have the right "to seek, receive and impact information and ideas through any media and regardless of frontiers." John R. Crook ed., *Contemporary Practice of the United States; Secretary of State Addresses Human Rights and the Internet*, 104 AM. J. OF INT'L LAW 271, 291–293.

Chapter IV

Newly Emerging Rights & Fundamental Rights Recognized as Customary International Law

Many of the rights recognized in international agreements above are also recognized as customary international law. An early invocation of human rights as part of customary international law was found in the Nuremberg Charter, charging Nazi leaders with "crimes against humanity." A more recent acknowledgment of the rights recognized in customary law is found in *Filartiga v. Pena-Irala*, 630 F.2d 876, 884, 890 (2d Cir. 1980) (" . . . we conclude that official torture is now prohibited by the law of nations."): "[T]he torturer has become—like the pirate and slave trader before him—*hostis humani generis*, an enemy of all mankind."

A. Restatement § 702 of U.S. Foreign Relations Law

The comments following this section indicate that there is a list of human rights generally accepted as customary law. The comments further state that the list is neither complete nor closed and other rights may have also reached the status of customary law. "A state violates international law if, as a matter of state policy, it practices, encourages or condones genocide, slavery or slave trade, the murder or causing the disappearance of individuals, torture or other cruel, inhuman or degrading treatment or punishment, prolonged arbitrary detention, systematic racial discrimination, or consistent patterns of gross violations of internationally recognized human rights."

B. Creation of Customary Human Rights Law

The Reporter's Notes to Restatement 701 suggest that customary human rights law is established in a manner different from other customary law, because historically human rights have been a matter between a state and its own individuals. According to the notes, customary human rights law may be established through: virtually universal adherence to the UN Charter; virtually universal adherence to the Universal Declaration of Human Rights; widespread participation of states in preparation and adoption of international human rights agreements; widespread support for UN General Assembly resolutions applying international human rights principles; and frequent invocation and application of international human rights principles in both domestic practice and diplomatic practice.

On May 29, 2008, the Italian Court of Cassation ruled that states are not immune from civil jurisdiction when they are charged with international crimes under customary international law. Carlo Focarelli, *Deportation-forced labor—international crimes—jus cogens—state immunity in civil proceedings—tort exception—commercial exception,* 103 AM. J. INT'L L. 122, 122–123 (2009).

C. The Evolution of New Rights

Human rights law is constantly evolving from recognition of rights in treaties, UN resolutions, and domestic state practice to the level of custom and *jus cogens.* Many protections originate in internal domestic law, with gradual recognition as general principles of international law if common to most legal systems. A few examples of more recently developed rights include the rights in the 1989 Convention on the Rights of the Child and the right to development in the 1986 General Assembly Resolution on the Right to Development.

Emerging Law Regarding Sexual Orientation

Recent actions have been taken to address discrimination against sexual orientation. For example, the Yogyakarta Principles on the Application of International Human Rights Law in Relation to Sexual Orientation and Gender Identity were adopted in 2006.

1. Domestic Law

In *Lawrence v. Texas,* 539 U.S. 558 (2003), the Supreme Court struck down a statute that criminalized same-sex intimate conduct as an invasion of privacy and a violation of 14th Amendment Due Process rights.

2. International Law

In *Toonen v. Australia,* U.N. Doc. CCPR/C/50/D/488/1992 (Mar. 31, 1994)(Hum. Rts. Comm.), the Human Rights Committee held that a Tasmanian law criminalizing same-sex intimacy violated the Article 17 right to privacy.

In *X v. Colombia,* U.N. Doc. CCPR/C/89/D/1361/2005 (May 14, 2007)(Hum. Rts. Comm.), the Human Rights Committee found that a same-sex partner's Article 26 rights were violated when he was denied pension benefits following his partner's death. According to the Committee, the statute violated Article 26 due to its discriminatory distinction between heterosexual and homosexual couples. The Committee rejected the claim that Article 3 gender equality rights had been violated, as the statute also impacted female homosexual couples.

D. *Jus Cogens* & Peremptory Norms

The doctrine of *jus cogens* defines certain peremptory norms from which derogation is not permitted. This description is generally attached to a principle that, based on its importance, is accepted and recognized by the international community as one from which derogation is not permitted. While there is no agreement on the exhaustive list of these norms, it is generally agreed that it includes genocide, war crimes, torture, crimes against humanity, piracy, and slavery.

Chapter V

Derogation from Protection of Rights

Treaties ensuring protection of fundamental human rights often allow derogation from the rights in times of *"war or other public emergencies."* A wide margin of appreciation is given to countries to determine whether such a "public emergency" exists in their state. Human rights conventions with derogation clauses include the International Covenant on Civil and Political Rights (Article 4), Convention Relating to the Status of Refugees (Article 9), Convention Relating to the Status of Stateless Persons (Article 9), European Convention for the Protection of Human Rights and Fundamental Freedoms (Article 15), and the European Social Charter (Article 30). The derogation provisions of the Covenant on Civil and Political Rights and the European Convention serve as key examples, demonstrating the necessary circumstances and limitations to derogation.

A. The International Covenant on Civil & Political Rights

There are limitations on, and procedures regulating derogation under this Convention.

1. Requirements for Derogation

Article 4 provides derogation from the Covenant's obligations under the following circumstances. It must be a "time of public emergency which threatens the life of the nation." The existence of such dire circumstances must be "officially proclaimed." Derogation is permitted "only to the extent strictly required by the exigencies of the situation." The measures may not be "inconsistent with their other obligations under international law." The measures may not "involve discrimination solely on the ground of race, colour, sex, language, religion or social origin."

2. Limitations to Derogation Under the Covenant

Certain rights may not be derogated from, even in times of public emergency. Article 4(2) states that no derogation is permitted from the rights accorded by Articles 6, 7, 8 (paragraphs 1 and 2), 11, 15, 16 and 18.

a. Article 6 protects the inherent right to life, prohibits genocide, restricts the death penalty to only the most serious crimes, requires rights to seek pardon or commutation of death penalty, and prohibits the death penalty for persons under eighteen and pregnant women.

b.   Article 7 prohibits torture and cruel, inhuman, or degrading treatment of punishment.

c.   Article 8, Paragraph 1 prohibits slavery and slave trade. Paragraph 2 prohibits holding anyone in servitude.

d.   Article 11 prohibits imprisonment for failure to fulfill contractual obligation.

e.   Article 15 prohibits conviction for an act or omission not a criminal offense under either national or international law at the time it was committed. It also prohibits imposition of a heavier penalty than was applicable at the time the crime was committed.

f.   Article 16 states that everyone has a right to recognition as a person before the law.

g.   Article 18 protects rights of religious freedoms and prevents imposition of religion.

3.   Procedure

Article 4(3) requires a state availing itself of the right of derogation to follow specific steps. For instance, a state must immediately inform other state parties to the Covenant of the provisions from which it has derogated, using the UN Secretary-General as intermediary; it must provide the reasons for derogation; and it must communicate the date on which it terminates the derogation.

B. European Convention for the Protection of Human Rights & Fundamental Freedoms

The derogation provision of the European Convention is similar to that of the Covenant on Civil and Political Rights.

1.   Requirements for Derogation

Article 15(1) permits derogation: "[i]n time of war or other public emergency threatening the life of the nation"; "[o]nly to the extent strictly required by the exigencies of the situation;" and "[p]rovided such measures are not inconsistent with its other obligations under international law." European Convention for the Protection of Human Rights and Fundamental Freedoms, Nov. 4, 1950, Art. 15, & 1, Europ. T.S. No. 5 [hereinafter European Human Rights Convention]. The European Court of Human Rights has given states a wide "margin of appreciation" in determining whether the first condition exists, but has been more demanding in determining whether the second condition has been satisfied.

2.   Limitations to Derogation

Article 15(2) prohibits derogation from Articles 2, 3, 4 (paragraph 1) and 7.

a.   Article 2 protects the right to life, except for executions resulting from conviction of a crime for which the death penalty is provided by law. Deprivation of life does not violate this article if it occurs as a result of self-defense; in the course of attempts to make a lawful arrest or prevent escape from lawful detention; or from lawful action taken to quell riots or insurrections.

b.   Article 3 prohibits torture or inhuman or degrading treatment or punishment.

c.   Article 4 prohibits slavery or servitude.

d.   Article 7 prohibits ex post facto criminal law.

3.   Procedure

Article 15(3) requires the derogating party to fully inform the Secretary-General of the Council of Europe of measures taken and the reasons therefor and further inform the Secretary-General when derogation has ceased and provisions of the Convention are once again fully executed.

4.   Clauses of Limitation

A number of the rights enumerated in the European Convention on Human Rights also have their own clauses of limitation, which allow restrictions on the right as necessary to protect national security, safety, and health or morals (*see* p. 55 *supra*).

Chapter VI

The International Courts

There are five generally recognized, established international courts with a major role in human rights law. They are: the International Court of Justice, Court of Justice of the European Communities (now European Union), European Court of Human Rights, and the Inter-American Court of Human Rights. In 2002 the International Criminal Court was also established.

A. The International Court of Justice

The International Court of Justice (ICJ), successor to the Permanent Court of International Justice, is the *principal judicial organ* of the United Nations (UN). Its Statute is annexed to the UN Charter. All members of the UN are automatically parties to the ICJ Statute, and under certain circumstances parties not members of the UN may appear before the Court and may also be parties to the Statute. UN Charter Art. 93. Being a party to the statute does *not* mean that the state has submitted itself to the Court's jurisdiction. The ICJ hears relatively few cases because only states may be parties in contentious proceedings before the Court. Stat. of the I.C.J. Art. 34, & 1. States must consent to jurisdiction. This limitation is further compounded by the fact that historically states often have chosen to settle disputes through political and diplomatic channels rather than through the ICJ. Regional international courts, therefore, have been more frequently utilized for international law claims of private parties. Nevertheless, the cases the ICJ has decided have had a major impact on the development of international law.

1. Structure and Composition

Article 3(1) of the Statute requires that the Court, with its seat in the Hague, be composed of fifteen judges elected by both the Security Council and the General Assembly. Judges serve for nine-year periods but may be, and often are, re-elected. The terms are staggered so that elections for five of the fifteen judges take place every three years. In practice, several considerations, including the following, determine the composition of the court. For instance, members of the Security Council almost always have a judge on the court. Judges are elected with regard for distribution. A balanced distribution, as exemplified in the 1986 Court, was four judges from Western Europe, two judges from Eastern Europe, three judges each from Africa and Asia, two judges from Latin America and one judge from the U.S. No more than one national of a state may sit as a judge at any one time. Stat. of the I.C.J. Art. 3, & 1. If a state appearing before the Court does not have one of its own nationals as a judge, it may appoint an *ad hoc* judge to ensure that its views will be fully considered. This practice is not easily reconciled with the view of judges as impartial decision makers. *See* Stat. of the I.C.J. Art. 20.

2. Contentious & Advisory Jurisdiction

The Court may only hear cases *governed by international law*. Stat. of the I.C.J. Art. 38. The ICJ has two types of jurisdiction: contentious jurisdiction and advisory jurisdiction. Contentious jurisdiction is based on either the express or implied consent of the parties, and only states party to the ICJ Statute may be parties in a contentious case. Decisions in contentious cases are binding on the parties. The Court also may issue non-binding, advisory opinions at the request of bodies so authorized by the UN Charter. Article 36 provides three ways for a state to consent to the jurisdiction of the ICJ. First, states may refer an existing dispute on an ad hoc basis. Second, a treaty may provide that any disputes arising from it be settled by the ICJ. Stat. of the I.C.J. Art. 36. Third, the ICJ may have jurisdiction under the so called "optional clause" of Art. 36(2).

3. Compulsory Jurisdiction Under the Optional Clause

Article 36(2) provides states parties to the present Statute may at any time declare that they recognize as compulsory *ipso facto* and without special agreement, in relation to any other state accepting the same obligation, the jurisdiction of the Court in all legal disputes concerning: the interpretation of a treaty; any question of international law; the existence of any fact which, if established, would constitute a breach of an international obligation; and the nature or extent of the reparation to be made for the breach of an international obligation. In 1986, in response to *Nicaragua v. United States, infra,* the United States withdrew its acceptance of the Court's compulsory jurisdiction under Article 36(2), but remains a party to many treaties conferring jurisdiction to the Court under Article 36(1).

a. Reciprocity

A state accepting the jurisdiction of the ICJ, under the optional clause of Article 36(2), does so only with respect to other states which have made a similar declaration. Thus, a respondent state may assert not only whatever reservations it has declared on the Court's compulsory jurisdiction, but also any reservations of the petitioner state. *See* Case of Certain Norwegian Loans (Fr. v. Nor.) 1957 I.C.J. 9.

b. *Nicaragua v. United States*

In 1946, when the U.S. accepted the ICJ's jurisdiction under Art. 36(2), it accepted jurisdiction for a period of five years and "thereafter until the expiration of six months after notice may be given to terminate this declaration." In 1984, however, the U.S. sought to amend the declaration to exclude disputes with Central American states, with the amendment to take effect immediately. In *Military and Paramilitary Activities in and Against Nicaragua (Nicaragua v. U.S.),* 1984 I.C.J. 392, the ICJ agreed with Nicaragua and ruled that the U.S. was bound to its original six months' notice provision and was thus precluded from escaping the ICJ's jurisdiction on such short notice. The Court so held even though Nicaragua's declaration had no advance notice requirement.

The Court refused to apply reciprocity to excuse compliance with a state's own declaration "whatever its scope, limitation, or conditions." Withdrawal precludes future cases but not cases which have already been started. Nottebohm *(Liecht. v. Guat.)*, 1953 I.C.J. 111.

4. Duration of Declaration Under Article 36(2)

Some declarations state no time limits, while others remain in effect for specific periods (usually five or ten years) and often include automatic renewal clauses. Many declarations include a right to terminate effective upon receipt by the UN's Secretary-General of a notice of withdrawal.

5. Reservations to Compulsory Jurisdiction

Article 36(3) authorizes reservations conditioned on other states' accepting the Court's compulsory jurisdiction or for a certain time. In fact, a wide variety of reservations have been utilized.

a. Disputes to be Settled by Other Means

The most common reservation is to exclude disputes which the parties had already agreed to settle in other tribunals or by other means.

b. Disputes Within Domestic Jurisdiction

Another common reservation is the so called self-judging reservation, such as the Connally Amendment, a reservation to the United States' acceptance of compulsory jurisdiction from 1946 to 1986. This reservation excluded from the jurisdiction of the ICJ "disputes with regard to matters which are essentially within the domestic jurisdiction of the United States of America as determined by the United States of America." It has been argued (most notably by ICJ judge and eminent scholar Hersch Lauterpacht) that such clauses violate Article 36(6), which provides that the ICJ rather than domestic courts shall determine whether it has jurisdiction over a dispute.

c. Disputes Under Multilateral Treaties

Other reservations exclude disputes arising under a multilateral treaty "unless all parties to the treaty affected by the decision are also parties to the case before the Court", or "unless all parties to the treaty are also parties to the case before the Court."

d. Specific Disputes

Also excluded may be specific disputes, such as those concerning law of the sea issues and territorial disputes.

e. Rwanda & the Genocide Convention

In *Case Concerning Armed Activities on the Territory of the Congo (New Application: 2002) (Democratic Republic of the Congo v. Rwanda)*, 2006 I.C.J. 126 (Feb. 3), the ICJ considered whether Rwanda's reservation to Art. IX of the Genocide Convention (regarding submission of disputes to ICJ) precluded its jurisdiction over proceedings instituted by the Democratic Republic of the Congo against Rwanda for alleged violations of the Convention. The ICJ determined that Rwanda's reservation was not "incompatible with the object and purpose" of the Genocide Convention, and therefore that Art. IX could not constitute the basis for the ICJ's jurisdiction over the dispute.

6.   Reservations Concerning National Security and Self Defense

A number of states have modified their acceptance of compulsory jurisdiction to exclude matters related to national security and defense. The ICJ itself, however, does not adhere to the view that such matters are *ipso facto* unsuitable for adjudication in its Court.

7.   Effect and Enforcement of Judgments

Article 94 of the United Nations Charter and Article 59 of the Statute provide that judgments of the ICJ are *binding* upon the parties. Article 94 authorizes the Security Council to "make recommendations or decide upon measures to be taken to give effect to the judgment." Recommendations under Chapter VI or enforcement measures under Chapter VII are substantive and subject to the veto power. When Nicaragua sought enforcement of the ICJ decision against the United States, the United States vetoed the proposed resolution. *See* 25 I.L.M. 1352 (1986).

In *Medellin v. Texas,* 552 U.S. 491 (2008), the U.S. Supreme Court found that U.N. Charter Article 94's obligations upon the U.S. did not make an ICJ ruling go into immediate effect domestically. The ICJ ordered the United States not to execute Jose Ernesto Medellin Rojas until the dispute between the United States and Mexico could be resolved. Texas executed Rojas on August 5, 2008. 43 INT'L LAW. 425, 430 (2009).

8.   Advisory Jurisdiction

Article 65 of the ICJ Statute authorizes the Court to give advisory opinions "on any legal question at the request of whatever body may be authorized by or in accordance with the charter to the UN to make such a request." Article 96 of the UN Charter authorizes the General Assembly or the Security Council to request advisory opinions, as well as "[o]ther organs of the UN and specialized agencies, which may at any time be so authorized by the General Assembly." Examples of other authorized bodies are the International Labour Organization, the World Health Organization, the International Bank for Reconstruction and Development, the International Monetary Fund and the International Atomic Energy Agency.

In October 2008, the resolution initiated by Serbia asking the International Court of Justice to give an advisory opinion on whether "the unilateral declaration of independence by the Provisional Institutions of Self-Government of Kosovo [is] in accordance with international law?" was approved by the UN General Assembly. John R. Crook, ed., *Contemporary Practice of the United States Relating to International Law: United States Opposes Request for ICJ Advisory Opinion on Kosovo,* 103 AM. J. OF INT'L L. 140, 140 (2009). Seventy-seven members voted to pass the resolution and six voted against the resolution. *Id.* at 140–141. The countries that voted against the resolution included Albania, Marshall Islands, Federated States of Micronesia, Nauru, Palau, and the United States. *Id.* at 141. The United States respected the ICJ's position to issue advisory opinions but felt it was not appropriate in this situation. *Id.* at 141.

Example: **Israeli-Palestinian Wall:** In 2004, the ICJ released a controversial opinion holding that Israel's construction of a wall on occupied Palestinian territory impeded the liberty of the Palestinian inhabitants, violated Israel's international obligations, and that Israel was obligated to cease construction of the wall.

9. Legal Effect

Although advisory opinions are legally *non-binding*, they are, nevertheless, very influential in the development of international law. Some international agreements do provide that disputes arising from the agreement will be submitted to the ICJ for an advisory opinion which will be "accepted as decisive by the parties." The Convention on the Privileges and Immunities of the UN is one such example.

10. Preliminary Relief

The ICJ under Article 41 may provide preliminary relief "if the circumstances so require . . . to preserve the respective rights of either party." Examples include the preliminary prohibition on mining of Nicaraguan harbors in *Nicaragua v. United States*, and the preliminary order against Yugoslavia to take measures to prevent genocide in *Bosnia v. Yugoslavia*.

B. The International Criminal Court

Despite the growing recognition of crimes under international law, after the Nuremberg and Tokyo tribunals there was no international court dedicated to adjudication of these offenses until the establishment of the International Criminal Court in 2002. As of January 2009, the Statute of the ICC had been ratified by 108 governments and would permit the prosecution of war crimes, genocide, crimes against humanity. The ICC has jurisdiction when the government fails to prosecute individuals for crimes against humanity when the government is unable to do so. It has eighteen judges who are elected for nine-year terms by the state parties. *Stare decisis* does not apply in the ICC. Recently, the ICC has allowed victims to apply to participate in trials.

A victim must have personally suffered harm, the crime alleged by the applicant must fall within the jurisdiction of the court, and there must be a causal link between the crime and the harms. Elizabeth Bingold et al., *International Criminal Law*, 43 INT'L LAW. 473, 473–75 (2009).

1. Jurisdiction

In 1998, the Rome Statute calling for the establishment of an International Criminal Court was adopted at a UN sponsored conference. The Statute received the necessary ratifications to go into effect in April 2002. The ICC has jurisdiction over genocide, war crimes and crimes against humanity. The statute also authorizes future jurisdiction over crimes against peace once the Parties have agreed on a definition. The Court's jurisdiction is complementary to that of states; that is, the ICC may only address a case if states with jurisdiction are unable or unwilling to prosecute. As of February 2012, the Statute of the ICC had been ratified by 120 governments and would permit the prosecution of war crimes, genocide, and crimes against humanity. The ICC has jurisdiction when the government fails to prosecute individuals for crimes against humanity when the government is unable to do so. It has eighteen judges who are elected for nine-year terms by the state parties. *Stare decisis* does not apply in the ICC.

2. *Mens Rea* Under Article 30 of the ICC Statute

Article 30 of the ICC Statute requires that the material elements of crimes must have been committed with intent and knowledge. In addition, they have specified that intent can take three forms: *dolus directus*, *dolus indirectus* and *dolus eventualis*. Dolus directus is a scenario in which the perpetrator foresees and desires the consequences of the act. Dolus indirectus refers to a situation in which the perpetrator foresees as "almost inevitable", certain harmful or illegal consequences in addition to those specifically desired consequences, and he/she commits the act resulting in the foreseen secondary consequences. Finally, dolus eventualis refers to a situation in which a perpetrator foresees a harmful or illegal consequence, other than the one desired, as a possibility and commits the act which does result in the foreseen undesired consequence. Johan D. Van Der Vyver, *Prosecutor v. Jean-Pierre Bemba Gomb*, 104 AM. J. INT'L LAW 241, 241 (2010).

3. The U.S. Position

Although the United States played a key role in promoting such a court in the fifty years prior to its establishment, the United States has refused to become a party to the treaty based on concern that U.S. forces acting abroad might be subject to politically motivated prosecutions.

However, in November 2008, Department of State Legal Adviser John Bellinger said that the United States considers Darfur a situation in which the ICC should have a role. John R. Crook, ed., *Contemporary Practice Of the United States Relating to International Law: United States Eases Opposition to International Criminal Court, Opposes Efforts to Thwart ICC Proceedings Involving Darfur*, 103 AM. J. OF INT'L LAW 152, 152 (2009). U.S. Ambassador Zlamay Khalilzad had also recognized the need for the ICC in June 2008. *Id.* at 153.

4. The African Union

The Organisation of African Unity (OAU) was formed in 1963 as a loose association of African nations. The many conflicting points of view held by the member states were reflected by the limited power given to the OAU in its charter. Each nation retained autonomy as recognized by the OAU charter. In 2002, the OAU was succeeded by the African Union (AU).

C. Other International Courts of European Jurisdictions

Since World War II there have been a growing number of regional and specialized tribunals, particularly in Western Europe. Three regional courts sitting in Europe are: the Court of Justice of the European Union, the Benelux Court of Justice, the European Court of Human Rights.

1. Court of Justice of the European Union

This court is the *judicial organ of the European Union*.

a. Functions

The European Court of Justice was established to ensure that the laws of the EC are enforced, to act as referee between disputing member states and between the Community institutions and the member states, and to guard against infringement of individual rights by the Community institutions.

b. Structure

Judges are appointed for staggered six year terms and are eligible for re-appointment. Traditionally, there is a judge from each member state with an additional judge appointed to complete the bench with an odd number. The

Court may sit in plenary session, or it may sit in Chamber to consider preliminary rulings or actions instituted by individuals. The judges issue a single "judgment of the court" and have been sworn to uphold the secrecy of their deliberations. The judges are thus protected from the pressure of national interests. In addition to the judges, the European Court of Justice has six advocates general, whose function it is to make "reasoned submissions on cases brought before the Court of Justice, in order to assist the Court . . . "

c. Jurisdiction

The European Court of Justice has only the jurisdiction conferred on it by the treaties. There is a fundamental division between direct actions, which are those actions initiated in the European Court of Justice, and actions begun in a national court but referred to the Court of Justice for a preliminary ruling. Direct actions begin and end in the European Court of Justice, and are usually the result of an agreement between the parties assigning disputes to the Court of Justice. On the other hand, actions begun in national courts also end in national courts, which apply the preliminary ruling obtained from the Court of Justice. The Court of Justice issues preliminary rulings only when requested to do so by a national court seeking clarification of Community law before coming to its own decision.

d. Precedence

Although there is no legal doctrine of *stare decisis* in the European Court of Justice, the Court often follows earlier decisions. Instances in which prior rulings have not been followed are often the result of changed circumstances or changed opinions amongst the judges. In such instances, the Court does not follow the common law practice of formally overruling the earlier decision, but rather ignores it altogether.

e. Sources of Law

The European Court of Justice relies on "primary legislation," "secondary legislation" and international agreements concluded by the Union. Primary legislation includes the Union's constitutive treaties with all their amendments, protocols, etc. Secondary legislation consists of the laws created by the Union institutions. The European Court of Justice also relies on the European Union's Charter of Fundamental Rights as a source of law. This charter draws together all of the human rights norms from the treaties of the European Union into one document.

f. The Court of First Instance

The Single European Act called for the addition of this new court to relieve the European Court of Justice of its heavy caseload. It has a more limited jurisdiction than the Court of Justice, but otherwise has similar structures and procedures.

g. Application of the European Convention on Human Rights

The European Union legal system is separate and distinct from that of the Council of Europe. The treaties applied by the European Court of Justice were not addressed to human rights concerns, and did not include the European Convention on Human Rights.

In several decisions, however, the European Court of Justice has stated that human rights principles are general principles of law which the Court must apply, in interpreting Community treaties, and that the European Convention on Human Rights is evidence of these principles which are to be applied.

In December 2000, the EU formulated a European Charter of Fundamental Rights as a non-binding source of interpretation of human rights. The rights in the Charter go beyond those in the European Convention on Human Rights particularly with respect to rights of democratic governance. Although not adopted as a treaty and not technically binding, it is likely to be influential in the interpretation of EU human rights obligations. The present EU Treaty requires its members to respect human rights, with "serious and persistent" breach of human rights being grounds for suspension of membership.

The Andean Community is a pact between the countries of Bolivia, Colombia, Ecuador, Peru, and Venezuela to harmonize the region and promote economic growth. While the community has only been mildly successful, the Tribunal of Justice, which is remarkably similar to the European Court of Justice, is the third most active international court in the world. Their docket is concentrated on intellectual property and the Tribunal has managed to create stable law by using repetitive rulings and staying insulated from the political pressure within their community and from foreign nations.

Laurence Helfer, Karen Alter, Florencia Guerzovich, *Islands of Effective International Adjusdication: Constructing an Intellectual Property Rule of Law in the Andean Community*, 103 AM. J. INT'L L. 1 (2008).

2. European Court of Human Rights

See p. 78 *infra*.

3. The African Union

The OAU was traditionally concerned with noninterference and peaceful resolution of disputes among member states. The AU, however, has taken a much more active role, intervening in regional conflicts in Sudan, Somalia, and Anjouan (Comoros). The OAU and the AU have made a point of promoting African unity on issues like human rights.

4. Uganda

The ICC issued its first arrest warrants in 2005 in response to alleged human rights violations perpetrated by the Lord's Resistance Army, a rebel group in Uganda. The ICC has been criticized for still being unprepared to handle the situation.

5. Sierra Leone

In 2008, the Appeals Chamber of the Special Court for Sierra Leone found Armed Forces Revolutionary Council (AFRC) political leaders and military commanders Brima, Kamara, and Kanu "guilty of eleven counts of . . . crimes against humanity of extermination, murder, rape, and enslavement, and of the war crimes of acts of terrorism, collective punishments, murder, outrages upon personal dignity, mutilation, pillage, and enlisting children under the age of fifteen or using them to participate actively in hostilities." Valerie, Oosterveld, *International Decisions:*

Special Court for Sierra Leone—international criminal law—forced marriage—recruitment and use of child soldiers, 103 AM. J. OF INT'L L. 103, 104 (2009). Crimes against humanity of sexual slavery and forced marriage were dismissed. *Id.* In the case against Civil Defence Forces (CDF), Fofana and Kondewa were convicted of murder, cruel treatment, pillage, and collective punishments as war crimes. *Id.* Kondewa was also convicted of the crime of enlistment of children under fifteen into an armed force or group. *Id.* The appeals chamber ruled that forced marriage should not have been considered only as a sexual crime by the trial chamber. *Id.* at 108. The appeals chamber held that forced marriage is "forced conjugal association with another person resulting in great suffering, or serious physical or mental injury on the part of the victim." *Id.* at 108 (quoting AFRC Appeals Judgment para. 195). The AFRC convictions for recruitment and use of child soldiers were upheld on appeal while the CDF conviction was reversed. *Id.* at 109.

On March 2, 2009 judgment was issued in *Prosecutor v. Issa Hassan Sesay, Morris Kallon & Augustine Gbao*, also known was the *Revolutionary United Front* case. This judgment was the first to enter a conviction in an international criminal tribunal for the war crime of attacking peacekeeping personnel, and for the crime of sexual slavery and forced marriage. *See* Section III(J)(2)(c) *supra.* The charge for crimes against peacekeeping personnel came from RUF attacks on UNAMSIL personnel in May 2000, in which the peacekeepers were abducted and killed. The trial chamber identified four elements of the crime: 1) the accused directed an attack against the personnel, material, vehicles, installations or unity involved in a humanitarian or peacekeeping mission in accordance with the UN Charter; 2) the accused intended for such personnel, installations, units, material, or vehicles to be the object of the attack; 3) the personnel, installations, units, material or vehicles were entitled to give protection to civilians or civilian objects under the international law of armed conflict; and 4) the accused knew or had reason to know that the personnel, installations, units, materials or vehicles were protected. The totality of circumstances at the time of the offense must also be examined to determine whether the peacekeepers were taking a part in the hostilities when the attacks occurred. Under this evaluation the court held that the RUF launched a deliberate campaign against the ANAMSIL peacekeeping personnel. Valerie Oosterveld ed., *Prosecutor v. Issa Hassan Sesay, Morris Kallon & Augustine Gbao*, 104 AM. J. INT'L L. 73, 80–81 (2010).

Chapter VII

Regional Organizations

"Regional organization" is a term of art under the UN Charter that refers to international associations established under Chapter VIII. Each of these institutions is created through an agreement between the member states that outlines the structure, functions, and authority of the organization. "Regional organization" is not defined in the UN Charter. Unlike other international organizations, however, regional organizations are concerned with problems within a specific region. Some handle only specific concerns such as economic, military or political issues, while others deal with any matter that concerns the nations in that region.

Note: These Chapter VIII organizations for peaceful dispute resolution should not be confused with Article 51 regional self-defense alliances, such as the North Atlantic Treaty Organization (NATO). Chapter VIII organizations may only use force if authorized by the Security Council to do so. Article 51 alliances may only use force in the event of an "armed attack" on one of its members.

A. Basic Characteristics

Some regional organizations are loose associations of member states with little or no legislative authority. These organizations may only provide a forum for nations to meet and discuss matters of common interest. Other regional organizations have legislative power and take significant actions in fulfilling their mandates. The organizations with the most legislative authority are supranational organizations such as the European Union, *see* p. 73 *infra*.

B. Major Organizations

The Organization of American States (OAS), Council of Europe, and the Organization of African Unity (OAU) (now known as the African Union) are three of the most prominent regional organizations.

1. The Organization of American States

The OAS was created in 1948 to promote unity and cooperation among nations in the Western Hemisphere. One of the primary influences on the formation of the OAS was the Cold War. As a result, its charter emphasized security through a common defense.

2. The Council of Europe

The Council of Europe was created in 1949 to promote unity in Europe after World War II. All members of the European Union are members of the Council of Europe, but not all members of the larger Council of Europe are members of the European Union.

3. The African Union

The OAU was formed in 1963 as a loose association of African nations. The many conflicting points of view held by the member states were reflected by the limited power given to the OAU in its charter. Each nation retained autonomy as recognized by the OAU charter. In 2001 the OAU was designated the African Union.

C. Functions

The primary function of each of these regional organizations is to promote cooperation between the member states. The specific areas, methods, and extent of cooperation, however, differ among regional organizations.

1. The Organization of American States

The OAS has concentrated its efforts on responding to political developments and furthering political cooperation. The OAS charter outlines the functions of the organization as strengthening security, ensuring peaceful settlement of disputes, coordinating common defense, and promoting economic, social and cultural development. Although the OAS has drafted a number of human rights treaties, it has been somewhat less successful than the Council of Europe in winning the acceptance of those treaties particularly due to the refusal of the United States to ratify. The OAS has made significant progress in the development of regional human rights, including notably the establishment of the Inter-American Court of Human Rights in 1969.

2. The Council of Europe

The Council of Europe has focused on human rights and economic cooperation with the European Union, and has been influential in incorporating human rights obligations into the essentially economic focus of the European Union.

3. The African Union

The OAU Charter is primarily concerned with noninterference and peaceful resolution of disputes among member states. It has promoted African unity on issues including human rights, but has played a more limited role in dealing with regional conflicts.

D. Relationship to UN

Chapter VIII of the UN Charter describes the relationship between the UN and regional organizations. Article 52(1) in the UN Charter allows UN members to participate in any regional arrangement with principles consistent with the UN. The UN encourages its members in regional organizations to attempt to settle "local disputes" in those organizations before referring them to the Security Council. U.N. Charter Art. 52, ¶ 2.

Regional organizations have a duty to inform the Security Council of any actions the organization is undertaking or contemplating for the maintenance of international peace and security. U.N. Charter Art. 54. Regional organizations must seek Security Council authorization for any enforcement action. U.N. Charter Art. 53.

1. Jurisdictional Issues

Chapter VIII is unclear concerning regional jurisdiction and the often overlapping authority of the Security Council. Although it has been argued that regional organizations have primary or exclusive jurisdiction over regional matters, *see* U.N. Charter Art. 52, ¶ 2, neither of these arguments has been accepted given the Security Council's "primary" responsibility for the maintenance of international peace and security. *See* U.N. Charter Art. 52, ¶ 4 and Art. 24. The UN Security Council, however, has chosen to defer to regional organizations in a number of instances. The Security Council also may choose to exercise concurrent jurisdiction, but these decisions are founded more on pragmatic considerations than any legal requirements in the UN Charter.

E. The Organization for Security and Cooperation in Europe

The OSCE membership includes not only all of Europe, but also the United States. It was created in 1975 by the Helsinki Final Act which established a political rather than a legal system to promote human rights and national security.

The Helsinki Act has four "baskets" of rights, of which the most important currently is Basket IV, which established conferences to assess development and implementation of human rights. These conferences and their concluding documents have created an expansive catalog not just of human rights, but of principles relating to democratic governance. Pursuant to the "Human Dimension Mechanism" a state complaint that another state is not fulfilling its obligations progressively leads to diplomatic exchanges between states, placement on the conference agendas, and OSCE expert missions or rapporteurs. In 1992 the OSCE also established the High Commissioner on National Minorities largely in response to the Yugoslavian conflict.

Chapter VIII

Regional Human Rights Law & Institutions

The longest standing and most well developed regional system of human rights law is in Europe. Outside of Europe, the inter-American system has also established a judicial system for regional enforcement of human rights. Unlike these systems, the African system relied more on mediation and political remedies to enforce regional human obligations until 1998, when the African Court on Human and People's Rights was created.

A. The European System

European human rights law is contained primarily in the European Convention for the Protection of Human Rights and Freedoms and subsequent protocols for civil and political rights, and the European Social Charter for economic and social rights. These treaties were promulgated by the Council of Europe, first established in 1949. The Statute of the Council requires that "every member of the Council of Europe accept the principles of the rule of law and of the enjoyment by all persons within its jurisdiction of human rights and fundamental freedoms."

1. The European Convention on Human Rights

The organization and content of the European Convention, which entered into force in 1953, is similar to the International Covenant on Civil and Political Rights. Every member of the Council of Europe has ratified the Convention and now membership requires its ratification. The European Convention and its protocols include: the right to life; freedom from torture and "inhuman or degrading treatment"; freedom from slavery, servitude or forced labor; rights to a fair and public hearing to determine civil rights and criminal charges; freedom of expression and religion; rights of privacy; rights of assembly and association; and rights must be granted free from discrimination based upon "sex, race, color, language, religion, political or other opinion, national or social origin, association with a national minority, property, birth or other status." Protocol 6, entered into force in 1986, prohibits capital punishment in time of peace. The Convention differs from the International Covenant by failing to recognize a people's right of self-determination or make any reference to the rights of people belonging to ethnic, religious or linguistic minorities (dealt with in separate treaties). The Convention also differs by not making any reference to the rights of the child or to prohibitions on war propaganda or propaganda inciting discrimination. Non-citizens who are in states under the Convention also fall within its reach. The Convention's work is reinforced by individual nations' laws that fall in line with the document.

a.   States may derogate from their obligations under the Convention in times of "war or other public emergency" (Art. 15).

   i.   Such derogation must be only "to the extent strictly required by the exigencies of the situation."

   ii. The derogating party must inform the Secretary General of the intent to derogate and the reasons therefore, as well as its resumption of its obligations of the Convention after the emergency has passed.

   iii. Parties may not derogate from the right to life (Art. 2) "except in respect of deaths resulting from lawful acts of war"; the prohibition of torture (Art. 3); prohibition of slavery (Art. 4(1)); or the prohibition of punishment without law (Art. 7).

b.   Under Article 16, States may restrict the political activity of aliens in disregard to the rights of Freedom of Expression (Art. 10); Freedom of Assembly and Association (Art. 11); and the Prohibition of Discrimination (Art. 14).

   i.   In *Demir v. Turkey*, a unanimous Grand Chamber of the European Court of Human Rights ruled that Turkey had violated Article 11 of the European Convection for the Protection of Human Rights and Fundamental Freedoms. Ragnar Nordeide, European Convention on Human Rights—right to form a trade union—right to bargain collectively—interpretation of Convention in light of other international law, 103 Am. J. Int'l L. 567, 568 (2009). The court held that the trade union Tum Bel Sen, founded in 1990, should legally be recognized because the applicants had a right to form a trade union and bargain collectively. Ragnar Nordeide, European Convention on Human Rights—right to form a trade union—right to bargain collectively—interpretation of Convention in light of other international law, 103 Am. J. Int'l L. 567, 568 (2009).

c.   Key rights conferred by Protocols subsequently added to the Convention, and a separate Convention on Action Against Trafficking in Humans.

   i.   Protection of Property (Protocol 1)

   ii. Right to Education (Protocol 1)

   iii. Right to Free Elections (Protocol 1)

       In *Mathieu-Mohin and Clerfayt v. Belgium*, the European Court of Human Rights heard a case brought by two French-speaking legislators who challenged Belgium's system of national election.

       The applicants were prohibited by national law from being members of the Flemish council that controlled regional matters in their district on the grounds that they had, in their capacity as members of the national Parliament, taken the parliamentary oath in French. The Court found no violation of Article 3 of Protocol 1 of the Convention because when considered in historical and political context, the electoral system allowed for the free expression of the opinion of the people in the choice of the legislature.

iv. Prohibition of Imprisonment for Debt (Protocol 4)

v. Freedom of Movement (Protocol 4)

vi. Prohibition of Expulsion of Nationals (Protocol 4)

vii. Prohibition of Collective Expulsion of Aliens (Protocol 4)

viii. Abolition of the Death Penalty (Protocol 6) with a limited exception for the death penalty in time of war

ix. Procedural safeguards relating to the expulsion of aliens (Protocol 7)

x. Right of appeal in criminal matters (Protocol 7)

xi. Compensation for wrongful conviction (Protocol 7)

xii. Right not to be tried or punished twice (Protocol 7)

xiii. Equality between spouses (Protocol 7)

In the Austrian case of *Schalk & Kopf v. Austria*, App. No. 30141/04, Eur. Ct. H.R. (June 24, 2010), the European Court of Human Rights found that acts that allowed domestic partnership or marriage of homosexuals that granted similar rights as a heterosexual partnership does not violate Article 12.

xiv. General prohibition of discrimination (Protocol 12)

In June of 2009, the European Court of Human Rights decided the landmark case of *Opuz v. Turkey*. The Court held that under the European Convention of Human Rights, gender-based domestic violence is considered to be discrimination.

xv. Total abolition of the death penalty (Protocol 13)

The Council of Europe has also adopted a separate Convention for the Prevention of Torture and Inhuman or Degrading Treatment or Punishment.

d. The European Court of Human Rights has recognized that the right to life under the European Convention creates a positive obligation on states to safeguard life in activities "in which the right to life may be at stake." *Oneryildiz v. Turkey*, App. No. 48939/99, 2004–XII Eur. Ct. H.R. (2004).

The European Court of Human Rights held that Article 13 of the Hague Convention on the Civil Aspects of International Child Abduction and Article 8's protections in the European Convention of Human Rights, addressing the risks of returning abducted children, can be brought into conformity with each other.

In *Abbott v. Abbott*, 560 U.S. 1 (2010), the Supreme Court ruled that a non-custodial father who held a *ne exeat* right over his son could use the Hague Convention on the Civil Aspects of Child Abduction to sue the custodial mother for taking his son out of the country. The Court ruled that the *ne exeat* right counted as a "right of custody" for the purposes of the Child Abduction Convention, bringing the United States' interpretation in line with many other countries' interpretations.

The European Court of Human rights denied Greek North-Cypriot claims for restoration of property in *Demopoulos & Others v. Turkey*. The claims for seized property by expatriate Greek North-Cypriots were rejected because the plaintiffs had not applied through the Turkish Republic of North Cyprus's Immovable Property Commission (IPC) first. The court adhered to the "Namibia Principle," which states that even if the legitimacy of the administration of a territory is not recognized by the international community (as The Turkish Republic of Cyprus is not), "international law recognized the legitimacy of certain legal arrangements and transactions in such a situation,. . .the effects of which can be ignored only to the detriment of the inhabitants of the territory." Simply put, mere unrecognized occupation does not invalidate all the laws of the occupying government. There were four reasons behind the courts holding that the IPC provides the necessary redress:

i. There is no formal *indicia* of unlawfulness or breach of rights despite the harsh criteria for economic redress. These harsh standards are partially justified, in the courts view, by amount of time that has elapsed since the initial causation for the claims.

ii. Independence and impartiality of the redress

iii. Adequacy of the compensation

iv. Accessibility and efficiency of the remedy

These factors led the court to the conclusion that the rule of exhaustion of domestic remedies stands in this matter (whereby the plaintiffs must first show that they have exhausted all remedies available to them within the Turkish Republic of Cyprus before any redress is available on the international level). Alexia Solomou, *Demopoulos & Others v. Turkey*, 104 AM. J. INT'L L. 628, 628–636 (2010).

In July of 2010, the European Court of Human Rights ruled in *Gäfgen v. Germany*. The case concerned a threat of torture used by German police to elicit information about the whereabouts of an abducted child from the abductor. The Court ruled this tactic was illegal under Article 3 of the Convention for the Protection of Human Rights, but allowed evidence gleaned under the threat of torture to stand because there was no overall Article 6 violation of a right to a fair trial. The Court found that "threat of conduct prohibited by Article 3, provided it is sufficiently real and immediate, may fall foul of that provision," and demonstrated a willingness to apply the doctrine of fruit of the poisonous tree without reserve. Extending past a forced confession to include hard evidence, any evidence obtained through an Art. 3 violation can therefore be barred. The court upheld the conviction however because the Defendant gave a full confession at trial while under no threat of torture. This confession was found to be sufficient evidence for the jury to convict. Much depends on how relevant and crucial the evidence acquired through a breach of Art. 3 is in the context of finding an Art. 6 violation—if inconsequential, there will be no problem with the "fair trail" guarantee of Art. 6. Heijo Sauer and Mirja Trilsh, *Gäfgen v. Germany*, 105 AM. J. INT'L L. 313, 313–318 (2011).

2. The European Social Charter

In addition to the European Convention's protection of political and civil rights, there is promotion and protection of economic and social rights under the European Social Charter. As of 2011, thirty-two of forty-seven members of the Council of Europe have signed on to the original Charter. Five of these members have not ratified the Charter. The Charter's recognition of economic, social and cultural rights includes: the right to work, the right to fair compensation, the rights of children, the rights of employed women to protection, and the right to social and medical assistance. States have some latitude in selecting which of the enumerated rights they will accept. European Social Charter, Oct. 18, 1961, Art. 20, Europ. T.S. No. 35. A Protocol with Additional Rights went into force in 1992. Its lack of adjudicative machinery (implementation is through a reporting system like many human rights treaties) makes it less prominent than the Convention in the enforcement of human rights in Europe. An Amending Protocol in 1991 revised the implementation process.

Note: In 1998 an additional protocol went into effect which allows for collective complaints. Collective complaints of "unsatisfactory application of the Charter" may be brought by specifically recognized international and national organizations. Complaints are made to the European Committee of Social Rights, which issues a report to the Committee of Ministers. Their recommendations in turn go to the European Parliament, the ECSR report is made public, and states must report on their implementation of any recommendations made.

In 1999 a revised Charter went into effect which progressively replaced the prior Charter system. Under the revised Charter, states must accept six out of nine enumerated rights in Part II, and an additional number of rights from those not selected. Reports must be sent to the newly established European Committee of Social Rights to assess compliance. In turn it sends its recommendations to the Governmental Committee, which sends a report to the Committee of Ministers. The Committee of Ministers may make recommendations for compliance to the states concerned. As of 2011, twenty-seven of the forty-seven members of the Council of Europe had ratified the revised Charter.

3. European Union Agency for Fundamental Rights

In 2007, the European Council created the European Union Agency for Fundamental Rights as an information-gathering and advice-giving body. Its goal is to aid member states with questions on human rights as considered in the Treaty on European Union, also known as the Maastricht Treaty.

4. Other European Entities and Human Rights

The European Court of Justice and the European Parliament have also had some experience with human rights concerns: the former through its interpretation of European Union law in cases and the later through resolutions and publications. As of 2011, the European Union as a whole has considered signing on to the European Convention on Human Rights, although this would require significant changes to be made to the Maastricht Treaty. The ECHR permits the EU to consider doing so through Protocol 14.

The Organization for Security and Cooperation in Europe (OSCE) also engages in work involving election monitoring and minority concerns.

B. The Institutions of the European Regime

The European Convention on Human Rights has established an effective human rights regime, enforcing rights through the European Commission on Human Rights, the European Court of Human Rights, and the Committee of Ministers of the Council of Europe. The system was changed substantially by Protocol 11, which took effect in 1998.

1. European Commission of Human Rights

The Commission was composed of a number of members equal to the number of state parties to the Convention. The Commission was vested with both compulsory and optional jurisdiction. During its tenure, the Commission ranged widely in its caseload: at first it only took a fraction of its cases, but then it became overburdened with its number of cases prior to Protocol 11 taking effect.

a. Compulsory Jurisdiction

It could hear cases filed by one state against another state as long as both states have ratified the Convention. European Human Rights Convention, p. 73 *supra*, Art. 24, Europ. T.S. No. 5.

b. Optional Jurisdiction

The Commission had optional jurisdiction with respect to individual petitions. The optional jurisdiction was invoked only if a state had ratified the Convention and declared its acceptance of the Commission's right to hear individual petitions. European Human Rights Convention, p. 73 *supra*, Art. 25, Europ. T.S. No. 5. Most states had made such a declaration.

2. European Court of Human Rights

The Court was comprised of a number of members equal to the membership of the Council of Europe. The Court's jurisdiction was optional and was not invoked by mere ratification of the Convention. Most state parties had made the necessary special declaration accepting the jurisdiction of the Court. Originally cases could be referred to the Court only by states or by the Commission, and the Court's judgments are final and binding. The Court was vested with the power to award damages. The Court also has limited authority to issue advisory opinions. Decisions of the Court were enforced by the Committee of Ministers.

The European Court of Human Rights has found violations of Convention Article 8 (right to respect for private life and family life) in situations where governments have failed to take actions necessary to counter substantial risks of harm to individuals due to pollution. With each case the Court has given further details to what the state's obligations are to prevent or mitigate the risk of harm from hazardous activities. The Court looks to international environmental law, as opposed to the state's law, to determine whether the measures taken by the state were sufficient. Dinah Shelton, *International Decisions: Tatar C. Roumain, App. No. 67021/01*, 104 AM. J. OF INT'L LAW 247, 247–253.

3. Committee of Ministers of the Council of Europe

The Committee is made up of one representative for each member state of the Council of Europe. It appoints the members of the Human Rights Commission and at one time decided those cases which the Commission failed to settle and which were not referred to the European Court within three months after the Commission's report.

C. The Process of Implementation and Enforcement

The process discussed below is the adjudicative process under the European Convention before and after 1998, followed by a brief description of the reportorial system under the amended European Social Charter.

1. Enforcement Process Prior to Protocol 11

Consideration of claims submitted by either states or individuals began with the Commission. The Commission's work involved *three stages*.

a. Stage 1

The Commission considered the admissibility of the case, determined among other factors by whether the petition presents a prima facie case for violations of specific provisions of the Convention and by whether all available domestic remedies have already been exhausted.

b. Stage 2

If the case is admissible, the Commission ascertained the facts and attempted to resolve the case with a friendly settlement. Reports on friendly settlements were sent to the states concerned and to the Council of Europe for publication.

c. Stage 3

Finally, the Commission prepared a report regarding unsettled cases, including findings of facts and its opinions with regard to violations of the Convention. This report was submitted to the Committee of Ministers of the Council of Europe. During the three month period following submission of the report to the Committee, the Commission or any interested state party could refer cases to the Court, provided the Court had jurisdiction.

Note: Before 1998, individual claims came before the court only through submission by the Commission because only states or the Commission could bring cases before the Court. Individuals did not have the same rights as did states to submit their claims to the Court.

2. Committee of Ministers

Cases not submitted to the Court within three months were decided on by the Committee of Ministers, and states were obliged to take measures to satisfy the decision of the Committee. The Commission typically left to the Committee only those cases in which the Commission believed there had been no violation of the Convention. The Committee could find a violation of the Convention only by a two-thirds vote, short of which it decides to take no action.

3. European Court of Human Rights

The European Court of Human Rights is the judicial organ of the Council of Europe, an organization distinct from the European Union. The member most frequently before the Court has been the United Kingdom which for many years had no constitution and no formal domestic guarantee of individual rights, which often forced individuals to seek protection for individual rights in this forum. The number of judges was equal to the number of members to the Council and there was usually one judge from each member state. No two judges can be nationals of the same state. Judges served for staggered nine-year terms, with one third of the judges being elected every three years.

Note: Before 1998, a case was first dealt with by the Commission of Human Rights.

4. The European Court of Human Rights & the Enforcement Process After Protocol 11

a. Creation and Structure

A newly constituted European Court of Human Rights was established pursuant to Protocol 11 on November 1, 1998.

i. Organization

The Court, located in Strasbourg, France, now operates full time. Qualification requirements of judges remain the same as under the old system; however, an age limit of seventy now exists, as well as the expectation that the judges not engage in activity incompatible with their full time obligation to the Court and that the judges reside in Strasbourg. It is the first permanent, full-time human rights court.

ii. Jurisdiction

The Court hears all cases alleging violations of individual rights. The initial review and mediation function of the Commission, and the Commission itself, has been terminated. All applicants, including individuals, have direct access to the Court. The right of individual application is mandatory. The Court continues to have jurisdiction with respect to all interstate cases, although actions filed by one state against another rarely take place.

In *Bankovic v. Belgium*, the European Court of Human Rights heard a case brought by citizens of the Federal Republic of Yugoslavia against NATO member countries that had allegedly violated European human rights instruments. Because Serbia had not yet become a member of the Council of Europe, in the instant case there was no jurisdictional link between the persons who were victims of the act complained of and the respondent states. The applicants and their deceased relatives were not capable of coming within the jurisdiction of the respondent states on account of the extra-territorial act in question. Accordingly, the impugned action of the respondent states did not engage their convention responsibility.

iii. Adjudicatory Structure

Frivolous, "unfounded" cases may be dismissed by a unanimous decision by a three judge committee. Most cases not dismissed as unfounded will be heard by a seven-judge chamber. Exceptional cases will be heard by the Grand Chamber, consisting of seventeen judges.

b. Process for Hearing and Adjudicating Cases

Individual and interstate applications may be made to the Court. Contact with applicants established by the Registry of the Court; the Registry will request additional information from applicants if necessary. A chamber of the Court will register the application, and the application will be assigned to a judge rapporteur. The judge rapporteur may refer the application to a three-judge committee, which may include the judge rapporteur, to determine whether the application is inadmissible. If the three-judge committee unanimously decides that the application is inadmissible, this application is dismissed. The committee's decision in final. If the committee does not unanimously decide that the application is inadmissible, the application is referred to a seven-judge chamber. If the judge rapporteur believes that the application is admissible in that it raises a question of principle, then the application is referred to a seven-judge chamber. The seven-judge chamber will decide on the merits of the application and, if necessary, determine its competency to hear the case. Appeals may be heard by a seventeen-member Grand Chamber, with five members deciding on whether the case is deserving of an appeal; individual cases rarely reach this stage, while interstate cases are automatically sent there. The Committee of Ministers will oversee the execution of the Court's judgment, which in the case of a violation can include damage awards usually limited to allowing the recovery of the complaining party's expenses, but which can also include damages for harm or for emotional suffering in more serious cases.

5. Protocol 14

In 2009 the Council of Europe put forward Protocol 14, which streamlines the Convention system in several key areas. These changes include, among other things, reducing the three-judge inadmissibility process to one judge. As of January 6, 2010, all forty-seven member states had ratified Protocol 14.

6. The European Social Charter

The Charter does not provide an adjudicative process similar to that of the European Convention. Rights are promoted and protected primarily by reporting. European Social Charter, Arts. 21–29, Europ. T.S. No. 35. State Parties "undertake to consider the economic, social and cultural rights enumerated [in the Charter]" and to pursue such aims with appropriate measures. States reported on their progress in biennial reports submitted to the Council of Europe's Secretary-General. The reports were examined by the Committee of Experts; then passed on with the Committee of Expert's conclusions to the Governmental Social Committee and finally to the Council's Parliament. The Committee of Ministers may, on the basis of reports and consultation with the foregoing bodies, make necessary recommendations to the state.

7. Specific Enforcement Action

In *Imakayeva v. Russia,* App. No. 7615/02, 2006–XIII Eur. Ct. H.R., the European Court of Human Rights determined that Russia violated Article 2 of the European Convention with respect to the government detention and disappearance of Said-Khuseyn Imakayev, a Chechen civilian, during a rebel uprising in 1999. The Court presumed Imakayev's death following Russia's prolonged refusal to cooperate with the investigative proceedings, and found that Russia violated Article 2 by failing to protect Imakayev's life and conduct an adequate investigation of his disappearance.

In *Kosovo v. Latvia,* App. No. 26276/04 (Eur. Ct. H.R. May 17, 2010) (Grand Chamber), the European Court of Human Rights upheld Latvia's recent conviction of a former Soviet leader for World War II war crimes. This precedent allows the laws of war to be applied retroactively.

D. Inter-American System—Human Rights Law

Outside of Europe the most developed regime of human rights law is in the Americas. The primary sources for human rights law in the Americas are the Charter of the Organization of American States (OAS) and the 1969 American Convention on Human Rights. These two systems of Inter-American human rights law overlap and interact, and although they are separate entities, they often seem to act as one.

1. The Organization of American States: A Historical Overview

On April 30, 1948, twenty-one countries met in Bogota, Colombia, to adopt the Charter of the Organization of American States (OAS). The OAS Charter affirmed a hemisphere wide commitment to common goals and respect for national sovereignty. A long history of regional cooperation contributed to the successful evolution of the OAS. Some important milestones in the eventual development of the OAS include Simon Bolivar's Congress of Panama convention at which he expressed his vision of an association of states within the Western hemisphere, the First International Conference of American States that was held in Washington, D.C. in 1890, and the establishment of the Commercial Bureau of the American Republics (the forerunner to the OAS). The Commercial Bureau of the American Republics was renamed in 1910 to the Pan American Union, which subsequently became the OAS. The first Secretary General of the OAS was Alberto Lleras Camargo.

2. Modern OAS Membership

Since its inception, the OAS has expanded to include Canada and the nations of the Caribbean.

a. The Twenty-One Original Members of the OAS Are

Argentina, Bolivia, Brazil, Chile, Colombia, Costa Rica, Cuba (although the Castro government was expelled in 1962), Dominican Republic, Ecuador, El Salvador, Guatemala, Haiti, Honduras (membership suspended in 2009), Mexico, Nicaragua, Panama, Paraguay, Peru, United States, Uruguay, and Venezuela.

b. Fourteen Additional Members Have Been Added to the OAS Since Its Inception in 1948

1967:   Barbados & Trinidad & Tobago

1969:   Jamaica

1975:   Grenada

1977:   Suriname

1979:   Dominica & Saint Lucia

1981:   Antigua & Barbuda; Saint Vincent & the Grenadines

1982:   The Bahamas

1984:   St. Kitts & Nevis

1990:   Canada

1991:   Belize & Guyana

3. The OAS Charter

The OAS charter serves as the constitution of the OAS, and was signed by member states in 1948. The OAS charter went into effect three years later. There have been several amendments to the charter, including the 1993 Protocol of Managua, in part because the original OAS Charter itself made little mention of human rights and provided no machinery for the protection of human rights. However, an enumeration of substantive rights was embodied in the American Declaration of the Rights and Duties of Man, which was also proclaimed in 1948. Charter based human rights obligations apply to all members of the OAS.

4. The American Declaration of the Rights & Duties of Man

Until 1960 the American Declaration served only as a nonbinding resolution of the OAS. In 1960, however, the OAS formed the Inter-American Commission on Human Rights to promote respect for human rights. Today, the American Declaration is considered the instrument that defines the fundamental rights of the individual which are proclaimed and mandated of all members in Article 3(*l*) of the OAS Charter. The American Declaration includes two main sets of proclamations: a proclamation of rights and a proclamation of duties. The spirit under which the Declaration was proclaimed was emphasized in the first few passages of the document:

The American States have on repeated occasions recognized that the essential rights of man are not derived from the fact that he is a national of a certain state, but are based upon attributes of his human personality.

The international protection of the rights of man should be the principal guide of an evolving American law.

a. Rights

The American Declaration, adopted just a few months before the Universal Declaration of Human Rights, proclaims a list of twenty-seven human rights. These include but are not limited to the right to life, liberty, and security of person; the right to equality before the law; the right to freely profess and practice a religious faith; the right to freedom of investigation and opinion; the right to residence and movement; the right to preservation of health and well-being; the right to education (at a minimum primary education); the right to a fair trial; the right to nationality; the right to humane treatment while in custody; the right to free association; the right to assemble; the right to establish a family; and the right to asylum.

b. Duties

The American Declaration also outlines ten duties of every individual. These include: Duties to society; duties to children and parents; the duty to vote; the duty to serve the community and the nation; the duty to pay taxes, and the duty to work.

c. Reach

The Inter-American Commission has consistently held that the U.S. is responsible for duties under the Declaration as a result of ratifying the OAS Charter despite U.S. efforts to reject its jurisdiction. *See The Haitian Centre for Human Rights et al. v. United States,* Case 10.675, Report No. 51/96, Inter-Am.C.H.R., OEA/Ser.L/V/II.95, doc. 7 rev. at 550 (1997).

5. The Relationship Between the Inter-American Commission on Human Rights (IACHR) & the OAS

The 1948 OAS Charter did not provide for the establishment of the Inter-American Commission. However, when the establishment of the IACHR was mandated in 1959, the OAS needed to determine how the new commission would fit within the existing rubric. The OAS determined that the IACHR would be an autonomous entity of the OAS given the task of promoting respect for human rights. Human rights were understood to be those spelled out in the American Declaration of the Rights and Duties of Man. In the 1960 Statute, the OAS outlined various powers of the IACHR, including the power to prepare studies and reports (including country studies that are still an important power of the Commission today) and to make recommendations to countries in relation to the study findings. Specifically, the recommendations would relate to, "the adoption of progressive measures in favor of human rights in the framework of legislation, constitutional provisions and international commitments, as well as appropriate measures to further observance of those rights." (1960 Commission Statute, Article 9; Revised 1979 Commission Statute, Article 18).

In 1965, the IACHR was authorized to accept individual petitions regarding specifically designated human rights violations in the Declaration. Under the current system the Commission's rules allow for individual petitions to enforce any of the rights in the American Declaration. The IACHR has received and processed thousands of petitions. The reports of the IACHR regarding these individual cases are published in the Annual Reports of the Commission, and are also often independently published by the specific country (www.oas.org). Exclusively Charter based petitions may not be brought before the Court, however, because only state parties to the American Convention can be brought before the Court.

In 1970, the status and role of the IACHR changed again. The Commission was elevated to the status of a formal organ of the OAS in order to further implementation of the American Declaration of the Rights and Duties of Man. The principal function of the Inter-American Commission became, "to promote the observance and protection of human rights and to serve as a consultative organ of the Organization in these matters." (OAS Charter, amended, arts. 52 and 111(1)) The specific structure and procedures of the Commission were to be determined by the Inter-American Convention on Human Rights (OAS Charter, amended, 111(2)).

6. The Commission as an OAS Charter Organ

With the adoption of the Inter-American Commission as a charter organ in 1970, the functional role of the IACHR broadened. The IACHR helped the OAS establish the American Convention on Human Rights. The IACHR is often consulted concerning any human rights issues that emerge. The Commission still publishes reports and studies, and the individual country studies and on site investigations compose a large function of the IACHR. Due to the frequency and importance of the on-site investigations, the IACHR has established a set of rules and regulations regarding the visits, which are now codified in Articles 55–59 of the IACHR Regulations. On a few occasions, the Commission has also served as mediator in situations where human rights were at issue in civil war conflicts (Dominican Republic, 1965; El Salvador and Honduras, 1969–1970; Colombia, 1981). A more detailed analysis of the Commission generally will follow in the Inter-American Convention section. The Commission, therefore, has two roles: the oversight of the human rights obligations of *all* OAS members under Article 41(a)–(e) and (g) of the American Convention, and oversight of the obligations of the Convention parties under Articles 41(f), 44–51.

7. The American Convention on Human Rights

The second main source of Inter-American human rights law is the American Convention on Human Rights, which was opened for signature at the Inter-American Specialized Conference on Human Rights in San Jose, Costa Rica, November 22, 1969. The Convention went into force on July 18, 1978.

a. Ratification

The Convention has been ratified by twenty-five OAS Member States, including: Argentina; Barbados; Bolivia; Brazil; Chile; Colombia; Costa Rica; Dominica; Dominican Republic; Ecuador; E1 Salvador; Grenada; Guatemala; Haiti; Honduras; Jamaica; Mexico; Nicaragua; Panama; Paraguay; Peru; Suriname; Trinidad and Tobago; Uruguay; and Venezuela.

President Jimmy Carter signed the Convention and referred it to the Senate for ratification, but the Senate has yet to act upon it. The Inter-American Commission, established originally under the OAS Charter, has also been incorporated into the institutional framework established by the American Convention, as discussed previously (IACHR section above).

b. Protection of Civil & Political Rights

The American Convention is similar to the European Convention and has a similar institutional structure. The American Convention focuses on the broad protection of political and civil rights that are enumerated through twenty-four categories of protected rights. These categories include:

i.   The right to be recognized as a person under the law

ii.   The right to life

iii.   The right to humane treatment

iv.   The right to freedom from slavery

v.   The right to liberty

vi.   The right to a fair trial

vii.   The right to freedom from ex post facto laws

viii.   The right to compensation for a miscarriage of justice

ix.   The right to privacy

x.   The right to free exercise of conscience and religion

xi.   The right to freedom of thought and expression

xii.   The right to reply to inaccurate or offensive statements

xiii.   The right to peaceful assembly

xiv.   The right to freedom of association

xv.   The right to a family and protection of that family

xvi.   The right to a name

xvii.   The right for children to be protected

xviii. The right to nationality

xix.   The right to the use and enjoyment of property

xx.   The right to freedom of movement and residence

xxi.   The right to participate in government

xxii. The right to equal protection under the law

xxiii. The right to judicial protection

The right to life has been interpreted to include *"vida digna"* (dignified life.) *Vida Digna* includes positive duties to provide "minimum living conditions that are compatible with the dignity of the human person," especially for persons at risk. *Yakye Axa Indigenous Community v. Paraguay,* 125 Inter-Am. Ct. H.R. (ser. C.) (2005), para. 162.

The General Assembly of the OAS adopted the Inter-American Democratic Charter, which declares that the peoples of American have a right to democracy and an obligation to promote and defend democracy. The Charter allows the OAS to suspend a state's membership as a result of an "unconstitutional interruption of the democratic order" and may undertake diplomatic measures to support democracy.

A protocol to abolish the death penalty went into effect in 1993. Unlike the Declaration, the American Convention does not include the right to an education or other economic and social rights. Economic and social rights are to be achieved "progressively by legislation or other appropriate means." American Convention on Human Rights, Nov. 22, 1969, Art. 26, 9 I.L.M. 673 (1970). An Additional Protocol on Economic, Social, and Cultural Rights entered into force in 1999.

The duties imposed on countries that ratify the Convention are both enumerated and unenumerated. Article 1 of the Convention states that "The States Parties to this Convention undertake to respect the rights and freedoms recognized herein and to ensure to all persons subject to their jurisdiction the free and full exercise of those rights and freedoms, without any discrimination for reasons of race, color, sex, language, religion, political or other opinion, national or social origin, economic status, birth, or any other social condition." Art. 1(1). In this respect, ratifying States have the affirmative duty to not violate the rights enumerated within the Convention, but also the unenumerated duty to take whatever other unwritten measures are necessary to ensure free and full exercise of those rights.

Article 1(2) defined person to mean "every human being," which therefore limits the Convention to human application, as opposed to Corporate or National entities that might be referred to as "persons."

The requirements undertaken by ratifying countries can be suspended in "time of war, public danger, or other emergency that threatens independence or security." (Art. 27). However, the Convention sets forth certain non-derogable rights that cannot, in any circumstance, be suspended. The non-derogable rights include any discrimination, "on the ground of race, color, sex, language, religion, or social origin." Art. 27(1).

More specifically, Article 27(2) states that: "The foregoing provision does not authorize any suspension of the following articles: Article 3 (Right to Juridical Personality), Article 4 (Right to Life), Article 5 (Right to Humane Treatment),

Article 6 (Freedom from Slavery), Article 9 (Freedom from *Ex Post Facto* Laws), Article 12 (Freedom of Conscience and Religion), Article 17 (Rights of the Family), Article 18 (Right to a Name), Article 19 (Rights of the Child), Article 20 (Right to Nationality), and Article 23 (Right to Participate in Government), or of the judicial guarantees essential for the protection of such rights."

c. Institutions of the Inter-American System

The two organs established under the Convention for the purpose of overseeing State fulfillment of the requirements of the Convention are the Inter-American Commission on Human Rights and the Inter-American Court of Human Rights. Today, the Inter-American Commission on Human Rights and the Inter-American Court of Human Rights, together provide recourse to people who have suffered human rights violations.

d. Inter-American Commission on Human Rights

The Inter-American Commission is an organ of both the OAS and the American Convention on Human Rights. It consists of seven members elected for four year, once renewable terms by the OAS General Assembly to "represent all member countries." The Inter-American Commission complaint system is also available to U.S. residents.

i. Functions Under the OAS Charter

Its principal function under the OAS is to ensure compliance by OAS member states to their obligations under the OAS Charter. Note that states, such as the U.S., which have not ratified the Convention are nevertheless obliged under the Charter to promote human rights. In addition to receiving individual communications, preparing country studies, and reporting on the status of human rights in various states, the Commission may investigate human rights conditions without awaiting formal individual or interstate complaints. The Commission also works on developing and proposing new drafts to be evaluated for inclusion in the OAS body of laws.

ii. Functions Under the Convention

The Commission's principal function under the Convention is to consider charges of violations of the rights guaranteed by the American Convention on Human Rights. The functions are outlined in Article 41 of the Convention, and its authority to act in order to further these functions is outlined in Articles 44–51.

(a) <u>Process of Petition Examination</u>: The commission is entrusted with the authority to act not only on formal, individual petitions, but also on other interstate communications. Arts. 44 and 45. The American Convention differs from other international human rights regimes by making the right of individual petition mandatory and interstate petitions optional. If a state has accepted Convention Membership, then they have also acknowledged the authority of the Commission to inspect any private petitions made against that state. Private groups that may make petitions include, "[a]ny person or group of persons, or any nongovernmental entity legally recognized in one or more member states of the Organization." Art. 44. The situation is different with a complaint of one member state against another member state. In this case, the states must not only have accepted Commission Membership, but must also have specifically accepted the interstate jurisdiction of the Commission. Art. 45. Thus the Commission has authority to deal with individual petitions against any state which has ratified the Convention, but may only consider interstate claims if both states have made a special declaration in addition to ratification of the Convention. For a petition to be admitted into the OAS system, there must be a prima facie case (Art. 47) and the following requirements, outlined in Article 46(1), must be met:

(1)   "that the remedies under domestic law have been pursued and exhausted in accordance with generally recognized principles of international law;

(2)   that the petition or communication is lodged within a period of six months from the date on which the party alleging violation of his rights was notified of the final judgment;

(3)   that the subject of the petition or communication is not pending in another international proceeding for settlement;

(4)   that, in the case of Article 44, the petition contains the name, nationality, profession, domicile, and signature of the person or persons or of the legal representative of the entity lodging the petition." Art. 46 (1)(a)B(d)

However, the above limitations are not applicable in the following conditions, which are outlined in Article 46(2):

(1)   "the domestic legislation of the state concerned does not afford due process of law for the protection of the right or rights that have allegedly been violated;

(2)   the party alleging violation of his rights has been denied access to the remedies under domestic law or has been prevented from exhausting them; or

(3)   there has been unwarranted delay in rendering a final judgment under the aforementioned remedies. Art. 46(2) (a)–(c)."

After deciding which petitions are admissible, the Commission must then begin the process of examining the allegations. To do so, the Commission will request information from the government of the state against which the petition was made. Art. 48(1)(a). If the Commission, after receiving the requested information, decides that there is no ground for the petition, the Commission will order the petition record closed. Art. 48(1)(b). If the investigation proceeds, the Commission may hold hearings, receive oral and written statements, and will also, "place itself at the disposal of the parties concerned with a view to reaching a friendly settlement of the matter on the basis of respect for the human rights recognized in this Convention." Art. 48(1)(f). If a friendly settlement is reached, then the Commission will draw up a report, transmit it to the petitioner and to the State members, and communicate the settlement to the Secretary General of the OAS. Art. 49. If a settlement is not reached, the Commission will still draw up their report containing both findings and conclusions, and will transmit this to the "concerned states." Art. 50(2). Any member of the Commission may attach a separate opinion to the Commission report. Art. 50(1).

The final step in the process is the vote of the Commission in the case of an unresolved dispute, which is outlined in Art. 51: "If, within a period of three months from the date of the transmittal of the report of the Commission to the states concerned, the matter has not either been settled or submitted by the Commission or by the state concerned to the Court and its jurisdiction accepted, the Commission may, by the vote of an absolute majority of its members, set forth its opinion and conclusions concerning the question submitted for its consideration." The Commission then will outline recommendations and set a timeline for the necessary measures to be taken. Art. 51(2).

iii. Remedies Available

The Court can order the payment of damages, ask for a state apology, or request actions to be taken by the state to address the fallout from the breach, but only if the state has granted the Court contentious jurisdiction. The parties may seek enforcement of the ruling in their own state governments as well, in contrast to the European Convention.

e. Inter-American Court of Human Rights

The Commission, in addition to State Parties, has the right to refer cases to the Inter-American Court. Art. 61. In addition, "The Commission shall appear in all cases before the Court." Art. 57. Under Commission rules which took effect in 2001, it must refer all cases to the Court unless the Commission votes otherwise by an absolute majority. The Court is composed of seven judges elected by state parties to the American Convention to six year, once renewable terms. Art. 52, 54. The judges are not elected by the OAS General Assembly, because the Court was not established under the OAS Charter, as was the Commission. Only state parties and the Commission have the right to bring cases before the Court, which has both contentious and advisory jurisdiction. Under the 2001 Commission rules, individuals may appear before the Commission seeking submission to the Court, and under new Court rules may appear in Court on a submitted petition.

i. Contentious Jurisdiction

Under its contentious jurisdiction, the Court has authority to decide claims that a state party violated rights guaranteed by the American Convention. Contentious jurisdiction is optional and cases may be filed by or against only those states which have accepted such jurisdiction. As of 2012, twenty-one of the twenty-four OAS Convention-ratifying states had accepted contentious jurisdiction. Peru attempted to withdraw from contentious jurisdiction in 1999, but the Court found that there was no mechanism for withdrawal from its contentious jurisdiction and that the act was invalid. The Court's contentious jurisdiction is outlined in Article 62 of the Convention:

(a) A State Party may, upon depositing its instrument of ratification or adherence to this Convention, or at any subsequent time, declare that it recognizes as binding, ipso facto, and not requiring special agreement, the jurisdiction of the Court on all matters relating to the interpretation or application of this Convention.

(b) Such declaration may be made unconditionally, on the condition of reciprocity, for a specified period, or for specific cases. It shall be presented to the Secretary General of the organization, who shall transmit copies thereof to the other member states of the organization and to the Secretary of the Court.

(c) The jurisdiction of the Court shall comprise all cases concerning the interpretation and application of the provisions of this Convention that are submitted to it, provided that the States Parties to the case recognize or have recognized such jurisdiction, whether by special declaration pursuant to the preceding paragraphs, or by a special agreement.

The above provisions provide that the contentious jurisdiction of the court is not automatically accepted by the Member States solely because they ratified the Convention. Rather, one of the above three mechanisms must be utilized.

f. The Scope and Power of Contentious Jurisdiction

i. Jurisdiction

"The jurisdiction of the Court shall comprise all cases concerning the interpretation and application of the provisions of this Convention that are submitted to it, provided that the States Parties to the case recognize or have recognized such jurisdiction, whether by special declaration pursuant to the preceding paragraphs, or by a special agreement. Art. 62(3)."

ii. Judgment Rendered

When the Court finds that there has indeed been a violation of the Convention after evaluating preliminary motions, considering the merits of the case, and holding a testimony hearing, the Court will mandate that the injured party be ensured the right of which he/she was deprived.

iii. The Power of the Court Ruling

For each judgment made by the Court, the Court must outline their reasons for that decision. Art. 66(1). However, once the Court has ruled, "[t]he judgment of the Court shall be final and not subject to appeal." Art. 67. Member States must comply with the judgment of the Court. Art. 68.

iv. Enforcement of the Court's Judgments & Court Recommendations

Each year, at the General Assembly meeting of the OAS, the Court reports on the cases they have tried in the previous year, including instances where States have not complied with Convention guidelines, and have also failed to comply with Court orders. The Court then makes their recommendations to the OAS as how to best proceed in these situations. Art. 65.

v. Provisional Measures

Article 63(2) provides "In cases of extreme gravity and urgency, and when necessary to avoid irreparable damage to persons, the Court shall adopt such provisional measures as it deems pertinent in matters it has under consideration. With respect to a case not yet submitted to the Court, it may act at the request of the Commission." In essence, the Convention allows the Court to issue temporary restraining orders in cases of emergency. This is a unique power that has been given to the Court.

g. Advisory Jurisdiction

The Court may request that a state which has not accepted the Court's jurisdiction to do so for a certain situation, but the state is under no obligation to honor the request. The Court's authority is broader under its advisory jurisdiction than under its contentious jurisdiction. It may render opinions interpreting not only the American Convention but also other human rights treaties of the Inter-American regime. This may include human rights provisions in treaties that were not created for the primary purpose of interpreting human rights, and it may also include treaties not limited to the Inter-American system. All OAS member states and all OAS organs may invoke the advisory jurisdiction of the court. Article 64 states:

i.   The member states of the Organization may consult the Court regarding the interpretation of this Convention or of other treaties concerning the protection of human rights in the American states. Within their spheres of competence, the organs listed in Chapter X of the Charter of the Organization of American States, as amended by the Protocol of Buenos Aires, may in like manner consult the Court.

ii. The Court, at the request of a member state of the Organization, may provide that state with opinions regarding the compatibility of any of its domestic laws with the aforesaid international instruments.

iii. The Court has recently interpreted international human rights agreements as evaluated within its own governing documents. In the 2000 case *Las Palmeras v. Columbia*, the Court issued an opinion on how it interpreted the American Convention on Human Rights when considered in tandem with the Geneva Conventions, but did not want to issue an opinion solely based on the Geneva Conventions without the OAS document.

In contrast to the contentious jurisdiction cases, under advisory jurisdiction, the opinion of the Court is not binding.

h. Specific Enforcement Actions of Inter-American Court of Human Rights

The Court interpreted the American Convention's obligations with respect to mentally disabled citizens and found that Brazil violated the Convention by failing to regulate and supervise a private psychiatric clinic, whose "inhuman and degrading hospitalization conditions" led to the death of a thirty-one year-old patient. The Court emphasized the "special attention the States must give to persons with mental disabilities for they are particularly vulnerable." *Ximenes-Lopez v. Brazil*, 2006 Inter-Am. Ct. H.R. (ser. C) No. 149.

In *Moiwana Village v. Suriname*, 2005 Inter-Am. Ct. H.R. (ser. C) No. 124, the Court found Suriname legally responsible for a violation of the American Convention, predicated on a massacre of an N'djuka rainforest community forty years earlier during a period of civil war. The survivors of the community were entitled to material and moral damages and additional forms of reparation for the massacre, their forcible displacement from their traditional homeland, and their subsequent poverty and deprivation.

E. African Regional System—Human Rights Law

The primary source of law is the African Charter on Human and People's Rights, which entered into force in 1986. All fifty-three members of the Organization of African Unity now known as the African Union have thus far ratified the Charter. It guarantees economic, social and cultural rights as well as political and civil rights; it is concerned with the rights of "peoples" as well as individuals; and it proclaims the duties as well as rights of individuals. The emergence of the African human rights system means that many provisions of the Charter have yet to be interpreted and applied. The Charter also differed significantly from the European and American human rights regime, because it *did not provide originally for a human rights court*.

The Charter does establish an African Commission on Human and People's Rights to consider state and individual petitions. In 2008 the African Union passed a protocol creating the African Court of Justice and Human Rights as the primary judicial branch of the AU, merging two earlier entities—the African Court of Justice Rights and the African Court of Justice. AU member states which are parties to the protocol, as well as other African Union organs, are able to submit cases to the Court. Individuals and NGOs may only do so if the member state has granted the Court such jurisdiction. The African Court on Human and People's Rights was established in January 2004. There are eleven judges who are nationals of the member states of the African Union. It hears cases by the AU states, African intergovernmental organizations, and other nongovernmental organizations.

1. The African Court of Justice & Human Rights

In 2008 the African Union passed a protocol creating the African Court of Justice and Human Rights as the primary judicial branch of the AU, merging two earlier entities—the African Court of Justice Rights and the African Court of Justice. AU member states which are parties to the protocol, as well as other African Union organs, are able to submit cases to the Court. Individuals and NGOs may only do so if the member state has granted the Court such jurisdiction. The African Court on Human and People's Rights was established in 2004 thirty days after fifteen states ratified the protocol. Notably, there is no appellate review. Robert Gaudet, Jr., *Human Rights*, 43 INT'L LAW. 861, 870 (2009).

On December 15, 2009 the African Court on Human and Peoples' Rights (sitting in Tanzania) rendered its first-ever judgment, concerning the extradition of former Chadian president Hissein Habre by Michelor Yogogombaye. The court still has significant weaknesses; individuals and NGO's are only able to bring direct complaints against governments after convincing the court to exercise its discretion to hear the case and showing that the relevant state had filed a declaration accepting the court's jurisdiction. Problematically, as of 2010, only Burkina Faso and Malawi have filed such declarations.

2. The African Commission on Human & People's Rights

The African Commission on Human and People's Rights has eleven members with a maximum of one per member state. It evaluates how member states are following human rights laws through a report process. Timely and non-redundant individual petitions can be accepted once all local remedies have been used.

F. Emerging Regional Systems

The Arab world and southeast Asia do not have the human rights systems available to those living in Europe, the Americas, and now Africa. Arab nations have moved closer to creating one by establishing the Arab Charter on Human Rights and the League of Arab States' Human Rights Commission. Southeast Asia is further behind, but the Association of Southeast Asian Nations (ASEAN) in 2007 formed the ASEAN Human Rights Commission and created the ASEAN Charter of Human Rights.

Other Asian attempts at a core human rights document include the Asian Human Rights Charter, put forward by the Asian Human Rights Commission, and the Pacific Charter on Human Rights.

1. Asian System

The Association of Southeast Asian Nations (ASEAN) is made up of ten member states: Brunei, Cambodia, Indonesia, Laos, Malaysia, Myanmar, Philippines, Singapore, Thailand, and Vietnam.

ASEAN established the ASEAN Intergovernmental Commission on Human Rights in 2009 and adopted the in November 2012. The Declaration was welcomed by many, but it has also faced criticism for language that limits or qualifies important rights, including concern from the U.S. Department of State. The State Department issued a statement, noting that the Universal Declaration on Human Rights (UDHR) lays out universal principles of human rights and establishes a minimum baseline for the protection of human rights. While regional declarations can be useful to reinforce human rights commitments and obligations, there is concern "that many of the ASEAN Declaration's principles and articles could weaken and erode universal human rights and fundamental freedoms as contained in the UDHR." U.S. Dep't of State Press Release No. 2012/1826, ASEAN Declaration on Human Rights (Nov. 20, 2012), https://2009-2017.state.gov/r/pa/prs/ps/2012/11/200915.htm. The U.S. State Department urged ASEAN to take steps to revise the Declaration through a process involving civil society, bringing the document in line with UDHR and ICCPR standards. Major concerns about the ASEAN Declaration include cultural relativism, since universal human rights are not subject to regional or national limitation; the role of domestic law and international rights, as universal human rights are not subordinate to domestic law and making them so would depart from 50 years of established international practice of human rights; novel limits to rights, as the ASEAN Declaration seeks to introduce illegitimate limitations on universal rights, claiming that some must be balanced against an individual's duties—a notion that undermines the very values that the Declaration purports to uphold in affirming its commitment to international human rights instruments; and the notion that individual rights could be subject to group veto, as the Declaration notes that rights can be held by both "persons" and by "peoples." Similarly, the UN High Commissioner for Human Rights welcomed the renewed commitment and noted that other regions have demonstrated how regional systems can evolve and improve over time. She also, however, expressed concern that the Declaration retains language inconsistent with international standards.

Chapter IX

Humanitarian Intervention by the UN

A. Historic Development of the Security Council

1. Background

a. Council Organization

The Security Council was first established in 1945 in the Charter of the United Nations as one of the five major organs of the UN.

i. The Council has fifteen members, five permanent members and ten elected by the General Assembly. The permanent members are the United States, China, France, the Russian Federation, and the United Kingdom.

ii. According to Article 28, the Security Council is organized so that it functions continuously, and its members must be represented at all times at UN Headquarters.

iii. Presidency of the Council

    (a) The presidency rotates monthly, in an English alphabetical rotation of member States.

b. Council Responsibility

i. Chapter VII of the UN Charter sets forth the authority of the Security Council to act with respect to "threat[s] to the peace, breach[es] of the peace, or act[s] of aggression." UN Charter Art. 39. These critical terms are not defined in the Charter. If the Security Council finds that such circumstances exist, it may take enforcement action in accordance with Articles 41 and 42 of the Charter in order to "maintain or restore international peace and security."

ii. In fulfilling this responsibility with respect to human rights, the Security Council must balance the conflicting goals of respecting state sovereignty and promoting fundamental human rights.

(a) Respecting state sovereignty: Article 2(4) of the UN Charter addresses the need to protect state sovereignty by limiting the use of force in international conflicts. Article 2(4) provides that: "All members shall refrain in their international relations from the threat or use of force against the territorial integrity or political independence of any state or in any other manner inconsistent with the Purposes of the United Nations."

(b) Promoting Human Rights: Chapter VII of the UN Charter provides exceptions to Article 2(4) and exceptions to the prohibition against the use of force. Article 42 authorizes the Security Council to take "action by air, sea, or land forces as may be necessary to maintain or restore international peace and security."

c. Request for Consideration of a Dispute

i. Article 35(1) states that "[a]ny member of the United Nations may bring any dispute, or any situation of the nature referred to in Article 34, to the attention of the Security Council or of the General Assembly."

ii. Article 35(2) states that "[a] state which is not a Member of the United Nations may bring to the attention of the Security Council or of the General Assembly any dispute to which it is a party if it accepts in advance, for the purposes of the dispute, the obligations of pacific settlement provided in the present Charter."

iii. The Security Council has the discretion to deny the request or accede to it by placing the dispute on its agenda. Once on the agenda, only the Security Council may remove it.

d. Unique Power of Security Council

i. Under the Charter, all Members of the UN agree to accept and carry out the binding decisions of the Security Council. Art. 25. While other organs of the UN make recommendations to the Council, the Council alone has the power to take binding decisions which Member States are obligated under the Charter to carry out.

B. Chapter VI: Pacific Settlement of Disputes

1. When a dispute is brought before the Security Council, the first step the Council takes is to seek a peaceful means of reconciliation.

   a. "The parties to any dispute, the continuance of which is likely to endanger the maintenance of international peace and security shall, first of all, seek a solution by negotiation, enquiry, mediation, conciliation, arbitration, judicial settlement, resort to regional agencies or arrangements, or other peaceful means of their own choice." Art. 33(1).

   b. The Security Council may itself undertake the mediation process, may appoint mediators, or may ask the Secretary General to appoint special representatives as a matter of **preventive diplomacy**.

      i. Preventive Diplomacy is an effort to deal with potential conflict situations before they explode into crisis. One of the ways the UN engages in this type of activity is through the good offices of UN personnel, especially the Secretary-General.

> **Example:** The UN has been able to provide useful mediation on occasion, as in the Congo, Zaire, and Angola. Special representatives have also headed larger operations authorized under Chapter VI, involving responsibility for large scale government transitions as in Mozambique (ONUMOZ), Cambodia (UNTAC), Namibia (UNTAG), Western Sahara (MINURSO), and elsewhere.

C. Chapter VII: Action with Respect to Threats to the Peace, Breaches of the Peace, and Acts of Aggression

1. An Alternative When Pacific Settlement Is Ineffective

a. Aware of the limits to pacific settlement and of the failure of 'automatic sanctions' during the League of Nations, the drafters of the UN Charter gave the Security Council powerful means to counter aggression and threats to peace. Chapter VII of the Charter authorizes the Security Council to go beyond recommendations and to make binding decisions which may ultimately involve the use of armed force. In order to do so, the Council must first determine that a threat to peace, breach of the peace, or act of aggression has occurred. (Art. 39). That finding implies that subsequent Council decisions have the quality of a legal obligation. Should the Security Council consider that peaceful measures "would be inadequate, or have proved to be inadequate, it may take such action by air, sea, or land forces as may be necessary to maintain or restore international peace and security. Such action may include demonstrations, blockades, and other operations by air, sea or land forces of Members of the United Nations." Art. 42. It should be noted that the Security Council is not required to take peaceful measures under Article 41 before proceeding under Article 42; the Security Council need only find that peaceful measures would be inadequate.

2. Definition of Aggression

The General Assembly Resolution Definition of Aggression is a clarification of the UN Security Council's jurisdiction over "any threat to the peace, breach of peace, or act of aggression." Article 1 defines aggression as the "use of armed force by a State against the sovereignty, territorial integrity, or political independence of another State, or in any other matter inconsistent with the Charter of the United Nations. . . ." Article 2 provides that the first use of armed force by a state in contravention of the UN Charter is prima facie evidence of an act of aggression, defined in Article 3 to include the invasion of armed forces of another state. Article 3 lists acts that qualify as acts of aggression, and includes the sending of armed bands to carry out acts of armed force against a state of sufficient gravity to be tantamount to an invasion or attack against the state itself. Finally, Article 5 adopts the Nuremberg Principles, which make armed aggression a "crime against peace," and prohibit territorial acquisition by virtue of such aggression.

3. Provisions of Forces for Enforcement

Article 43 provides that a state is not required to take part in military operations authorized under Article 42 unless it has concluded a special agreement with the UN.

At this time, no such agreements have been concluded. However, Article 43 generally is not considered to prohibit the Security Council from assembling military forces by other means. The Security Council may not order states actually to take part in military operations, but it can authorize them to do so.

4. Humanitarian Intervention Under Chapter VII

During the Cold War, the Security Council did not utilize Chapter VII for humanitarian intervention. After the Cold War, however, the UN gradually adopted Chapter VII to provide the legal basis for humanitarian intervention. The key issue is how broadly the term "threat to peace" can be construed to include dire humanitarian crises which do not involve or realistically pose a threat of violence.

5. Specific Enforcement Actions Under Chapter VII

a. Kurds

i. After the defeat of Iraq's army by the coalition forces in February of 1991, Saddam Hussein's military forces began to stage attacks on the civilian populations in northern and southern Iraq in order to quell uprisings against his regime. The Kurds of northern Iraq had been seeking autonomy in the region for decades. In 1988, the Kurds had been attacked with chemical weapons by Saddam's regime. The severity of the attacks led nearly two million Kurds to leave the region, fleeing into Turkey and Iran.

(a) On April 5, 1991, at the initiation of Turkey and France, the Security Council adopted Resolution 688 which "condemned the repression of the Iraqi civilian population" and demanded that Iraq . . . "immediately end this repression" . . . What became known as 'Safe Havens' operation began with the deployment of unarmed guards on May 19, 1991 and the addition of armed guards on May 20, 1991. These forces began to build camps for the Kurds so that they would return from the mountains of northern Iraq.

(b) Controversy Over the Resolution 688: Yemen and China argued that the intervention based on humanitarian grounds contravened Article 2(7) and would lead to a 'dangerous precedent." Supporters of the resolution pointed to the threat to international peace and security from mass exodus of refugees into other states and the humanitarian nature of the operation. Although there is no mention of Chapter VII in the resolution, the use of the word "demand" in reference to terminating repression indicates that the Security Council was acting pursuant to its decision making authority under Chapter VII. The resolution allowed the relief operation without the consent of Iraq.

(c) The groundbreaking effect of UNSC 688: The resolution had an exclusively humanitarian objective in its insistence on an immediate end to repression of the Kurdish population of Iraq by the Iraqi government. It led to the establishment of 'safe havens' in northern Iraq to allow Kurdish exiles to return to Iraq under international protection. For the first time, the Security Council had clearly linked humanitarian concerns to international peace and security.

b. Somalia

The overthrow of President Said Barre in January of 1991 by combating rival factions, and the lack of an effective government in Somalia, led to a UN authorized humanitarian relief effort. Civil war in Somalia prevented the transport of food and humanitarian aid to millions of starving Somalis. By January of 1992, the situation had deteriorated to such a degree that the Security Council unanimously enacted a weapon embargo on the country. The Security Council sent a team to observe the administration of humanitarian aid and deployed fifty UN observers through the creation of the United Nations Operation in Somalia or UNOSOM. By the summer of 1992, invoking Chapter VII of the UN Charter, the Security Council increased the troop levels of the UNOSOM peacekeepers and approved the transport of humanitarian aid through airlifts.

Citing violence against relief workers, the Secretary General, Boutros Boutros-Ghali, called upon the Security Council to take action under Article 42 of the Charter. In November 1992, after the United States offered to lead a military operation in order to deliver humanitarian aid to Somalis, the Security Council unanimously adopted Resolution 794. The resolution "authorized the Secretary-General and Member States cooperating to . . . use all necessary means to establish as soon as possible a secure environment for humanitarian relief operations in Somalia. . . ." The legal basis under Chapter VII was an Article 39 determination that the humanitarian situation in Somalia and the continuing civil war constituted a threat to international peace and security. Note that Somalia was without a government fully able to consent to the UN sponsored intervention due to the civil war.

c. Bosnian "No-Fly Zones"

i. Background

The Security Council Resolution referred in part to "blatant violations of the ban on military fights in the airspace of the Republic of Bosnia and Herzegovina and recalling in this regard the . . . reference to the bombing of villages in the Republic of Bosnia and Herzegovina."

ii. Call to Action

The broad call for action to member states within the Resolution authorized "[m]ember states . . . acting nationally or through regional organizations or arrangements, to take . . . all necessary measures in the airspace of the Republic of Bosnia and Herzegovina, in the event of further violations, to ensure compliance with the ban on flights . . . and proportionate to the specific circumstances and the nature of the flights." UNSC 816.

d. Rwanda

i. Situation

Approximately 800,000 people were killed during the 1994 genocide in Rwanda, including men, women, and children. Despite this massive human rights violation, the UN, and the international community as a whole, failed to act, prompting an intense investigation into how such events could be prevented in the future.

(a) In the UN *Report of the Independent Inquiry into the Actions of the United Nations During the 1994 Genocide in Rwanda (December 15, 1999)* the committee wrote that, "The international community did not prevent the genocide, nor did it stop the killing once the genocide had begun. This failure has left deep wounds within Rwandan society, and in the relationship between Rwanda and the international community, in particular the United Nations. These are wounds which need to be healed, for the sake of the people of Rwanda and for the sake of the United Nations. Establishing the truth is necessary for Rwanda, for the United Nations and also for all those, wherever they may live, who are at risk of becoming victims of genocide in the future."

ii.   Criticism of Inaction

One of the key systematic failures of the UN that was addressed in the UN Report, as well as by other commentators, was the role Rwanda played on the Security Council during the crisis.

e.   Haiti

i.   Situation

The UN was called to intervene in Haiti due to the reluctance of the Haitian military junta to restore power to the democratically elected government of President Jean-Bertrand Aristide.

(a) In the Security Council resolution, the Council outlines their motivation in part due to "the continuing escalation by the illegal de facto regime of systematic violations of civil liberties, the desperate plight of Haitian refugees and the recent expulsion of the staff of the International Civilian Mission (MICIVIH) . . . "

ii.   Call to Action

(a) General Assembly: On October 11, 1991, the UN General Assembly adopted resolution 46/7, condemning the illegal replacement of the President of Haiti, the use of violence and military coercion, and the violation of human rights. The General Assembly affirmed as unacceptable any entity resulting from that illegal situation; demanded the immediate restoration of the legitimate Government of President Aristide, and the full observance of human rights in Haiti.

(b) Security Council: On July 31, 1994, the Security Council, acting under Chapter VII, adopted resolution 940. The Council authorized Member States to "form a multinational force under unified command and control and, in this framework, to use all necessary means to facilitate the departure from Haiti of the military leadership, . . . the prompt return of the legitimately elected President, and the restoration of the legitimate authorities of the Government of Haiti . . . " (UNSC 940)

iii. Multinational Force

Under the terms of the resolution, the multinational force would terminate its mission and an expanded, strengthened UNMIH would "assume the full range of its functions when a secure and stable environment had been established . . . and UNMIH has adequate force capability and structure to assume the full range of its functions." That determination would be made by the Council, on the basis of recommendations from Member States participating in the multinational force and from the Secretary-General. (UNSC 940)

Note: How a government assumes power, even if by force, is ordinarily not a matter of international law absent human rights violations. In part, the Security Council's action may be attributed to the fact that Aristide was elected in a UN sponsored election.

f. The International Tribunals for the Former Yugoslavia (ICTY) & Rwanda (ICTR)

The Security Council, acting under Chapter VII, established both of these tribunals with jurisdiction over the international criminal offenses of crimes against humanity, genocide, and the most serious of war crimes. The ICTR was expected to complete its work, including all trials and appeals by 2010, but as of 2011 had not done so. The Tribunals are examples of the broad discretion the Council has in authorizing action short of the use of armed force when the necessary conditions for Chapter VII enforcement action have been found. The legality of the ICTY was upheld under Chapter VII in *Prosecutor v. Tadic*, No. IT–94–1–AR72 (Oct. 2, 1995), *reprinted in* 35 I.L.M. 32 (1996).

Note: Unlike the ICC, these tribunals have primary jurisdiction which allows them to proceed regardless of whether a state proceeding was initiated. Notice also that the offenses covered by the Rwanda statute are limited to those occurring during a non-international conflict.

The ICTR appeals chamber ruled that media leaders can be liable for inciting genocide and persecution through their acts in *The Media Case*. Catharine A. MacKinnon, *International Decisions: Prosecutor v. Nahimana, Barayagwiza, & Ngeze. Case No. ICTR 99–52*, 103 AM. J. OF INT'L L. 97, 97–99 (2009). The media must "contribut[ ] substantially to the commission of the crime but [it] need not be a *sine qua non* condition for its commission." *Id.* at 99. The appeals chamber upheld the convictions of three media leaders for crimes of speech in the 1994 Rwandan genocide. *Id.* at 97.

g. Sudan

i. Background

Beginning in 2003, the government of Sudan began arming, training, and assisting local Arab militias, known as the Janjaweed. The Janjaweed proceeded to target minority African tribes in the Darfur region of Sudan, clearly committing war crimes and crimes against humanity.

ii. Question of Genocide

(a) In the UN *Report of the International Commission of Inquiry on Darfur to the United Nations Secretary-General* (January 31, 2005), the Commission concluded that although there had been mass murders and rapes of civilians in Darfur, they could not classify the situation as genocide because the government lacked genocidal intent.

(b) Despite a peace agreement brokered in mid-2006 between the government of Sudan and one faction of the Sudan Liberation Movement, the situation in Sudan continued to grow worse.

iii. Call to Action

Beginning in 2004, a small peacekeeping force (AMIS) operated in Sudan under the direction of the African Union. UN Security Council Resolution 1706, adopted August 31, 2006, was aimed at strengthening AMIS's efforts by establishing a joint African Union—United Nations Hybrid Mission (UNAMID) in Darfur.

iv. Sudan and the International Criminal Court

In March 2005, the Security Council issued Resolution 1593, referring the violence in the Darfur region to the International Criminal Court. This marks the Security Council's first referral to the ICC. In May 2007, the ICC issued its first arrest warrants for persons wanted in connection with the violence in Darfur.

h. Ad Hoc International Criminal Tribunals

Although an international tribunal would ordinarily be established by treaty, in order to save time and ensure all UN Member States are bound by its decisions, in the 1990s the Security Council acted under Chapter VII in establishing the International Criminal Tribunal for the former Yugoslavia (ICTY) and the International Criminal Tribunal for Rwanda (ICTR). The legality of the ICTY was upheld under Chapter VII in *Prosecutor v. Tadic*, No. IT–94–1–AR72 (Oct. 2, 1995), *reprinted in* 35 I.L.M. 32 (1996). After 2000, the Security Council continued to act under Chapter VII in establishing the Special Court for Sierra Leone, the Cambodian Tribunal on the Khmer Rouge, and the Special Tribunal for Lebanon. In general, such tribunals have had jurisdiction over the international criminal offenses of crimes against humanity, genocide, and the most serious of war crimes.

In December 2010 the U.S. supported adoption of Resolution 1966. This Resolution establishes a new institution, the International Residual Mechanism for Criminal Tribunals, through which to complete the work done by the ICTR and ICTY. The Resolution was passed with fourteen votes. Russia abstained from the voting. The Resolution urges the ICTY and the ICTR to complete their work by December 2014 and to ensure a smooth transition. In addition, the Resolution recalls the obligation of the States to cooperate with the Tribunals and the Mechanism, and sets an operation period for the Mechanism for four years from the commencement date. John R. Crook ed., *Contemporary Practice of the United States: United States Supports New Mechanism to Conclude Work of UN Criminal Tribunal for Rwanda and the Former Yugoslavia*, 105 AM. J. OF INT'L L. 354, 354–56.

Chapter X

Humanitarian Intervention by States

Are humanitarian concerns justification for state intervention? Some scholars argue that military actions undertaken for humanitarian purposes by states in response to gross violations of human rights are permissible under a narrow reading of Article 2(4).

A. Pro-Interventionist

Under a narrow reading of UN Charter Article 2(4), collective or individual humanitarian intervention is defended as, not being a force *directed against* the territorial integrity or political independence of the state concerned. It has also been argued that the UN Charter did not totally displace the legally accepted grounds for intervention prior to the Charter, leading to a mostly historical debate over the instances and legal recognition of humanitarian intervention prior to 1945.

B. Anti-Interventionist

This view is predicated on the Charter reflecting the only presently recognized legal grounds for the use of force, and that none of the narrow exceptions for the use of force include humanitarian intervention. Armed intervention in the territory of a state is necessarily force against the state's territorial integrity and political independence.

Although scholars differ as to legitimacy of humanitarian intervention, it is generally agreed that a state or states using force would have to act from humanitarian motives (not "against the territorial integrity or indecence" of the target state), act proportionally, and cease military operations as soon as the humanitarian objective was achieved. Opponents argue that the use of force is inherently disproportionate.

1. Federal Republic of Yugoslavia-Kosovo

The UN Security Council resolution was in response to the "excessive and indiscriminate use of force by Serbian security forces and the Yugoslav Army" which resulted in civilian casualties and, according to the estimate of the Secretary-General, "the displacement of over 230,000 persons from their homes." UNSC 1199.

2.   Call to Action

Unlike resolutions regarding Kuwait, Somalia, Haiti, and Bosnia, the UN did not authorize the use of armed forces in any of their resolutions. Rather, the Security Council affirmed the need for state sovereignty by stating that this resolution "reaffirmed the commitment of all Member States to the sovereignty and territorial integrity of the Federal Republic of Yugoslavia." UNSC 1199. Despite the fact there was no threat of force, the Security Council did call for a ceasefire in accordance with Chapter VII. UNSC 1199.

3.   NATO Bombing

After NATO began their bombing raids on Kosovo, the Security Council authorized "Member States and relevant international organizations to establish the international security presence in Kosovo . . ." In so doing, the United Nations did nothing to prevent future use of force against the Former Republic of Yugoslavia. UNSC 1244.

4.   International Criticism

The action, or inaction of the UN in the Kosovo situation, particularly the Security Council's handling of the NATO bombings, was met with great criticism. The effects of this criticism may be a reevaluation of the scope of humanitarian intervention. Kosovo faces the difficult task of approaching the legality of its declaration of independence from Serbia in 2008, which the ICJ was to consider in the form of a nonbinding advisory opinion in 2009. ("Indisputably, the NATO intervention through its bombing campaign violated the UN Charter and international law. As a result, the intervention risked destabilizing the international rule of law that prohibits a state or group of states from intervening by the use of force in another state, absent authorization by the UN Security Council or a situation of self-defense. The NATO actions, regardless of how well intentioned, constitute an unfortunate precedent for states to use force to suppress the commission of international crimes in other states grounds that easily can be and have been abused to justify intervention for less laudable objectives. As now conceived, the so called doctrine of humanitarian intervention can lead to an escalation of international violence, discord, and disorder and diminish protections of human rights worldwide." Jonathan Charney, *Anticipatory Humanitarian Intervention in Kosovo*, 32 VANDERBILT J. OF TRANSNATIONAL LAW, 1231, 1232 (1999).

5.   Kosovo Mission

On February 4, 2008, the Council of the European Union adopted a joint action creating the European Union Rule of Law Mission in Kosovo (EULEX). Erika de Wet, *The Governance of Kosovo: Security Council Resolution 1244 and the Establishment and Functioning of EULEX*, 103 AM. J. OF INT'L L. 83 (2009). EULEX was mainly legalized on November 26, 2008 when the Security Council endorsed the UN Mission in Kosovo (UNMIK) through the adoption of a Presidential Statement. *Id.* at 89. The European organization is supported by the United States which agreed to pay 25 percent of operating costs. *Id.* at 83. EULEX was originally created for two years. *Id.* at 93.

Since UNMIK was still in place when EULEX was created, there was controversy over whether the creation of EULEX could be allowed under Resolution 1244. *Id.* at 84. Russia argued that EULEX was not rooted in Resolution 1244 like the EU member states and the United States said it was. *Id.* at 85.

EULEX's actions must be consistent with UNMIK's responsibilities and UNMIK's power in the area of rule of law. *Id.* at 91. When EULEX was created, the UN limited its international responsibility and placed this operation's responsibility on the European Union. This was a result of the *Behrami* case in which the European Court of Human Rights said that international responsibility could be placed on the UN for EULEX's actions because of the Security Council's control and Resolution 1244. *Id.* at 94–95. However, the court continued in its reasoning to conclude that member states of the NATO Kosovo Force should first take responsibility for human rights violations because of their effective control when the violations took place.

6. The Sudan

The Sudan faces a humanitarian crisis in the Darfur region as of 2012. Alleged violations of the International Covenant on Civil and Political Rights and the Convention on the Rights of the Child due to the civil war in that area have resulted in calls for humanitarian intervention by the international community. In 2008, the International Criminal Court indicted Sudanese President Omar al-Bashir for war crimes and crimes against humanity, the first one against a current president; in 2009, an arrest warrant was issued.

C. The World Bank & Human Rights

1. The World Bank does not have an "operational policy on human rights," which means human rights are not considered in the everyday work of the Bank. Human rights have been supported in reports and speeches from the World Bank but there is no mention of human rights in policy, provisions, or safeguards in programs. Galit A. Sarfaty, *Why Culture Matters in International Institutions: The Marginality of Human Rights at the World Bank*, 103 AM. J. OF INT'L L. 647, 648 (2009). The Bank's "private-sector arm," the International Finance Corporation, has considered human rights when managing risk but it has also been selective when determining which human rights are considered, which has led to criticism from nongovernmental organizations. *Id.* at 649.

2. One of the main reasons why a World Bank human rights policy has not been created is that countries disagree on the approach that should be taken because of the diversity of the organization. *Id.* at 656. An alternative to using the board to make changes has been to make small changes in operations. *Id.* Many scholars argue that although the Bank is an international body operating under its Articles, it has obligations under customary international law. *Id.* at 657.

   The Bank is also a special agency of the UN and must respect the UN Charter including Article 55 and the UN Security Council decisions. *Id.* at 658. However, the Bank is not required to follow UN human rights agencies' decisions and recommendations. *Id.*

3. In 2006, General Counsel Dañino presented his staff with "Legal Opinion on Human Rights and the Work of the World Bank" in which he said human rights violations should be considered when the Bank makes decisions. *Id.* at 663. This opinion removed some of the "legal restrictions in the Articles of Agreement" but its effect was limited because its legal status was disputed and it was uncertain whether the opinion was "official." *Id.* at 665. Senior bank management, not the board, asked the general counsel for an opinion on human rights and Dañino bypassed the board when presenting the opinion because of the board's conflicting opinions over human rights issues and the Bank's involvement. *Id.*

The executive directors decide the Articles' interpretation and general counsel provides guidance but there is no policy for opinions which are not approved by the board but written as guidance from a general counsel on his departure. *Id.* at 666.

4.   The Nordic Trust Fund (originally the Justice and Human Rights Trust Fund) was put into effect in 2009. The purpose of the fund is to "provide effective support" and "include human rights considerations in the analytical and operational activities of the World Bank Group." *Id.* at 678–79. The fund is managed by the Bank's Operations Policy and Country Services.

Chapter XI

The Humanitarian Law of Armed Conflict

The humanitarian law of armed conflict attempts to place limitations upon the conduct of warfare in order to prevent unnecessary suffering of civilians and combatants. It applies to international armed conflict and, to a more limited degree, internal conflicts or civil wars.

A. Sources of the Law of Armed Conflict

Customary law and international treaties are the primary sources of armed conflict law. Many treaties, including the Hague and the four Geneva Conventions, reflect or have evolved into customary law. Whether a treaty reflects custom becomes very important when the treaty limits its coverage to certain conflicts or parties to a conflict.

1. Customary Law

The humanitarian laws of war were articulated by some of the earliest scholars such as Grotius and de Vattel, among others. Many of the principles laid down by these scholars have entered into customary international law are the foundation of the landmark treaties of the 20th century.

2. International Treaties

Many international treaties regulate the conduct of warfare. Among the most important of these treaties still in force are:

a. The Hague Conventions and Declarations of 1907, especially the Convention Respecting the Law and Customs of War on Land (Hague Convention IV), with Annex of Regulations (referred to as the Hague regulations);

b. The Nuremberg Charter of 1945, the inter allies agreement for the prosecution and punishment of Nazi leaders;

c. The Geneva Conventions of 1949:

    i. Convention for the Amelioration of the Condition of the Wounded and Sick in Armed Forces in the Field;

ii. Convention for the Amelioration of the Condition of Wounded, Sick and Shipwrecked Members of Armed Forces at Sea;

iii. Convention Relative to the Treatment of Prisoners of War;

iv. Convention Relative to the Protection of Civilian Persons in Time of War;

d. The Protocols Additional Of 1977:

i. Protocol Additional to the Geneva Conventions of August 12, 1949, and Relating to the Protection of Victims of International Armed Conflicts;

ii. Protocol Additional to the Geneva Conventions of August 12, 1949, and Relating to the Protection of Victims of Non international Armed Conflicts.

B. Protections Provided by the Hague and Geneva Conventions

Certain protections are provided to specific categories of people and property.

1. Protection of the Individual

The degree of protection the laws of armed conflict extend to any given individual depends largely upon that individual's characterization under the Hague and Geneva Conventions and the Additional Protocols.

a. Protections Extended to Combatants

The primary sources of protection to combatants are the Annex to Hague Convention IV of 1907 and the first three Geneva Conventions. Under the laws of armed conflict, a combatant is *any individual legally entitled to take part in hostilities*. Combatants include not only members of the armed forces of a state involved in a conflict, but also citizens who rise in a levee in masse and members of organized resistance groups who fulfill the criteria of being commanded by a responsible superior, wearing some type of uniform, carrying arms openly, and obeying the laws and customs of war. Third Geneva Convention. Under the laws of armed conflict, a combatant is *subject to attack at any time*. The protections extended to active combatants are minimal; in general, the only protections consist of the limitations on weapons and tactics. The laws of armed conflict also extend certain additional protections against attack to medical personnel, clergy, and the like.

b. Protections Extended to Wounded, Sick and Shipwrecked Combatants

While an active combatant is accorded minimal protection, a combatant who is wounded, sick, or who has surrendered is accorded *considerable protection* under international law; they may not be subjected to further attack. The primary sources of protection to these individuals are the Hague Convention IV, the Geneva Convention for the Amelioration of the Condition of the Wounded and Sick in Armed Forces in the Field, and the Geneva Convention for the Amelioration of the Condition of Wounded, Sick and Shipwrecked Members of Armed Forces at Sea. An individual who is injured or sick is not only protected from further attack but *must be provided with medical care*. Information about the wounded individuals must be forwarded to the central prisoner of war information agency.

c. Protections Extended to Prisoners of War

Any lawful combatant who falls into the hands of the enemy is entitled to prisoner of war status. These protections are extended *whether or not the detaining power recognizes the authority of the organization or group which they represent*. The primary source of international law relating to the treatment of POWs is the 1949 Geneva Convention Relative to the Treatment of Prisoners of War. Essentially, the Convention provides for the *humane and decent treatment* of POWs and expressly forbids torture, biological experimentation, and other invasions of personal dignity. POWs may be used as a labor force, but noncommissioned officers may only be employed in supervisory roles and commissioned officers cannot be forced to work at all. If POWs are employed as a labor force, they must be compensated, the tasks may not be unhealthy or unreasonably dangerous, and due regard must be given to their physical capabilities. POWs are subject to the disciplinary regulations of the detaining power and may be tried, within limits set forth in the Convention, for violations of such regulations. The protecting power may oversee all trials and punishments. During a conflict, POWs must be repatriated if they have suffered substantial mental or physical impairment or if they need medical attention which will last more than one year. Upon the conclusion of active hostilities, all POWs must be released and repatriated without delay.

d. Protections Extended to Civilians

In the nineteenth century, the protection of civilians was not a major concern of the laws of war. The Hague Convention provided protection to some civilians and undefended areas. With the advent of the concept of total war, (involvement of both the military and civilian populace in the conflict) in World War II, and developments in military technology, the protection of civilians became a prime concern.

This concern is reflected in the fourth Geneva Convention of 1949, the Convention Relative to the Protection of Civilian Persons in Time of War. This Convention protects civilians both during active hostilities and during time of enemy occupation of a state by providing for the creation of various protected zones in which hostilities may not be carried out. An occupying power may take security measures, but torture, murder, corporal punishment, and the like are prohibited, as are collective punishments and hostage taking. While internment of civilians is permitted, the Convention required that internees be provided treatment which roughly corresponds to that of POWs. Perhaps most importantly, while an occupying power may set up a government, the rights of the people under occupation are delineated.

The Ottawa Convention, finalized in 1997, continued to reflect this concern for civilians by requiring the discontinuance of all landmine use, the cessation of the development and acquisition of landmines, the destruction of all landmines in a state party's possession or control, and abstention from aiding other actors' development or use of landmines. The U.S. is not a party to the Ottawa Convention, but the treaty has widespread international support, with 164 states parties. The Obama administration promulgated a previous U.S. policy limiting the use of landmines, concluding that any military advantage generated by use of landmines was outweighed by the harm to civilians that these instruments of war have the potential to cause. In contrast, the Trump administration, in January 2020, moved the U.S. further away from alignment with the Ottawa Convention, allowing the universal use of "non-persistent" landmines, i.e., those that have self-destruction mechanisms and self-deactivation features. Previously, the use of such landmines had only been permitted on the Korean peninsula.

2. Protection of Property

As with individuals, the degree of protection extended to any particular piece of property depends largely upon its nature. As a general rule under both the Hague Conventions of 1907 and the Geneva Conventions of 1949, the destruction or confiscation of enemy property is forbidden except for situations of military necessity. In no event is looting of enemy property permissible, although enemy military equipment may be seized as war trophies.

a. Military Installations

All military installations, including industries and facilities which directly contribute to the war effort, are *subject to attack*. Article 26 of the Annex to Hague Convention IV provided that the commander of attacking forces must attempt to notify the enemy before such an attack. While often impracticable, this rule still applies, especially if civilians may be at risk.

b. The Civilian Populace

The 1907 Hague Conventions provided that undefended buildings, towns, and the like were *not to be attacked*. However, with the increasing involvement between civilian personnel and military industries, this provision is becoming increasingly difficult to enforce or obey.

c. Areas with Special Protection

The 1949 Geneva Conventions extended special protections to *medical facilities* (both military and civilian) and provided for the establishment of hospital, neutralized, and safety zones in which attacks are forbidden. *Works of art* are also entitled to special protection from attack under both the Annex to Hague Conventions IV and the 1954 Hague Convention on the Protection of Cultural Property in the Event of an Armed Conflict.

Cultural property includes both movable and immovable property having special cultural significance. The United States ratified the Hague Convention in 2008, excepting four understandings and one declaration. As of 2011, 123 states were parties to the Convention.

C. Conflicts Encompassed by the Geneva Conventions & Protocols

Which provisions of the Geneva Conventions and protocols apply depends upon whether the conflict is an international conflict, non-international conflict or a war of self-determination.

1. International Conflicts

Under common Article 2, the Geneva Conventions in their entirety apply to *international conflicts*. Protocol I of 1977 also applies to international conflicts and "wars of national liberation."

2. Civil Wars

For "armed conflict not of an international character" only common Article 3 of the Geneva Conventions applies. The protection it provides is general and *much more limited* than the protection provided in international conflicts. Article 3 requires all parties to the conflict to treat humanely "persons taking no active part in the hostilities, members of armed forces who have laid down their arms and those placed *hors de combat* by sickness, wounds, detention, or any other cause"

Discrimination on the basis of race, color, religion or faith, sex, birth or wealth, or similar criteria is prohibited. Specifically prohibited are:

a. Violence to life and person, in particular murder of all kinds, mutilation, cruel treatment and torture

b. Taking of hostages

c. Outrages upon personal dignity, in particular humiliating and degrading treatment

d. The passing of sentences and the carrying out of executions without previous judgment pronounced by a regularly constituted court affording all the judicial guarantees which are recognized as indispensable by civilized peoples

Because governments and opposing factions alike had resisted application of common Article 3 to civil wars, Protocol II relating to "non-international armed conflict" was adopted in 1977. It contains detailed provisions for humane treatment in conflicts between a state's armed forces and dissident armed forces or other organized armed forces which meet a specified level of control and command.

Article 1 states, however, that the protocol supplements Article 3 without modifying the existing conditions of application for Article 3. Some internal conflicts which fall under the broad coverage of common Article 3 will not qualify for coverage under the more restrictive conditions for coverage in Protocol II. The protocol also does not apply to "internal disturbances and tensions, such as riots, isolated and sporadic acts of violence and other acts of a similar nature. . . ." Under this provision, the issue is at what point hostilities reach an intensity that qualifies for coverage under Protocol II. Although Secretary of State Hillary Clinton called for the U.S. Senate to approve Protocol II in 2011, the U.S. has refused to ratify Protocols I or II.

3. Wars of Self-Determination

Protocol I applies not only to international conflicts but also to:

a. "armed conflicts in which people are fighting against colonial domination and alien occupation and against racist regimes in the exercise of their right of self-determination, as enshrined in the Charter of the UN and the Declaration on Principles of International Law concerning Friendly Relations . . ."

b. Protocol I makes the four Geneva Conventions applicable to such conflicts. It also extends protections to guerilla fighters and mercenaries in such conflicts not covered by the Conventions or Protocols. The U.S. has refused to ratify Protocol I for this reason.

Note: Despite its failures to ratify, the United States recognizes many provisions of both protocols as customary international law.

D. Applicability of General Human Rights Obligations During Armed Conflict

See pp. 55–57 *supra.*

E. Sanctions & Enforcement: Several Treaties & Conventions Contain Sanctions & Enforcement Provisions

1. The Hague Conventions of 1907

The Hague Conventions of 1907 provided that a state might be required to pay reparations if it, or any member of its armed forces, violated the Convention. However, the Conventions established no procedural framework through which a nation might press its claims that a violation had occurred. The Hague Conventions by their terms were only binding as between parties to the Conventions, and then only if all of the states involved in a conflict were also parties to the Convention. The International Military Tribunal at Nuremberg concluded that the provisions of the Hague Conventions are *customary international law.*

2. The Geneva Conventions of 1949

Parties have a general obligation to ensure respect for the Geneva Conventions in all circumstances. The Conventions provide that once a violation has been established, the parties shall "put an end to it and repress it with the least possible delay." The Geneva Conventions also contain provisions allowing a state to subject any individual, regardless of nationality, to *criminal* prosecution for violations of the Conventions. Unlike the Hague Conventions, the Geneva Conventions are not entirely self-administered; the Conventions provide that the interests of each party to the conflict are to be safeguarded by a neutral "protecting power" or an impartial humanitarian organization such as the Red Cross. By their terms, the Geneva Conventions apply to "all cases of declared war or of any other armed conflict" between contracting states. The parties to the convention are bound to apply its terms between themselves, even if not all of the states involved in the conflict are contracting parties. In addition, if a non-party state accepts and applies the provisions of the Conventions, the contracting parties are required to abide by the Conventions as they pertain to that state. The Geneva Conventions are generally regarded as *custom.*

States are liable for grave breaches by its nationals for whom they are responsible. With respect to prosecution and enforcement against individuals, the Conventions provide:

The High Contracting Parties undertake to enact any legislation necessary to provide effective penal sanctions for persons committing, or ordering to be committed, any of the grave breaches of the present Convention defined in the following Article. Each High Contracting Party shall be under the obligation to search for persons alleged to have committed, or to have ordered to be committed, such grave breaches, and shall bring such persons, regardless of their nationality, before its own courts. It may also, if it prefers, and in accordance with the provisions of its own legislation, hand such persons over for trial to another High Contracting Party concerned, provided such High Contracting Party has made out a *prima facie* case. Each High Contracting Party shall take measures necessary for the suppression of all acts contrary to the provisions of the present Convention other than the grave breaches defined in the following Article.

Grave breaches which are listed under each Convention are generally recognized as *war crimes* under international law. The Conventions provide for enforcement by the states, although the parties are not precluded from conferring jurisdiction upon an international tribunal over those grave breaches which constitute war crimes under international law.

3. The 1977 Protocols to the Geneva Convention

Protocol II does not establish any methods of implementation or enforcement. Protocol I does establish a fact finding commission to investigate grave breaches if its jurisdiction to do so is recognized by the parties to the conflict.

Protocol I expands upon the substantive rules and procedural mechanisms of the Convention for repression of breaches.

4. The Nuremberg Principles

The Charter of the International Military Tribunal at Nuremberg, which was later recognized as custom by the General Assembly of the UN, provided for individual *criminal* responsibility for "crimes against peace," war crimes, or "crimes against humanity":

a. *Crimes against peace*: namely, planning, preparation, initiation or waging of a war of aggression, or a war in violation of international treaties, agreements or assurances, or participation in a common plan or conspiracy for the accomplishment of any of the foregoing.

b. *War crimes*: namely, violations of the laws or customs of war. Such violations shall include, but not be limited to, murder, ill treatment or deportation to slave labor or for any purpose of civilian population of or in occupied territory, murder or ill treatment of prisoners of war or persons on the seas, killing of hostages, plunder of public or private property, wanton destruction of cities, towns or villages, or devastation not justified by military necessity.

c. *Crimes against humanity*: namely, murder, extermination, enslavement, deportation, and other inhumane acts committed against any civilian population, before or during the war; or persecutions on political, racial or religious grounds in execution of or in connection with any crime within the jurisdiction of the Tribunal, whether or not in violation of the domestic law of the country where perpetrated.

Leaders, organizers, instigators and accomplices participating in the formulation or execution of a common plan or conspiracy to commit any of the foregoing crimes are responsible for all acts performed by any persons in execution of such plan.

Examples: In *Prosecutor v. Kunarac et al.*, Case No. IT–96–23&23/1–ES (Feb. 22, 2001), the ICTY held that systematic rape and sexual enslavement are crimes against humanity.

In *Application of Yamashita*, 327 U.S. 1 (1946), General Yamashita of Japan was tried by a special United States military commission applying the international laws of war as incorporated into United States domestic law. Yamashita was charged with war crimes, including the massacre of civilian populations in the Philippines, which also is a crime against humanity under the Nuremberg Principles. The gist of the charge was that Yamashita failed as commander to control the troops in his command and thereby prevent the alleged atrocities.

In holding Yamashita responsible for the alleged war crimes, the Court established that an official or commander who, through reports received by him or through other means, learns that troops or other persons subject to his control are about to commit or have committed war crimes, and fails to take the necessary and reasonable steps to ensure compliance with the law of war, is responsible for such crimes.

In *Prosecutor v. Mucic et al. (Celibici Camp)*, Case No. IT-96-21-A (Nov. 16, 1998), the ICTY held that civilians as well as military personnel are covered by the law of command responsibility based on de jure or de facto authority in a case in which a civilian with apparent authority in a concentration camp was involved in acts of rape constituting torture. *Id.*

In Eritrea's Damages Claims (Eritrea v. Ethiopia), Final Award, 2009 I.C.J. (Aug. 17) the ICJ ruled that under UN Charter Article 2, for jus in bello violations, compensation to victims is linked to the gravity of the violation. For jus ad bellum violations, compensation is linked to the magnitude and character of the use of force.

5. War Crimes Tribunals and the International Criminal Court

The Nuremberg Tribunal is an example of an international tribunal with jurisdiction conferred by agreement of the parties. Since 1993, the Security Council has authorized the establishment of a number of other special tribunals, including the International Criminal Tribunal for the former Yugoslavia (ICTY), the International Criminal Tribunal for Rwanda (ICTR), the Special Court for Sierra Leone, the Cambodian Tribunal on the Khmer Rouge, and the Special Tribunal for Lebanon. A permanent International Criminal Court (ICC) with jurisdiction over war crimes and other crimes under international law was also established in 2002. The fact that an individual before these tribunals acted pursuant to the orders of his government or superior is not a defense, but may be taken into consideration as a mitigating factor.

6. U.S. Military Commissions Act

In October 2012, the U.S. Court of Appeals for the D.C. Circuit vacated the conviction of Salim Ahmed Hamdan by a 2008 military commission at Guantanamo Bay. *Hamdan v. U.S.*, 696 F.3d 1238 (D.C. Cir. 2012). Hamdan was the driver for Osama bin Laden and was convicted of "material support for terrorism," a war crime under the Military Commissions Act of 2006. However, his conviction was based on actions taken between 1996 and 2001, before the Military Commissions Act was enacted. So while the Military Commissions Act did codify some new war crimes, including material support for terrorism, it was not a war crime at the time of the conduct in question. Further, no relevant international treaties make material support for terrorism an international-law war crime, nor does customary international law make it a war crime. Because of this, the D.C. Circuit reversed Hamdan's conviction, as his actions were not considered a war crime under the law at the time he took them.

F. September 11, 2001 and "Unlawful Combatant" Status

After the September 11 attacks on the World Trade Towers, President Bush issued a military order authorizing military commissions for the trial of non-citizen "unlawful combatants" with the Taliban and Al-Qaeda. 66 Fed. Reg. 57,833 (Nov. 16, 2001); implementing regulations at 41 I.L.M. 725 (Mar. 21, 2002) https://www.govinfo.gov/content/pkg/FR-2001-11-16/pdf/01-28904.pdf. Several human rights guarantees are applicable to trials of such combatants:

Executive Order 13,440 from the Bush Administration, which limited the application of Article III, was revoked by President Obama's 2009 order which banned torture and "degrading treatment" of detainees and included other limits on interrogation. John R. Crook, ed., *Contemporary Practice of the United States Relating to International Law,* 103 AM. J. INT'L L. 325, 331 (2009).

1. Article 14 Protections

Article 14 of the ICCPR prohibits discrimination in the legal process, and requires certain procedural guarantees including due process and a right of appeal to a "higher tribunal according to law." The U.S. has not formally claimed a right of derogation for "war . . . or other public emergency." Article 4.

2. Protections Under Third Geneva Convention

Third Geneva Convention Article III, Article 4 provides a number of substantial protections to prisoners of war and Article 5 provides that persons captured during an international armed conflict are entitled to the protections until a competent tribunal has determined their status. Army Field Manual 27–10 provides that a "competent tribunal" is a "board of not less than three officers acting according to such procedures as may be prescribed."

a. A country that does not respect Article 3 of the Geneva Conventions for the Protection of Victims of War regarding the conditions of confinement does not have the power to detain. Ryan Goodman, *Editorial Comment: The Detention of Civilians in Armed Conflict*, 103 AM. J. OF INT'L L. 48, 49 (2009).

b. International humanitarian law and the conditions set forth in Articles 5, 27, 41–43 and 78 of the Fourth Geneva Convention allow civilians to be detained if they "directly or indirectly participate[d] in hostilities." Ryan Goodman, *Editorial Comment: The Detention of Civilians in Armed Conflict*, 103 AM. J. OF INT'L L. 48, 57 (2009).

3. Types of Conflicts

The characterization of the conflict is critical to the provisions of humanitarian law which apply. The Geneva Conventions apply to international conflicts between states, regardless of whether a state of war is recognized by them. Protocol I applies to such international conflicts, as well as to wars of national liberation against colonial or racial domination.

For internal conflicts, Protocol II applies to narrowly defined internal conflicts under Article 1 where the dissident forces are under responsible command and control a part of the state's territory. Common Article 3 of the Geneva Conventions applies more broadly to armed conflicts "not of an international character" but more than isolated riots or sporadic acts of violence. If none of the above applies, dissident forces are protected by only those rights which have not been suspended or cannot be suspended under the derogation clauses in time of war or other public emergency.

4.   Types of Combatants

In international conflicts, the third Geneva Convention, Article 4, defines prisoners of war to include not only members of the regular armed forces, but also organized resistance movements which are commanded by a person responsible for his subordinates, carry a fixed distinctive sign recognizable at a distance, carry arms openly, and conduct their operations in accordance with the laws and customs of war. Protocol II contains a somewhat similar description of protected combatants for internal conflicts. In some circumstances a group such as Al-Qaeda might fall within these narrow definitions (e.g., while fighting against the US in Afghanistan) but not in other circumstances (while inflicting death and damage on civilian populations through terrorist attacks). Members of the Taliban, at one time the effective government of Afghanistan, may be entitled to full protection as members of a state's armed forces. As noted above, Article 5 states that prisoners of uncertain status are entitled to protection under the Conventions until their status is determined by a competent tribunal.

In 2008, the Supreme Court of Israel held in *A v. Israel* that "any tenuous connection with a terrorist organization" is not enough for detainment. A particular "connection and contribution to the organization" on the part of the individual must be shown in order to "include him in the cycle of hostilities in its broad sense." Ryan Goodman, *Editorial Comment: The Detention of Civilians in Armed Conflict*, 103 Am. J. of Int'l Law 48, 55 (2009).

In a March 2009 filing in the U.S. District Court of Columbia, the U.S. Department of Justice stated that the United States would no longer categorize detained Al Qaeda or Taliban members using the phrase enemy combatants. John R. Crook, ed., *Contemporary Practice of the United States Relating to International Law*, 103 AM. J. INT'L L. 325, 351–352 (2009). The government stated the congressional Authorization for the Use of Military Force based on the international laws of war would continue to give the government the right to detain those who provided "substantial support for Al Qaeda and the Taliban." John R. Crook, ed., *Contemporary Practice of the United States Relating to International Law*, 103 AM. J. INT'L L. 325, 352 (2009).

5.   Military Commissions

The regulations for the military commissions allow for some press coverage, provide government lawyers for defendants or civilian lawyers at the defendants' expense, and require a unanimous verdict by a seven member panel for the death penalty, a presumption of innocence, proof beyond a reasonable doubt, and access to incriminating evidence. The regulations, however, allow hearsay evidence and evidence convincing to a "reasonable person" and there is no independent appeal, keeping control of the tribunals in the military chain of command.

6.   Private Security Contractors

In December 2020, President Trump issued full pardons to four former Blackwater contractors convicted of killing Iraqi civilians in the 2007 Nisour Square incident, following a pattern he set in 2019 of issuing pardons to military personnel whose underlying offenses constitute war crimes. 31 Iraqi civilians were left dead or wounded following the 2007 Nisour Square incident. One of the four contractors was convicted of first-degree murder, and the other three men were convicted of manslaughter for their roles, alongside related charges. U.S. Dep't of Justice, Pardons Granted by President Donald Trump (2021), https://www.justice.gov/pardon/pardons-granted-president-donald-j-trump-2017-2021 (listing pardons). The incident sparked increased international scrutiny over the proper role of private security contractors operating in combat zones, and the pardons were condemned by human rights groups and independent human rights experts.

7. Guantanamo Bay & Habeas Corpus

In 2008, the U.S. Supreme Court found in *Boumediene v. Bush*, 553 U.S. 723 (2008) that military commissions under the Military Commissions Act, Pub. L. No. 109–366, 120 Stat. 2600 (2006) do not sufficiently protect the habeas corpus rights of detainees at Guantanamo Bay, Cuba. The Court did not suggest a substitute in its place, nor did it definitively settle the boundaries of habeas corpus for enemy combatants. *Hamdan v. Rumsfeld*, 548 U.S. 557 (2006) echoed the failure of the military commissions, adding an analysis of Article 3 of the Geneva Conventions as to why they were insufficient. In *Rumsfeld v. Padilla*, 542 U.S. 426 (2004), an American citizen was arrested as an "enemy combatant" on United States soil and then denied access to his family or an attorney. Before the Supreme Court made a decision in this case, the government filed criminal charges and transferred the detainee from military to civilian custody. In *Hamdi v. Rumsfeld*, 542 U.S. 507 (2004), an American citizen was again arrested and held as an "enemy combatant" by the military, but this citizen was arrested overseas. The government claimed that Congress had authorized this by enacting the Authorization of Use of Military Force. The Supreme Court held that the President did have authorization to hold enemy combatants during active hostilities in Afghanistan, but that U.S. citizens have an additional due process right to challenge their detention. In *Rasul v. Bush*, 542 U.S. 466 (2004), fourteen non-U.S. Citizens were held at Guantanamo Bay as enemy combatants. They attempted to file habeas corpus petitions challenging various aspects of their detention. The Supreme Court held that Guantanamo was effectively under U.S. sovereignty, and the federal courts, therefore, had jurisdiction to hear the habeas corpus challenges.

In January 2009, President Obama issued an executive order to close Guantanamo Bay detention facilities. John R. Crook, ed., *Contemporary Practice of the United States Relating to International Law,* 103 AM. J. INT'L L. 325 (2009). President Obama stated in the executive order that detainees had the constitutional right of the writ of *habeas corpus.* John R. Crook, ed., *Contemporary Practice of the United States Relating to International Law,* 103 AM. J. INT'L L. 325, 326 (2009).

In April 2009, U.S. District Court Judge John Bates ruled in *al Maqaleh v. Gates* that the Suspension Clause extends to three non-Afghan detainees from Yemen and Pakistan held for over six years at Bagram Air Base in Afghanistan. John R. Crook, ed., *Contemporary Practice of the United States Relating to International Law,* 103 AM. J. INT'L L. 575, 579–580 (2009). The court concluded that habeas corpus review was available to the three detainees by applying the "multi-factor functional test from *Boumediene.* John R. Crook, ed., *Contemporary Practice of the United States Relating to International Law,* 103 AM. J. INT'L L. 575, 580 (2009). This decision was reversed in May 2010 by the Court of Appeals for the District of Columbia. The unanimous court emphasized "Bagram's location within a zone of conflict . . . and saw significant differences between the character of U.S. presence there and the United States' more substantial rights at Guantanamo Bay."

In October 2009, the U.S. Supreme Court granted *certiorari* in *Kiyemba v. Obama*. John R. Crook, ed., *Contemporary Practice of the United States Relating to International Law,* 104 AM. J. INT'L L. 100, 117 (2010). This case involved the continued detention of Uighur detainees. *Id.* In 2008 Judge Ricardo Urbina of the U.S. District Court for the District of Columbia ruled that the Uighur detainees could not be lawfully detained by the United States and ordered their release because it was conceded that they were not enemy combatants. *Id.* The U.S. Court of Appeals for the D.C. Circuit reversed, claiming that they would be overstepping their boundary if they decided whether to admit aliens into the United States. *Id.* In March 2010, the Court vacated and remanded this case.

In December 2009, officials announced plans to purchase Thomas Correctional Facility in Thomas, Illinois to house detainees transferred from Guantanamo. John R. Crook, ed., *Contemporary Practice of the United States Relating to International Law,* 104 AM. J. INT'L L. 100, 115 (2010). However, this requires congressional approval, which Republicans and other opponents vowed to block. *Id.* In the meantime several of the detainees were transferred to other countries. *Id.*

In December 2009, following the transfer of several Guantanamo detainees, ninety Yemeni detainees remained at Guantanamo Bay. John R. Crook, ed., *Contemporary Practice of the United States Relating to International Law,* 104 AM. J. INT'L L. 100, 116 (2010). Despite the fact that several of the detainees were cleared for transfer, the United States was reluctant to release them due to concerns over the Yemeni government's ability to keep them from becoming threats to U.S. security. *Id.* In addition, the December 25 attack on a U.S. airliner by a terrorist trained in Yemen made the question of their release even less clear. *Id.*

The Department of Homeland Security Appropriations Act of 2010 became law on October 29, 2009 when President Obama signed it. The Act gives the Secretary of Defense authority to determine whether photographs of detainee abuse should be released. If the Secretary of Defense determines that their "disclosure 'would endanger citizens of the Unites States, members of the United States Armed Forces, or employees of the United State Government deployed outside the United States,' " he may choose to not disclose them.

In March 2011, Guantanamo trials reopened with the trial of Adb al-Rahim al-Nashiri (the leader of attack on USS Cole). John R. Crook, ed., *Contemporary Practice of the United States Relating to International Law,* 105 AM. J. INT'L L. 596, 596–97 (2011). President Obama concurrently issued Executive Order 13567, which prescribes standards for indefinite detentions, mandates periodic reviews of individual cases but also justifies indeterminate detentions in Guantanamo Bay. This order establishes a "Periodic Review Board" to assess whether an individual's continued detention meets this standard necessary. John R. Crook, ed., *Contemporary Practice of the United States Relating to International Law,* 105 AM. J. INT'L L. 598, 598–600 (2011).

No new detainees have been brought to Guantanamo since 2008. On the second day of his presidency, President Obama ordered the future closing of Guantanamo. He viewed the detention camp as contrary to American values and harmful to U.S. foreign policy. Under President Obama's direction, 196 detainees were transferred from the facility, leaving forty-one detainees by the end of his presidency. President Trump signed E.O. 13,823 on January 30, 2018, which directed officials to keep the Guantanamo Bay detention camp open and permitted additional detainees to be transported to the facility, revoking the order issued by President Obama. One inmate was transferred during Trump's term in office, bringing the total number of current detainees to forty. In early 2021, President Biden's administration announced its intent to shut down the facility.

8. The U.S. and Counterterrorism

a. Transfer of "Enemy Combatants"

In *Doe v. Mattis*, the U.S. Court of Appeals for the D.C. Circuit blocked the transfer of a dual U.S.-Saudi national, detained in Iraq as an alleged enemy combatant, to an unidentified third country. 889 F.3d 745 (D.C. Cir. 2018). In September 2017, "John Doe" was captured by Syrian Democratic Forces during clashes with the Islamic State of Iraq and the Levant (ISIL). He was transferred to U.S. custody and detained as an enemy combatant. In October of that year, the ACLU filed a petition for a writ of habeas corpus on his behalf, arguing that Doe either had to be criminally tried in a federal court or released. The ACLU asserted that U.S. domestic law does not authorize the military campaign against ISIL and does not grant the legal authority to detain an alleged member of ISIL. Under *Hamdi v. Rumsfeld*, Doe could potentially be transferred if the government demonstrated that it is legally authorized to use military force against ISIL and "affords Doe an adequate opportunity to challenge the Executive's factual determination that he is an ISIL combatant." Under the law of war, transfer of an enemy combatant is an option available to the military. National Defense Authorization Act for Fiscal Year 2012, Pub. L. No. 112–81, 125 Stat. 1298, § 1021(a) (Dec. 31, 2011). A U.S. citizen facing transfer, however, must be allowed to challenge the basis of this determination. The D.C. Circuit found that the government had failed to demonstrate their authority to wage war with ISIL and had failed to provide Doe with a meaningful opportunity to rebut the assertion that he is an ISIL combatant. In early June 2018, the government informed the district court that it planned to release Doe in Syria within seventy-two hours—the ACLU filed a motion against this move, arguing that "the government's proposal violates the requirement that military detainees be released to safety and not be exposed to hostile forces." Petition for a Writ of Habeas Corpus, at 8, *Doe v. Mattis*, 288 F. Supp. 3d 195 (D.D.C. 2018) (No. 1:17–cv–2069 (TSC)). In late October 2018, following negotiations with the ACLU, the government released Doe to an unnamed country under a confidential agreement.

b. ISIL

Further proceedings in the district court have the potential to address whether the U.S. military campaign against ISIL is lawful under U.S. domestic law. The D.C. Circuit did not address the merits of the legality of the military campaign against ISIL. The ACLU argued in *Doe v. Mattis* that the only possible legal bases for detaining a citizen without charge in military custody (the 2001 Authorization for Use of Military Force in junction with the 2012 National Defense Authorization Act (NDAA) or the 2002 Authorization for Use of Military Force) did not apply to individuals who were not "part of or substantially supported al-Qaeda, the Taliban, or associated forces engaged in hostilities with the U.S. or coalition partners." ISIL did not exist when the September 11, 2001 attacks took place and is distinct from al-Qaeda. The government argued that both the 2001 and 2002 AUMF justified the detention, noting the common roots shared between ISIL and al-Qaeda and invoked the president's Article II authority.

c. Yemen

Since 2011, the U.S. has carried out counterterrorism operations in Yemen aimed at Al Qaeda in the Arabian Peninsula (AQAP) and later at the Islamic State of Iraq and the Levant (ISIL). The U.S. continues to rely on the 2001 Authorization for the Use of Military Force against groups responsible for the terrorist attacks on September 11, 2001 as ground to continue these military actions. U.S. ground forces have conducted multiple ground operations and air strikes each year. Separate from U.S. military operations, the U.S. has supported the Saudi-led campaign against the Houthi movement in Yemen. President Obama authorized logistical and intelligence support in 2015 without involving direct military involvement. In 2016, the Obama administration began to scale back U.S. assistance to the coalition over concerns about the high rate of civilian casualties, as well as emphasizing the need for political settlement of the conflict. The Trump administration continued and enhanced the Obama administration's facilitation of the Saudi-led campaign, announcing an arms deal with Saudi Arabia that included the sale of precision-guided munitions.

Congressional concern for the Saudi-led coalition has grown as the conflict continues. The main objects of these concerns include thousands of civilian casualties, a cholera epidemic, and a country on the brink of famine. In 2017, Senators sought to prohibit the transaction, believing the coalition would use the weapons to target civilians, but was unable to block the $500 million sale with a vote of 53–47. This was a narrower margin than a similar resolution the previous fall, signaling a growing concern over the Saudi-led coalition's actions and the rise in civilian casualties. In August 2018, Congress passed the NDAA for Fiscal Year 2019, which contained multiple provisions relating to the humanitarian crisis in Yemen and to civilian casualties more generally.

An August 2018 report from the UN Office of the High Commissioner for Human Rights sharply criticized the coalition, identifying 6,475 civilian deaths from attacks in Yemen between March 2015 and June 2018, mostly carried out by coalition air strikes.

Relations between the U.S. and Saudi Arabia grew even more complicated following the brutal death of Jamal Khashoggi, a Saudi Arabian journalist who had moved to Washington D.C. and published columns in the Washington Post criticizing Saudi policy and the Saudi crown prince in the year before his murder. On November 15, 2018, the State Department announced sanctions pursuant to the Global Magnitsky Human Rights Accountability Act on seventeen Saudi government officials that the Department deemed to be implicated in Khashoggi's killing.

9. Regional Systems and Terrorism

a. Europe

The European Court on Human Rights has considered numerous cases regarding the limitation of rights to individuals labeled as terrorists. Common rights and practices such as detention periods, arrest procedures, extradition, and right to counsel have been evaluated by the Court. The states suspending or limiting the rights are usually given a very narrow interpretation of the rights, so they carry a heavy burden in proving why it was necessary to suspend or limit them. The Court has additionally ruled that the European Convention's Article 3 prohibition on torture exists regardless of the accused's crime.

In *Her Majesty's Treasury v. Ahmed et al.,* [2010] UKSC 2, a series of joint cases was decided by the U.K. Supreme Court regarding the implementation of UN Security Council decisions in U.K. law. Security Council Resolution 1373 (Sept. 28, 2001) required, among other things, an asset-freezing regime to prevent or suppress terroristic activities. The Treasury then implemented orders to turn the Security Council resolution into U.K. administrative law, under the authority of section 1(1) of the UN Act 1946, which authorizes the government to create orders to implement Security Council decisions. The Supreme Court quashed these orders, ruling that section 1(1) does not allow the treasury to freeze assets using only orders-in-council because the UN Act 1946 was never intended to impose limitations on individuals.

b. The Americas

The Inter-American Convention Against Terrorism was adopted by the OAS in 2002. It places heavy emphasis on member states' international role and compliance with international laws, and it also calls for greater cooperation within the OAS community in preventing acts of terrorism.

G. The United Nations & Terrorism

The UN has called upon member states to criminalize the collection of funds for use in terrorist acts, freeze related assets, prevent transfer of funds to be used in terrorist acts, and bring those to justice who are responsible for such acts via its Resolution 1373 (2001).

Terrorism & Counterterrorism

The International Convention for the Suppression of the Financing of Terrorism defines terrorism as any act:

Intended to cause death or serious bodily injury to a civilian, or to any other person not taking an active part in the hostilities in a situation of armed conflict, when the purpose of such an act, by its nature or context, is to intimidate a population, or to compel a government or an international organization to do or to abstain from doing any act.

The terminology in this definition suggests a relationship between terrorism and armed conflict, and therefore a relationship with international humanitarian law. Terrorism is often a method of waging war in violation of the rules of armed conflict, especially by targeting innocent civilians. In a technical sense, however, many terrorist acts do not violate particular human rights treaties, because those treaties do not impose obligations on non-state actors.

The European Court of Human Rights and the Inter-American Court of Human Rights have unequivocally stated that alleged terrorists, even undisputed terrorists, remain protected by human rights.

Saadi v. Italy

Saadi, a Tunisian national residing in Italy, was charged with involvement in international terrorism. The trial court convicted him of criminal conspiracy, forgery, and receiving stolen goods (in connection with alleged terrorist acts) and ordered him deported on completion of his sentence. Saadi challenged the deportation on grounds including the risk of torture or inhumane or degrading treatment that he would face if returned to Tunisia. The Court held that it is not possible to weigh the risk of ill-treatment against the reasons put forward for the expulsion in order to determine whether the responsibility of a State is engaged under Article 3, even where such treatment is inflicted by another state. The Court considered that the argument based on the balancing of the risk of harm if the person is sent back against the dangerousness he or she represents to the community if not sent back is misconceived. The Article 3 obligation not to deport an individual depends on a predictive judgment about the probability that the individual will suffer a violation of Article 3 in the receiving country.

Kadi v. Council of the European Union

The case concerns the freezing of the assets in the European Union of Yassiin Abdullah Kadi, a resident of Saudi Arabia, and the Al Barakaat International Foundation, established in Sweden, due to alleged connections to Al Qaeda. The Court ruled for Kadi because the Council neither communicated to Kadi the evidence used against them to justify the restrictive measures imposed on them nor afforded them the right to be informed of that evidence within a reasonable period after those measures were enacted. Kadi's rights of defense, in particular the right to be heard, were not respected. The imposition of the restrictive measures laid down by the contested regulation in respect to Mr. Kadi, constituted an unjustified restriction of his right to property.

Chapter XII

Sources of Human Rights Law

Along with treaty law, customary international law is one of the two principal sources of international law. Despite numerous treaties, there are many topics and many parties which are not covered by treaty law. Customary international law is important for its potentially general application to states not parties to treaties, as well as its ability to supplement areas of international concern not addressed in treaties. Despite its acknowledged importance, customary law is subject to much controversy for it eludes any definite formulation. First, the lack of sufficient consistency in state practices may make it difficult to establish a practice as customary. Secondly, customary law is ascertained by subjective analysis of whether states engaged in a certain practice are acting out of a sense of legal obligation (the *opinio juris* requirement) or for other reasons.

A. Two Approaches to Customary International Law

The two approaches are the objectivist/sociological approach and the participatory/voluntarist approach.

1. Objectivist/Sociological Approach

The objectivist/sociological approach is that customary law is *universal and therefore binding on every state* of the world community.

2. Participatory/Voluntarist Approach

The participatory/voluntarist approach is that customary law applies *only to those states which have participated in the custom*, and newly independent states have the right not to be bound by a previously established practice as customary international law. *See* S.S. "Lotus" *(Fr. v. Turk.),* [1927] P.C.I.J. (ser. A) No. 10, at 21 ("The rules of law binding upon States . . . emanate from their own free will as expressed in conventions or by usages generally accepted as expressing principles of law . . .").

a. Objections by Developing Nations

The former Soviet Union and many developing countries object to the universal application of customary law on the principle that countries outside the developed nations of the western hemisphere had little to do with the establishment of many customary laws and therefore ought not be bound by them.

b. Restatement § 102

The comments to Restatement 102 reject this position and view all states as bound by whatever customs are established at the time the state comes into existence.

B. Establishment of an International Custom

There are quantitative and qualitative elements to customary international law. Customary law follows the basic principle of international law that *acts are permitted unless expressly forbidden*. Therefore, prohibitions as well as affirmative practices must be proven by the state relying upon them. *See* S.S. Lotus *(Fr. v. Turk.)* [1927] P.C.I.J. (ser. A) No. 10.

1. Quantitative Factors

Quantitative factors include past state practice and duration of the state practice.

a. State Practice Generally

States in the *practice of their international relations* implicitly consent to the creation and application of legal rules. State practice may be ascertained from a wide variety of sources: treaties, executive agreements, legislation, regulations, court decisions, speeches and testimony before national and international bodies.

b. Duration of State Practice

The practice must have been followed for an *appreciable period of time*. The notion is that what began as a limited practice may, over time, ripen and widen in its adoption to become customary law. There is, however, no set standard to determine when practice is transformed into law.

i. Long-Term

Long-term practice was an important consideration of the Supreme Court in the case of *The Paquete Habana*, 175 U.S. 677 (1900). The court looked at the practices of England, France, Germany and the Netherlands from 1403 to 1898 to conclude that fishing vessels are recognized as exempt from capture as prizes of war.

ii. Short-Term

The ICJ held in the *North Sea Continental Shelf Cases*, 1969 I.C.J. 3 (Feb. 20), that a "passage of only a short period of time is not necessarily, or of itself, a bar to the formation of a new rule of customary international law," if the practice is "both extensive and virtually uniform."

c. Consistency of State Practice

More important than the duration of state practice is the *consistency with which it is applied*. Minor and infrequent inconsistencies do not necessarily negate a custom.

d. Number and Makeup of States Adhering to the Practice

To establish custom definitively, a practice must be followed by *a significant number of states representing diverse geographic, economic and social characteristics*. It has, however, been suggested that the consistent practice of only a handful of states may be sufficient to establish custom, particularly when those states are the only ones capable of engaging in the practice (*e.g.*, nuclear testing on the high seas in the 1950's). The question then becomes whether custom can be established and imposed over the objection of other states. *See* p. 128 *infra*.

2. Use of Regional Custom

Note, however, that customary law *may also be limited to a particular region* and therefore not be the practice of such a wide variety of states. A state may rely on regional custom but must show its existence by proving both quantitative and qualitative factors. Asylum Case *(Colombia v. Peru)*, 1950 I.C.J. 266 (Nov. 20).

3. Local Customary Rights

Local customary rights may develop from *constant and continual practice between two nations*, but such customary rights differ from, and are independent of, general international customary law principles. Right of Passage Over Indian Territory *(Port. v. India)*, 1960 I.C.J. 6 (Apr. 12).

4. Qualitative Factor—*Opinio Juris*

In addition to the quantitative factors, international lawyers often refer to the subjective element of *opinio juris sive necessitates* (called *opinio juris*). *Opinio juris* is the sense of *legal obligation compelling states to follow a certain practice*. The difficulty in ascertaining *opinio juris* is that states rarely acknowledge that they are acting under a sense of legal obligation rather than an as a matter of choice, comity, or convenience.

Examples: A ship was flying a French flag and collided with a Turkish ship. Criminal proceedings were brought in Turkey against the French captain of the French ship. The Permanent Court of International Justice held that there was no rule of international law at the time limiting criminal proceedings in a collision on the high seas to the exclusive jurisdiction of the state whose flag is flown on the offending ship. While the Court found that states in Turkey's position had often abstained from asserting criminal jurisdiction, there was no evidence that the abstentions were based on a sense of legal obligation. *S.S. Lotus (Fr. v. Turk.)*, [1927] P.C.I.J. (ser. A, No. 10).

In *North Sea Continental Shelf*, 1969 I.C.J. 3 (Feb. 20), the ICJ stated that "[t]he States concerned must therefore feel they are conforming to what amounts to a legal obligation. The frequency, or even habitual character of the acts is not in itself enough. There are many international acts . . . which are motivated only by considerations of courtesy, convenience or tradition, and not by any sense of legal duty."

C. Resolutions and Recommendations of International Organizations

The role of international organizations' resolutions and recommendations in establishing custom, in particular the General Assembly of the United Nations, is controversial. General Assembly resolutions are not a form of international legislation and accordingly are not legally binding. Indeed, the UN Charter itself refers to the "recommendations" of the General Assembly, in contrast to decisions of the Security Council which are binding on members of the UN Charter. U.N. Charter Art. 25. The resolutions are, however, frequently used as *evidence* of customary international law. The resolutions are useful as evidence because the votes of the world body may show a consensus (or lack of consensus) on a particular issue. A majority vote is more compelling evidence of custom when the majority represents a wide array of developed and developing countries. On the other hand, states vote in the General Assembly without expecting that they must act or have acted in accordance with their vote.

Example: The UN Declaration of Human Rights now has been recognized as expressing customary international law because it "create[d] an expectation of adherence" and that expectation was "gradually justified by State practice." *Filartiga v. Pena-Irala*, 630 F.2d 876, 883 (2d Cir. 1980).

D. Application of International Customary Law

The predominant view is that customary international law enjoys universal application, regardless of what nations participated in its formation. The issue then arises as to whether there is any way for a state to be exempt from application of a law. Two possible exceptions to application follow:

1. Clear & Consistent Objection

Dissent from a custom in the form of clear and consistent objections supported by action may prevent application of the custom to the objecting state.

2. Historic Departure

Historic departure from a customary rule and other states' acceptance of that deviation also provides an exception to the application of a custom. Note that wholesale departure from a custom by a large number of states may eventually result in the creation of a new custom.

E. Relationship Between Treaties & Customary International Law

Depending on the situation, treaties may be given equal weight with custom, prevail over custom, be proof of custom, or codify custom.

1. Equal Weight Standard

Although Article 38 of the Statute of the International Court of Justice places treaties first on the list of sources of international law, the order does not necessarily establish a hierarchy of sources. In fact, treaties and custom are generally given *equal weight in international law* (although a treaty which is more specific than a custom will prevail) and some peremptory norms of customs (*jus cogens*) preempt conflicting treaty law.

2. Treaty as Evidence of Custom

Treaty provisions may become so widely adopted that they are accepted as custom. Treaties can also serve to codify customary international law.

a. Multilateral Convention Provisions as Custom

Provisions of a multilateral convention which becomes widely adopted may be applicable as customary law, and therefore binding on non-party states, if the practice is uniform and widely recognized as a legal obligation. See *North Sea Continental Shelf Cases* 1969, I.C.J. 3 (Feb. 20).

b. Treaties as Codification of Custom

In recent years, treaties have been used to codify customary international law, as, for example, with the law of the sea treaties in 1958 and again in 1982, and with the Vienna Convention on the Law of Treaties. When utilizing such treaty provisions as evidence of custom, however, it is important to differentiate provisions which merely reiterate custom from provisions which expand upon custom or represent progressive development (*i.e.*, new) law.

Chapter XIII

General Principles of Law

A general principle of law "recognized by civilized nations" is one *so fundamental that it is a basic tenet in virtually every major legal system*. Unlike treaties or international customary laws, general principles are derived from domestic law and are not principles originating from international relations or obligations.

Example: General principles of law are rules concerning liability for damages, unjust enrichment, right of passage over territory, the doctrine of *res judicata*, some basic humanitarian rights, the prohibition against being a judge in one's own cause, and application of the principle of good faith.

A. Limited Application of General Principles

General principles of law primarily apply to fill in gaps left by treaties and customary law. As international law expands to encompass new subject areas, general principles of law from domestic legal systems may be utilized until custom is established or treaties are developed.

B. Decreasing Importance as a Source of International Law

General principles are losing importance in modern international law because many of the norms once recognized as general principles are now incorporated in treaties or are recognized as customary international law. The Restatement (Third) now classifies general principles as "a secondary source of international law."

C. Application of General Principles for Procedural Matters

Although generally decreasing in importance, general principles continue to be applied in procedural matters and problems of international judicial administration. General principles often relied on are the doctrines of *res judicata* and *laches*, as well as the rule that judges are to act with impartiality and independence. Corfu Channel Case *(U.K. v. Alb.)*, 1949 I.C.J. 4 (April 9).

Chapter XIV

Extradition

Extradition is the process by which an individual charged or convicted of a serious crime in one state (the requisitioning state) and found in a second state (the asylum state) is returned to the requisitioning state for trial or punishment. Extradition arises from bilateral and multilateral treaties and many issues of extradition are matters of treaty interpretation.

A. Obligation to Extradite

In the absence of a treaty *there is no obligation to extradite*. A state may volunteer to extradite an individual without the existence of a treaty but is obliged to extradite only by the terms of a treaty. The practice of the United States and the general modern trend is to disallow extradition in the absence of an applicable treaty.

B. Extraditable Offenses

Treaties employ one of two methods for specifying the grounds for extradition. The treaty may rely solely on the requirement of double criminality or it may list the indictable offenses for which extradition is available. In either case, treaties often prohibit extradition if prosecution of the offender would be barred in either state by the statute of limitations.

1. Double Criminality

Treaties often provide that extradition is available for any conduct which is an offense in both the requisitioning state and the asylum state punishable by a specified minimum term of imprisonment.

In December 2010, Julian Assange, founder of WikiLeaks, surrendered to British authorities in response to a Swedish extradition request for sexual offenses. He fought extradition on the grounds that extradition was politically discriminatory, based on insufficient evidence, and for the purpose of allowing the United States to extradite him for charges related to WikiLeak's release of sensitive classified national security information. The U.K. court found that "dual criminality," as required by the extradition treaty between Sweden and the United Kingdom, was satisfied because there was enough preliminary evidence of a violation of Swedish law.

2. List of Extraditable Offenses

A second method of listing extraditable offenses has fallen into disfavor, because it is considered clumsy and results in treaties being outdated as new crimes emerge.

C. Nationals of the Asylum State

State treaties sometimes provide that a state may not or cannot extradite its own nationals. A consequence of the latter type of treaty is that criminals may escape punishment altogether if their own state fails to prosecute them. Some treaties with such an exception obligate the asylum state to prosecute its own nationals for the crime if it refuses to extradite.

D. Process of Requesting Extradition

Although the process of requesting extradition varies, there are common characteristics. Requests for extradition are often initiated along diplomatic channels. The request is then subject to a judicial determination followed by consideration in the executive branch, which has some discretion in the final determination.

E. Standard Treaty Limitations on Extradition

Extradition treaties may include exceptions under which extradition by the asylum state is not required.

1. Discrimination

Extradition will not be granted if it would subject the fugitive to prosecution based on race, nationality, political opinion or other similar grounds that would prejudice the process.

2. Lack of Probable Cause

The request for extradition must include sufficient prima facie evidence of guilt attributable to the fugitive whose extradition is sought. This limitation is commonly found in treaties of English-speaking states. More generally, extradition does not apply to persons merely suspected of having committed an offense. Nor may extradition be utilized to obtain a person's presence as a witness or for the purpose of enforcing a civil judgment.

3. Political Offenses

Most treaties today exempt from extradition political offenses in either mandatory or discretionary terms. The exemption for political offenses is widely accepted by non-socialist states but the term itself is subject to several interpretations. While there is no generally agreed upon definition of political offenses, there are a few offenses which are generally recognized as *not* being political offenses, such as assassination of heads of state, war crimes, and genocide.

a. Purely Political Offenses

Purely political offenses are acts directed against the state which lack the essential characteristics of a common crime. Examples are treason, sedition, rebellion and espionage. Such acts are done with the purpose of damaging a political regime as such.

b. Related Political Offenses

Related political offenses are common crimes motivated by political goals. There are three approaches to related political offenses, requiring varying degrees of connection between the crime and the political act.

i. The "Political Incidence" Approach (the Anglo-American Approach)

This approach requires the criminal offense to be committed in the course of a dispute between a governing party and another party with political aims. The motive and purpose of the crime must be to further the aims of the party. Application of the test in U.S. courts has been inconsistent. *Compare Eain v. Wilkes*, 641 F.2d 504 (7th Cir. 1981), *cert. denied*, 454 U.S. 894 (1981) (extradition of PLO member for marketplace bombing) *with* Matter of Mackin, 668 F.2d 122 (2d Cir. 1981) (denied extradition of IRA member for attempted murder of British soldier); and *Quinn v. Robinson*, 783 F.2d 776 (9th Cir. 1986), *cert. denied*, 479 U.S. 882 (1986) (extradition of IRA member for murder of London police constable because relevant political uprising was in Northern Ireland, not Great Britain).

ii. The "Political Objective" Approach (the Franco-Belgian Approach)

Under this approach the means used to achieve the political objective may not be unlimited; the means used must relate to the political objective; and a degree of proportionality must exist between the political objective and the crime for which extradition is sought.

iii. The "Predominant Motive" Approach (the Swiss Approach)

This approach demands a close and direct link between the crime and the political act, thus making it more likely for a fugitive to be extradited. A crime is a political offense if it was committed in the course of preparing to perpetrate a purely political offense; there must be a direct link between the act and the political goal; and, the common law criminal element must be proportional to the political goal.

iv. Treaty Exceptions for Acts of Terrorism

There is an emerging trend in extradition treaties to exempt from treatment as political offenses, and thus require extradition for, acts of terrorism as defined by the relevant treaty. Such exceptions have been recognized in bilateral treaties (*e.g.*, the 1985 Supplementary Extradition Treaty between the United States and the United Kingdom) and in regional treaties (*e.g.*, the European Convention on Suppression of Terrorism). Use of this exception in extradition treaties has been criticized, particularly when done on a state-by-state basis (thus singling out certain political movements for less favorable extradition treatment) and when the extraditable offenses are broadly defined to include crimes against military and other non-civilian targets.

4. Doctrine of Specialty

The requisitioning nation cannot prosecute the extradited person for offenses other than those stated as the grounds for extradition. American extradition treaties expressly include such a provision, and the Supreme Court has also ruled that the doctrine of specialty may be implied from the "manifest scope and object of the treaty."

a. Re-Extradition to Third State

The doctrine of specialty may also prevent a state from extraditing the accused to a third state without first offering him the "right to return".

b. Exceptions

The requisitioning state may prosecute the extradited person for offenses committed after extradition. Other offenses committed before extradition may also be prosecuted if the accused first has a reasonable opportunity to depart the country.

5. Territorial Jurisdiction

Extradition treaties often rely on the principle of territorial jurisdiction so that the crime for which extradition is being requested must have been committed within the territorial jurisdiction of the requisitioning state. Difficulties often arise when a state is requesting extradition based on non-territorial jurisdictional grounds.

6. Other Non-Extraditable Crimes

A mandatory or discretionary exception for crimes of a religious, fiscal, or military nature is often included.

F. Methods Employed to Avoid the Safeguards of Extradition Treaties

1. Deportation (Also Referred to as "Disguised Extradition")

A potential asylum state may avoid the terms of an extradition treaty by either denying the fugitive permission to enter the state initially or by deportation as an undesirable alien.

2. Abduction

States occasionally recover fugitives by abduction from the asylum state. Although abduction is generally considered an affront to the sovereignty of the asylum state and widely considered a violation of individual human rights, U.S. courts nevertheless accept jurisdiction of defendants brought before them by such illegal means. *See, e.g., Ker v. Illinois*, 119 U.S. 436 (1886) (kidnapping by nongovernmental party); *United States v. Alvarez-Machain*, 504 U.S. 655 (1992) (kidnapping by government agents). Illegal recovery of a fugitive, however, will not be ignored by U.S. courts if the abduction, in addition to being illegal, was performed in a violent, brutal and inhumane manner. *See United States v. Toscanino*, 500 F.2d 267 (2d Cir. 1974).

3. Extraordinary Rendition

While *rendition* is a general term for "handing over" individuals to a foreign nation, *extraordinary rendition* refers to the extrajudicial capture and transport of terrorism suspects abroad for interrogation in countries known to practice torture. A highly publicized example involved a Syrian-born Canadian citizen who was mistakenly identified as a terrorist at JFK Airport and deported by the U.S. to Syria. He was tortured for nearly a year before being cleared of wrongdoing and returned to Canada. *See* Commission of Inquiry into the Actions of Canadian Officials in Relation to Maher Arar, *Report of the Events Relating to Maher Arar* (2006). A 2009 Second

Circuit opinion ruled that Arar could not sue for civil damages because the suit was not congressionally recognized. *Arar v. Ashcroft*, 585 F.3d 559 (2009), *cert. denied*, 560 U.S. 978 (2010).

Chapter XV

Enforcement of Human Rights Law in the U.S. & Other Domestic Courts

Before 1986, the only comprehensive human rights treaties ratified by the United States were the Refugee Protocol and the Convention on the Political Rights of Women. The Genocide Convention was ratified in 1986 with a number of reservations, declarations, and understandings, incorporated into the Genocide Convention Implementation Act (18 U.S.C. § 1091). In 1990, the United States Senate ratified the Torture Convention, but stated that the President should not ratify the Convention until implementing legislation had been passed. In 1992, Congress passed the Torture Victim Protection Act, 28 U.S.C. § 1350 (1992), which creates a civil action for damages from torture. The Act does not implement the Torture Convention, which requires criminal sanctions for violations. Also in 1992, the United States ratified the International Covenant on Civil and Political Rights, but as of 2012 had not passed any implementing legislation. In 1994 it ratified the Convention on the Elimination of All Forms of Racial Discrimination. As of June 2012, the United States had not ratified the International Covenant on Economic, Social and Cultural Rights, the American Convention on Human Rights, the Apartheid Convention, the Convention on Elimination of Discrimination Against Women, or the Convention on the Rights of the Child. Because the United States has failed to ratify so many human rights treaties, or to implement treaties characterized as non-self-executing, enforcement of human rights law in United States courts continues to be largely dependent on *incorporation of custom by courts into United States law* and *specific legislative provisions*, such as the Alien Tort Claims Act (28 U.S.C. § 1350) (ATCA).

A. The Alien Tort Claims Act

The Alien Tort Claims Act (sometimes referred to as the Alien Tort Statute or "ATS") confers district court jurisdiction over any "civil action by an alien for a tort only, committed in violation of the law of nations or a treaty of the United States." A claim may be barred, though, due to restrictions based on the political question doctrine or due to certain kinds of immunities, like those provided for in the Foreign Sovereign Immunities

Act (FSIA) and the Federal Tort Claims Act (FTCA). The ATCA has a companion law, the Torture Victim Protection Act (TVPA), that creates a cause of action for torture.

Examples: In *Filartiga v. Pena-Irala*, 630 F.2d 876 (2d Cir. 1980), the Second Circuit Court of Appeals held that *freedom from torture was part of customary international law* for which § 1350 provides federal jurisdiction. *See also Trajano v. Marcos*, 978 F.2d 493 (9th Cir. 1992) (reaffirming the *Filartiga* approach).

In contrast, the D.C. Circuit Court of Appeals in *Tel-Oren v. Libyan Arab Republic*, 726 F.2d 774 (D.C. Cir. 1984) took a much more restrictive approach to § 1350. In *Tel Oren* the plaintiffs sued the alleged perpetrators of an attack on a civilian bus in Israel. The three judge court dismissed the case with three separate opinions. Judge Robb held the case involved a non-justiciable political question. Judge Edwards endorsed *Filartiga*, but concluded that non-state, politically motivated acts of terrorism were not prohibited by customary international law. Judge Bork concluded that the Alien Tort Statute only provided jurisdiction over alien tort suits for which *international law* recognizes an individual cause of action (such as violation of safe conduct, piracy, and infringement of the rights of ambassadors).

Cases in the 1990's and 2000's opened up the possibility of ATCA liability for non-state actors. *See Kadic v. Karadzic*, 70 F.3d 232 (2d Cir. 1995).

In *Kadic v. Karadzic*, 70 F.3d 232 (2d Cir. 1995), the Second Circuit determined that the TVPA is complementary to the ATCA. In *Sosa v. Alvarez-Machain*, 542 U.S. 692 (2004), a Mexican national was forcibly transported into the United States at the request of Drug Enforcement Agency agents. Although the plaintiff's trial and subsequent acquittal occurred in the United States, the Supreme Court found that the root cause of action occurred in a foreign country, and therefore within an exception to that waiver of sovereign immunity in the ATCA.

Several significant decisions were made regarding the ATCA between 2009 and 2010. In *Samantar v. Yousuf*, 560 U.S. 305 (2010), the Supreme Court ruled that an individual is not immune from ATCA liability under the Foreign Sovereign Immunities Act, even if that person was working for a foreign government at the time. The court found that FISA only shields actions of a foreign state or their agents and instrumentalities, none of which were present in *Samantar*.

In *Abdullabi v. Pfizer, Inc.*, 562 F.3d 163 (2d Cir. 2009), *cert. denied*, 561 U.S. 1041 (2010), the Second Circuit held that Pfizer, Inc. violated the laws of nations by experimenting on non-consenting humans; Pfizer tested an antibiotic on Nigerian children without their knowledge or consent. To come to that determination, the court used a three prong analysis: first, the court would only recognize customs that were universally accepted ("universality"); second, it would only employ customs that were as definite and specific as the historical rules that were accepted when the ATCA was originally passed ("specificity"); and third, that countries must demonstrate, though treaties and international agreements, that the issue concerns all nations mutually.

In *Presbyterian Church of Sudan v. Talisman Energy, Inc.*, 582 F.3d 244 (2d Cir. 2009), *cert. denied*, 562 U.S. 946 (2010), the Second Circuit ruled that Talisman Energy Corporation was not liable under the ATCA for genocide, torture, war crimes, and crimes against humanity. The plaintiffs were alleging that Talisman Energy, Inc. aided and abetted the Sudanese government in committing the above crimes. The Second Circuit ruled, however, that though the crimes are universally considered actionable under the

ATCA, aiding and abetting is not universally recognized. In order for Talisman to be held liable, the court ruled that the company must not merely have knowledge of the Sudanese government's crimes, but must act with the purpose of aiding them.

In *Estate of Amergi v. Palestinian Authority*, 611 F.3d 1350 (11th Cir. 2010), the Eleventh Circuit held that single killings by non-state actors, including acts of terrorism, do not violate the ATCA, and that, even if the acts violate the Geneva Convention, not all violations of the Geneva Convention are cognizable under the ATCA.

In *Bowoto v. Chevron Corp.*, 621 F.3d 1116 (9th Cir. 2010), the Ninth Circuit decided that the ATCA applies in wrongful death claims on the high seas, but is preempted by the Death on the High Seas Act for survivor claims.

In *Kiobel v. Royal Dutch Petroleum Co.*, 621 F.3d 111 (2d Cir. 2010) (plaintiff's petition for rehearing en banc denied), the Second Circuit held that corporations are not liable under the ATCA. The court stated that, customarily, international tort liability does not extend to corporations, and thus, federal courts cannot decide those claims under the ATS. The Supreme Court granted certiorari in the case. *See* § XV.B.2 *infra*.

B. Alien Tort Claims Act (ATCA) Defendants

Alien plaintiffs have brought claims under the ATCA against corporate actors for violations of international human rights law. The ATCA also allows plaintiffs to sue individuals.

1. Individuals

Example: In *Lizarbe v. Hurtado*, 2008 WL 941851 (S.D. Fla. March 4, 2008), the court ordered the defendant, a Peruvian accused of taking part in a massacre in Peru, to pay $37 million to two survivors of the event. Robert Gaudet, Jr., *Human Rights*, 43 Int'l Law. 861, 893 (2009).

2. Corporate Liability

a. Courts Split on Corporate Liability

Examples: *Bowoto v. Chevron Corp.*, 557 F. Supp. 2d 1080 (N.D. Cal. 2008), *aff'd* 621 F.3d 1116 (9th Cir. 2010): In December 2008 a jury found that Chevron could not be liable for abuses committed by Nigerian governmental forces in 1998 and 1999.

Khulumani v. Barclay National Bank Ltd., 504 F.3d 254 (2d Cir. 2007): In this case plaintiffs brought suit against over fifty corporate defendants. They claimed that these corporate defendants aided and abetted the South African apartheid regime. The Second Circuit vacated a district court's dismissal of the lawsuit and supported the theory of aiding and abetting under the ATCA.

Wiwa v. Royal Dutch Petroleum: Plaintiffs alleged that Shell and other oil exploration companies aided and abetted Nigerian authorities in various human rights violations, including the execution of a group of activists in 1995. The Second Circuit eventually decided that the ATCA does not confer jurisdiction over claims against corporations. *Kiobel v. Royal Dutch Petroleum Co.*, 621 F.3d 111 (2d Cir. 2010). In December of 2011, the Supreme

Court granted certiorari to hear *Kiobel v. Royal Dutch Petroleum Co.*, 621 F.3d 111 (2d Cir. 2010). Oral argument was heard on February 28, 2012.

Kiobel comes to the Supreme Court from the Second Circuit, where the court held that oil companies in Nigeria could not be sued under the ATCA for aiding and abetting the Nigerian government in using violence to suppress local resistors. The court used *Sosa v. Alvarez-Machain,* 542 U.S. 692 (2004), which mandated looking to international norms in order to define "the law of nations" clause in the ATCA, to conclude that international norms must be examined not only when addressing the type of crime covered by the ATCA, but also when determining whom may be sued. Using that logic, the court looked to international military tribunals which had debated, but ultimately rejected, the idea of corporate liability. From this the court determined that corporate liability was not an international norm, and thus could not be read into the ATCA. The concurrence by Judge Leval agreed that *Kiobel*'s case was not pleaded sufficiently, but wrote separately to express his belief that looking to international criminal tribunals does not reveal whether there is support for international civil liability for corporations, a decision usually left up to individual nations.

Kiobel is an outlier case regarding ATCA liability; it has been rejected by other circuits. For example, *Sinaltrainal v. Coca-Cola Co.*, 578 F.3d 1252 (11th Cir. 2009), held that for the ATCA to be triggered, there must be a demonstrable state action; but that aiding and abetting liability could be extended to individuals and, importantly, to corporations.

After reargument, the Supreme Court affirmed the Second Circuit's judgment in a unanimous opinion. *Kiobel v. Royal Dutch Petroleum*, 569 U.S. 108 (2013). The Court held that there is a presumption against extraterritorial application of U.S. law under the ATCA. The Court found nothing within the text, history, or purpose of the statute that indicated that the ATCA was intended to apply extraterritorially. A petitioner's claim would need to touch and concern the territory of the U.S. with "sufficient force" in order to rebut this presumption. The Court did not address whether corporations are immune from tort liability for violations of the law of nations, as the statute was presumed not to apply.

Doe v. Exxon Mobil, 654 F.3d 11 (D.C. Cir. 2011) also supported the idea of extraterritoriality of the ATCA and the prospect of aiding and abetting liability, stating that there was support for a determination that aiding and abetting itself violates the law of nations, and was accepted by the international community post-World War II as an international criminal norm. The D.C. Circuit Court also recognized corporate liability under the ATCA.

The most recent precedent regarding corporate aiding and abetting liability, *Sarei v. Rio Tinto*, 671 F.3d 736 (9th Cir. 2011) (en banc), followed the D.C. and Eleventh Circuits, holding that

Sosa's reasoning expanded the reach of the ATCA to allow for corporate liability, and that a single purposeful action in furtherance of a war crime amounts to aiding and abetting as recognized under international law. *Rio Tinto* has also been appealed to the Supreme Court.

b. The Torture Victim Protection Act (TVPA)

The 1991 Torture Victim Protection Act (TVPA) establishes a civil action for damages from an "individual" who, under "actual or apparent authority, or color of law of any foreign nation," engages in "torture" or "extra-judicial killing." 106 Stat. 73, note following 28 U.S.C. § 1350. The definition of "torture" in the Act is not the same as that in the Torture Convention. TVPA § 3.

In *Mohamed v. Palestinian Authority*, 566 U.S. 449 (2012), a unanimous Supreme Court held that the TVPA did not extend liability for acts of torture to organizational entities such as the Palestinian Authority. The Court concluded that the term "individual," which was left undefined in the statute, referred only to natural persons because this was the ordinary meaning of "individual," as found in Webster's dictionary. The Court also noted that federal statutes routinely distinguish between individuals and persons, the latter being a term often used to encompass organizational entities. The Court acknowledged that other uses of the term individual exist that could be construed to cover organizational entities, but did not believe these other uses raised doubts as to the plain meaning of the statute. The Court also noted that the legislative history supported this interpretation of the statute, but given the clarity of the statute the history was not necessary to the holding. Justice Breyer, in his concurring opinion, argued that the legislative history ought to be determinative of the Court's interpretation because the word "individual" has different definitions.

c. State Tort Law

In August 2008, a federal district court allowed a case to continue against Exxon Mobil Corporation and Exxon Mobil Oil Indonesia (EMOI) under D.C. tort law. The plaintiffs alleged that the corporation supported killings and torture committed by the Indonesian military. Specifically, the court found that there was evidence suggesting that the atrocities occurred and that the security forces were paid for by EMOI, meaning that EMOI had some right to control the security forces. *Doe v. Exxon Mobil Corp.*, 573 F. Supp. 2d 16 (D.D.C. 2008).

d. Supreme Court Consideration of *Kiobel* and *Rio Tinto*

Less than a week after oral argument on corporate liability, the Supreme Court deferred to its October 2012 term the *Kiobel* case, ordering further argument on the additional issue of whether the ATCA allows U.S. courts to hear suits for violations of international law on foreign soil, a central issue in the *Rio Tinto* case. The Justices apparently chose to defer and expand the scope of hearing on the *Kiobel* case, rather than granting certiorari in the *Rio Tinto* case as well. The scope of the order also suggests that the Court will be addressing the question of recognition of aiding and abetting liability under international law for purposes of the ATCA. Thus these three critical issues under the ATCA will not be determined until the Court's next term, if then, in *Kiobel*.

C. United States Treaty Law

Article VI of the U.S. Constitution, the Supremacy Clause, declares treaties to be "the supreme law of the land" on par with federal legislation.

1. Conflicts

In the event of a conflict between federal legislation and a treaty, the last in time prevails as a matter of U.S. law. Restatement (Third) § 115. A treaty prevails over conflicting state or local law under the Supremacy Clause.

2. Self-Executing vs. Non-Self-Executing

Only self-executing treaties are directly enforceable in U.S. federal courts; non-self-executing treaties are only enforceable through implementing legislation. Whether a treaty is self-executing depends upon the language of the treaty and whether it seems to create direct, immediate obligations. Although many of the provisions of the human rights treaties the United States has ratified do just that, the Senate has characterized every human rights treaty ratified as non-self-executing. In *Medellin v. Texas*, 552 U.S. 491 (2008), the U.S. Supreme Court found that a presidential memorandum could not convert a non-self-executing treaty into a self-executing treaty, given the power allocated to the legislative branch to implement treaties.

3. Reservations, Understandings, and Declarations

Every human rights treaty ratified has been accompanied by a number of reservations, declarations and understandings. A reservation modifies the terms of the treaty between the state asserting the reservation and any state accepting the reservation. Vienna Convention on the Law of Treaties Art. 2. Understandings and declarations are a state's unilateral interpretation or view of a treaty's provisions but do not modify the state's obligations as a matter of international law. The Senate RUDs (reservation, understandings, or declarations) to human rights treaty generally declare the treaties to be non-self-executing (often done by a "proviso" that is not part of the ratification), that no treaty provision may conflict with the Constitution, that the treaty does not disturb the division between state and federal authority, and, in a few instances, specifically preserves a constitutional right or provision of U.S. law which conflicts with a treaty obligation. It is established U.S. constitutional law that a treaty may not derogate from a constitutional right. *Reid v. Covert*, 354 U.S. 1 (1957).

Example: *Ntakirutimana v. Reno*, 184 F.3d 419 (5th Cir. 1999), *cert. denied*, 528 U.S. 1135 (2000). The plaintiff, a Rwandan citizen residing in Texas and subject to surrender to the International Criminal Tribunal for Rwanda (the "Tribunal"), challenged the surrender order. The Fifth Circuit rejected Ntakirutimana's challenge. The Court held that surrendering a person to the Tribunal pursuant to an Executive-Congressional agreement did not offend the Constitution. The court determined that Ntakirutimana's challenges to the validity of the Tribunal's establishment, and to the compatibility of the Tribunal's procedures with the requirements of due process, were beyond the scope of habeas corpus review. This Senate practice has been criticized for allowing the United States to be a party to human rights treaties while ensuring that the treaty will make no changes in United States. law of any kind. Other states have also objected to United States reservations to the ICP as being incompatible with the object and purpose of the treaty, most notably with respect to the death penalty.

4. The Death Penalty Under International Law

With a growing number of states globally and regionally abolishing the death penalty, the question arises whether the death penalty, generally or in specific circumstances, violates international law. In 2007, the United Nations General Assembly reflected the current international consensus with a nonbinding resolution demanding a death penalty moratorium. The resolution passed over many nations' objections, most notably the United States.

a. Domestic Law

In *Stanford v. Kentucky*, 492 U.S. 361 (1989), the U.S. Supreme Court concluded that the prohibition of cruel and unusual punishment is determined by reference to United States norms only, not international norms. In *Gregg v. Georgia*, 428 U.S. 153 (1976), the Supreme Court held that the death penalty is not per se unconstitutional under the 8th Amendment prohibition against cruel and unusual punishment. In a more recent opinion prohibiting execution of the mentally retarded, however, the majority did take into consideration widespread international prohibition of such executions. *Atkins v. Virginia*, 536 U.S. 304 (2002).

In *Roper v. Simmons*, 543 U.S. 551 (2005), the U.S. Supreme Court declared that executing juvenile offenders constituted cruel and unusual punishment as forbidden by the Eighth Amendment to the U.S. Constitution. The Court evaluated trends in juvenile capital punishment from, among other sources, the United Kingdom.

In *Atkins v. Virginia*, 536 U.S. 304 (2002), the U.S. Supreme Court held that the Eighth Amendment does not permit the execution of criminals who are mentally disabled.

In *Baze v. Rees*, 553 U.S. 35 (2008), the Court held that Kentucky's three drug "cocktail" did not violate the Eighth Amendment. The Court determined that challenges to the prosecution's procedures must prove that the state's execution method creates a substantial risk of severe pain and feasible alternatives would reduce that risk. Notably, Justice Stevens renounced capital punishment procedures as unfair in his concurrence. *See id.* at 71–87 (Stevens, J., concurring).

In 2009, in the case of *Bobby v. Bies*, the Supreme Court unanimously held the Ohio Supreme Court could hear Bies' claim that he could not receive the death penalty because he is mentally disabled. The Double Jeopardy Clause and the issue preclusion doctrine did not bar the court from hearing the case.

In *Wood v. Allen*, 558 U.S. 290 (2010), the Supreme Court ruled that a capital conviction would stand for a man who displayed signs of mental retardation, but whose lawyers withheld that evidence as part of trial strategy. The Supreme Court agreed with an Eleventh Circuit ruling denying Wood's habeas claim of ineffective assistance of counsel.

In *Sears v. Upton*, 561 U.S. 945 (2010), the Court vacated a *Strickland* challenge and remanded the case to the Georgia Supreme Court because they did not apply the proper inquiry for evaluating whether counsel had properly investigated mitigating evidence about family trauma.

In *Jefferson v. Upton*, 560 U.S. 284 (2010), the Court vacated and remanded a habeas petition's claim of inadequate representation where the defendant alleged that counsel did not thoroughly investigate the potential significance of a childhood head injury.

In *Cullen v. Pinholster*, 563 U.S. 170 (2011), the Court reversed a Ninth Circuit ruling that had granted a habeas petition to a defendant who claimed that his counsel did not present evidence of his mental illness. The Court ruled that the California Supreme Court, who had originally decided the case, could have reasonably decided the case how they did, and the Supreme Court could not overturn their decision based on the evidence presented to them.

In *Smith v. Spisak*, 558 U.S. 139 (2010), the Court upheld a state court's jury instructions about the mitigation of "mental defect," ruling that they do not go against or unreasonably apply federal law. Using that same reasoning, the Court vacated and remanded a Third Circuit decision of a similar nature in *Beard v. Abu-Jamal*, 558 U.S. 1143 (2010).

In *Thaler v. Haynes*, 559 U.S. 43 (2010), the Court held that deference must be given to the second trial judge's decision that race had not been a factor in excluding a potential juror. This decision overturned a Fifth Circuit case.

In *Wellons v. Hall*, 558 U.S. 220 (2010), the Court overturned an Eleventh Circuit decision and allowed a federal habeas claim to be tried. Based on the reasoning in *Cone v. Bell*, 556 U.S. 449 (2009), the Court ruled that the merits of the defendant's improper jury communication claims must be heard.

In *Magwood v. Patterson*, 561 U.S. 320 (2010), the Court reversed a decision of the Eleventh Circuit and ruled that, if a defendant challenged a death sentence and was later resentenced to death for the same crime, that he could file a habeas petition challenging the new judgment without violating the "one opportunity" rule under the Antiterrorism and Effective Death Penalty Act of 1996.

In *Graham v. Florida*, 560 U.S. 48 (2010), the Court ruled that the 8th Amendment's "cruel and unusual punishment" language prohibits juveniles that are not being tried for homicides from being subjected to life imprisonment without the possibility of parole. In making this decision, the Court looked to capital jurisprudence.

In 2010, the American Law Institute disposed of its model capital law, citing structural and practical flaws in death penalty administration.

b. International Law

The United States has a specific reservation to the ICCPR preserving the death penalty. A number of states have contended that the reservation is invalid under international law as incompatible with the object and purpose of the treaty.

Example: In *State v. Makwanyane*, 1995 (3) SA391 (CC) (S. Afr.) the South African Constitutional Court invalidated the death penalty under the interim South African Constitution of 1993.

The UN General Assembly passed a nonbinding resolution for a moratorium on the death penalty in 2007, but many countries have continued to execute prisoners. Robert Gaudet, Jr., *Human Rights*, 43 INT'L LAW. 861, 873 (2009).

In 2010, Mongolian President Tsakhia Elbegdorj declared that he planned to pardon all inmates on death row because of fears that innocent people were convicted, and also based on growing international disfavor for the death penalty.

In 2010, the Kenyan Court of Appeals ruled that mandatory imposition of the death penalty for some crimes violated the right to life and was unconstitutional (*Mutiso v. Republic* [2010]). The same ruling also decided it was unconstitutional for a person to spend more than three years on death row.

c. *Jus Cogens*

Even if the prohibition on the death penalty generally is not yet *jus cogens* from which there may be no exceptions, a more compelling argument is that it is *jus cogens* in certain circumstances—*e.g.*, execution of juveniles.

Example: In *Domingues v. Nevada*, 114 Nev. 783, 961 P.2d 1279 (1998), *cert. denied*, 528 U.S. 963 (1999), the majority court concluded that the execution of a juvenile offender was specifically allowed by the Senate's reservation to the ICP. The dissents noted that the reservation was incompatible with the object and purpose of the ICP and that either the reservation or the U.S.'s ratification of the treaty might be invalid. In *Domingues v. United States*, the Inter-American Commission deemed that a consensus existed that offenders under eighteen at the time of the crime should not be executed. Case No. 12.285, Inter-Am. C.H.R., Rep. No. 62/02, OEA/Ser.L/V/II.117, doc. 1 rec. 1 (2002).

d. Extradition

In a 1989 European Court of Human Rights case, the Court found that the potential extradition of a person facing the death penalty in the U.S. violated the European Convention because of the circumstances facing the person on death row and other considerations surrounding the crime itself. *See Soering v. United Kingdom*, 161 Eur. Ct. H.R. (ser. A) (1989).

i.   In *Sanchez-Llamas v. Oregon*, 548 U.S. 331 (2006), the U.S. Supreme Court found that a foreign national in the process of being arrested could not suppress the incriminating statements he made to police even though he was not notified of his Article 36 rights.

ii. The Human Rights Committee held that a state party that had abolished the death penalty could not extradite a person to face the death penalty in compliance with the Covenant. *Judge v. Canada,* Comm. No. 829/1998, U.N. Doc. CCPR/C/78/D/829/1998 (2003).

iii. A violation of Articles 2 and 3 of the Convention may occur when a Contracting State deports a person who has been denied a fair trial, or is likely to be denied a fair trial, when the likely punishment is the death penalty. The European Court of Human Rights held that Sweden's efforts to deport a family to Syria violated Articles 2 and 3 of the Convention when the father had been convicted and sentenced to death in absentia. *Bader and Kanbor v. Sweden*, App. No. 13284/04, 2005–XI Eur. Ct. H.R.

e. Consular Notice

The Vienna Convention on Consular Relations, Article 36, provides an opportunity for notice to the counsel of any state whose national is detained or arrested, and requires that the person detained or arrested be informed of the rights accorded by the Convention. In *Germany v. United States*, 2001 I.C.J. 466 the ICJ held the United States had violated its obligations to Germany and the individual defendants under the Convention by not advising the defendants of their rights and by not permitting review and reconsideration of their sentences and convictions. In *Avena*, the ICJ held that the United States had violated the Vienna Convention on Consular Relations by failing to inform certain Mexican nationals of their Vienna Convention rights. In *Medellin v. Texas*, 552 U.S. 491 (2008), however, the Supreme Court held that this decision, while binding, was not directly enforceable domestic federal law that could preempt state limitations of filing of successive habeas petitions.

Although a President's Memorandum required state courts to give effect to the *Avena* decision, this requirement did not force states to disregard their procedural rules in reviewing the plaintiffs' claims. The courts are split on whether Article 36 creates an individual right.

f. Sovereign Immunity

The immunity of states in U.S. courts is governed by the Foreign Sovereign Immunities Act. 28 U.S.C. §§ 1339, 1605 *et seq*. Despite growing recognition that immunity should not preclude prosecution for certain international crimes, domestic courts continue to refuse consideration of such claims based on doctrines of sovereign immunity which are an inconsistent mix of international law, domestic law, and domestic court interpretation of international law.

The FSIA was amended by the 2008 National Defense Authorization Act, Pub. L. 110–181, 122 Stat. 3 (2008), which allows private parties to seek money damages against a foreign state designated as a state sponsor of terrorism. See *Gates v. Syrian Arab Republic,* 580 F. Supp. 2d 53 (2008) for an example of the amendment's use.

In March of 2011, the U.S. Court of Appeals for the District of Columbia held that the FSIA does not preclude contempt-of-court sanctions on foreign states for noncompliance with discovery orders. The Democratic Republic of the Congo (DRC) was held in civil contempt and made to pay a fine starting at $5000 and doubling every 2 weeks to a max of $80000 until it complied with discovery requests in a trial revolving around claims of government nonpayment of money due to a construction firm. The U.S. government filed a motion in support of the DRC but the Court of Appeals found nothing wrong with the lower court's ruling, and based this opinion on the principle that simply because sanctions are unenforceable, it does not follow that they should not be issued. John R. Crook, ed. *Contemporary Practice of the United States*, 105 Am. J. Int'l L. 578, 578–9 (2011).

i. The *Pinochet* Case, 2 All ER 97, [1999] 2 WLR 827 (House of Lords, 24 March 1999)

In 1998, police in London arrested the former president of Chile pursuant to a Spanish arrest warrant from 1973 and 1990. In a sharply splintered decision, the House of Lords denied immunity on narrow grounds. Utilizing the "dual criminality" rule of extradition law (*see* p. 133 *supra*), the panel concluded that both Great Britain and Spain had claimed jurisdiction over torture committed abroad only after December 8, 1988, when Great Britain became a party to the Convention Against Torture.

ii. The ICJ Decision in the *Congo* Case

In *Democratic Republic of the Congo v. Belgium*, Judgment, ICJ Reports 2002, p. 3 (Feb. 14, 2002) the ICJ gave a broad reach to sovereign immunity to international crimes which was immediately subject to criticism and a major setback to prosecution of gross human rights abuses. Rejecting Belgium's position of no immunity from war crimes and crimes against humanity as outside of official functions and the acts being committed before that position, the ICJ concluded that while acting as Minister for Foreign Affairs the individual had immunity from issuance of an arrest warrant pursuant to a Belgium law prescribing universal jurisdiction over these offenses and stating that "[i]mmunity attaching to the official capacity of a person shall not prevent the application of the present law." The Court concluded that the immunity was available with no distinction between "official" and "private" acts, and even for acts performed prior to assumption of the position accorded immunity. The Court was also unwilling to recognize a norm of custom of no immunity generally for war crimes or crimes against humanity, at least in state courts.

iii. *Belhas v. Ya'alon*, 515 F.3d 1279 (D.C. Cir. 2008)

In this case, an Israeli general was found to be protected by sovereign immunity for his actions during an Israeli military campaign in Lebanon because his actions were done as part of his duties as a general and not as a private individual.

D. Commission on Unalienable Rights

In July 2019, U.S. Secretary of State Pompeo established a Commission on Unalienable Rights, designed to "provide the Secretary of State advice and recommendations concerning international human rights matters . . . [and] provide fresh thinking about human rights discourse where such discourse has departed from our nation's founding principles of natural law and natural rights." Department of State Commission on Unalienable Rights, 84 Fed. Reg. 25109 (May 30, 2019). The Commission studied the Universal Declaration of Human Rights and Founding-era documents to produce a written guide. The Commission will automatically dissolve after two years unless formally determined to be in the public interest to continue it for another two years. Establishment of this Commission faced criticism and concern that the Commission was redundant, given the career, non-partisan human rights experts already at the State Department, and that the Commission could be used to denigrate LGBTQ+ and reproductive rights. Letter from 50 Democratic U.S. Representative to Mike Pompeo, Secretary of State (July 18, 2019), https://foreignaffairs.house.gov/_cache/files/2/9/294cc9ed-3391-4fa2-968a-424f8

e687dac/6B92FE10FE738FAEB3A6FB2BB7E69BC9.doc139.pdf [https://perma.cc/7XHZ-QY28].

The Commission released its final report in August 2020. Report of the Commission of Unalienable Rights, U.S. Dept. of State, Aug. 26, 2020.

Appendix A

Essay Exam Questions and Answers

Question 1: Santa Lucia, a Central American country bordered on the south by the state of Manatea, recently held elections in which Samuel Everyman of the Free People's Party was elected president. Shortly after assuming office, Everyman initiated steps toward a more socialist form of government, including broad social welfare programs and nationalization of Pan Am Fruit Company (a wholly owned subsidiary of a United States company, but incorporated in Santa Lucia). In addition, Everyman entered into a treaty to receive military weapons from the Soviet Union, similar to an earlier treaty with the United States.

At the same time Everyman began mass executions of members of the Right Party, the party of the previous repressive government led by Jean Dominique. Jean Dominique, hiding in exile and furious over the election results, claimed in several recent interviews that the election had to have been "fixed" by Everyman given his own broad based support among the people (although many sources have speculated that Dominique's reign of terror had led to popular support for Everyman). In fact, poverty and illiteracy in the state have been so extensive that no more than 10% of the population has ever voted in the two elections held since independence from colonial rule in 1954 in the first term of Dominique's seven terms in the presidency. Nevertheless, supporters of Dominique within Santa Lucia formed an "underground" group known as the White Guard, advocating the violent overthrow of the Everyman government. To this end, they staged destructive attacks on public utilities, railroad lines, and other major arteries of transportation from their base in the neighboring country of Manatea.

The United States, displeased with the turn of events in Santa Lucia, terminated its military aid treaty with the Everyman government citing the mass executions, nationalization of Pan Am Fruit and its own domestic law provisions governing military aid. The United States also severed diplomatic relations with the Everyman government. Relations between the United States and Santa Lucia steadily worsened. The U.S.S.R., North Korea, Cambodia, Cuba and approximately fifteen other countries which had previously refused to recognize the Dominique government quickly recognized the Everyman government to demonstrate their support.

Manatea, Santa Lucia's neighbor to the south, also claimed to have been the victim of "terrorist" activities by rebels (known as the Santanistas) within its borders. The

Santanistas opposed the Manatean government and received weapons from the Santa Lucia government. In a series of newspaper articles and in meetings of the House and Senate Intelligence Committees it had also come to light that the United States Central Intelligence Agency (C.I.A.) in Manatea, with the knowledge and approval of the President, had been advising the White Guard rebels from their bases in Manatea on their military activities over the border in Santa Lucia.

In a series of events, the violence in Santa Lucia and Manatea quickly escalated. The internal conflict in Manatea assumed the dimensions of full warfare, with the northern region under the control of the established government and the southern region under the control of the Santanistas. Trapped within the capital city in the southern region due to disruption of transportation was a substantial foreign population including United States nationals. Two United States journalists critical of the Manatean government, while covering the conflict at one of the fronts, disappeared and were afterward found dead in circumstances that indicated they were executed by a vigilante group of Manatean military officers fanatically opposed to any criticism of the Manatean government. Despite expressing its deepest regrets, the Manatean government made no further investigation of the incident. Many Manateans from the southern region of the state began fleeing from the destruction by boat and seeking refuge in the United States (To this time the United States has refused refuge). Thus far, however, the full scale conflict in Manatea has not spread to any of its neighboring countries.

In a chain of attacks, the Santanistas destroyed the main highway between the Manatean capital city in the south and the northern border. In retaliation, the Manatean government: (1) blockaded the southern ports with the Manatean navy 12 miles from shore and began searches from there of all foreign ships suspected of carrying weapons to the rebels; (2) staged a counter-attack on three Santanistan military installations in the southern region; (3) had Manatean forces cross the border into Santa Lucia to bomb indiscriminately two villages reasonably believed to be bases and refuges for the Santanista rebels; and (4) began executions without trial of all captured Santanista rebels.

Assume that Manatea and Santa Lucia are parties to and have ratified the Geneva Conventions of 1949 (and all subsequent protocols), the UN Charter, the Organization of American States (OAS) Charter, the Rio Pact, the Pact of Bogota, the International Covenant on Civil and Political Rights, the Genocide Convention, the Vienna Convention on the Law of Treaties and the Convention Relating to the Status of Refugees.

U.S. Senator Eagle, a full fledged supporter of the President's foreign policy in Manatea and Santa Lucia, comes to you, his aide, for preparation of a memo on the international law implications of the United States' actions in Manatea and Santa Lucia based on all of the above facts. Senator Eagle believes that U.S. actions in Santa Lucia and Manatea were justified under international law, but wants you to include in your memo all arguments that his opponents might advance that the United States acted in violation of international law, and on assessment of the legal grounds for Security Council intervention.

Question 2: India and Pakistan have experienced steadily worsening diplomatic relations between the two states for the past five years.

Disturbed by the worsening of relations and intensification of the nuclear arms threat between India and Pakistan, an Indian nuclear freeze group known as the Nuclear Liberation Front (NLF) decided to utilize information from several of its members that India had virtually no established security systems for its scientific and military installations. By breaking into the Indian Satellite Control System Building, the NLF members successfully interfered with the flight plan of a nuclear-powered weather satellite belonging to India in orbit around the earth, causing it to explode and several weeks later to shower several states with low level radioactive debris. The NLF members fled to Pakistan, where they were greeted as heroes by the government and applauded for their attack on the satellite control system.

India filed charges of criminal destruction of government property (punishable by three years imprisonment) against the members of the NLF, who were tried, convicted, and sentenced to three months imprisonment by a criminal court without their being present at the trial or sentencing. India is now seeking extradition. Assume that the treaties governing extradition between India and Pakistan contain standard extradition provisions.

Question 3: On February 23, 1993, a lawsuit was filed in a federal district court against the Bosnian Serbian leader, Radovan Karadzic. The suit is a multimillion-dollar civil class action lawsuit filed by three human rights organizations charging Karadzic with responsibility for systematic rape, forced pregnancies, murder, and torture allegedly carried out by Serbian forces under his command in Bosnia-Herzegovina primarily against Serbian Moslems. The class action was filed on behalf of two anonymous female plaintiffs—a sixteen-year-old raped and beaten by Serbian soldiers, and an eighteen-year-old raped by Serbian soldiers who also killed her mother. The suit is a class action on behalf of all "women and men who suffered rape, summary execution, other torture or other cruel, inhuman and degrading treatment inflicted by Bosnian Serb military forces under the command and control of the defendant."

Assume that you are a law clerk for the federal district court judge who will decide the case. The judge has asked you to write a memo addressing the jurisdiction of the court over the suit, its justiciability, and the decision on the merits (she wants you to evaluate the merits even if you conclude the court does not have jurisdiction).

Question 4: Assume that the following facts and law are contained in an application to the European Commission on Human Rights by Mr. Jens Soering.

Mr. Jens Soering is a German national. He is currently detained in prison in the United Kingdom pending extradition to the United States of America to face charges of murder in the Commonwealth of Virginia.

The homicides in question were committed in Bedford County, Virginia, in March 1985. The victims, William Reginald Haysom and Nancy Astor Haysom, were the parents of the applicant's girlfriend, Elizabeth Haysom, who is a Canadian national. Death in each case was the result of multiple and massive stab and slash wounds to the neck, throat and body. At the time the applicant and Elizabeth Haysom, aged eighteen and twenty respectively, were students at the University of Virginia. They disappeared together from Virginia in October 1985, but were arrested in England in April 1986 in connection with check fraud.

The applicant was interviewed in the United Kingdom between 5 and 8 June 1986 by a police investigator from the Sheriff's Department of Bedford County. In a sworn affidavit dated 24 July 1986 the investigator recorded the applicant as having admitted the killings in his presence and in that of two United Kingdom police officers. The applicant had stated that he was in love with Miss Haysom but that her parents were opposed to the relationship. He and Miss Haysom had therefore planned to kill them. The applicant went to the parents' house, discussed the relationship with them and, when they told him they would do anything to prevent it, a row developed during which he killed them with a knife.

On 13 June 1986 a grand jury of the Circuit Court of Bedford County, Virginia, indicted him on charges of murdering the Haysom parents. The charges alleged capital murder of both of them and alternatively the non-capital murders of each victim.

On 11 August 1986 the Government of the United States of America requested the applicant's extradition under the terms of the Extradition Treaty of 1972 between the United States and the United Kingdom. The applicant was subsequently arrested on 30 December at HM Prison Chelmsford after serving a prison sentence for check fraud.

On 29 October 1986 the British Embassy in Washington addressed a request to the United States' authorities in the following terms:

Because the death penalty has been abolished in the United Kingdom, the Embassy has been instructed to seek an assurance, in accordance with the terms of . . . the Extradition Treaty, that, in the event of Mr. Soering being surrendered and being convicted of the crimes for which he has been indicted . . ., the death penalty, if imposed, will not be carried out.

Should it not be possible on constitutional grounds for the United States Government to give such an assurance, the United Kingdom authorities ask that the United States Government undertake to recommend to the appropriate authorities that the death penalty should not be imposed or, if imposed, should not be executed.

On 1 June 1987 Mr. Updike swore an affidavit in his capacity as Attorney for Bedford County, Virginia, in which he certified as follows:

> I hereby certify that should Jens Soering be convicted of the offense of capital murder as charged in Bedford County, Virginia . . . a representation will be made in the name of the United Kingdom to the judge at the time of sentencing that it is the wish of the United Kingdom that the death penalty should not be imposed or carried out.

The assurance was transmitted to the United Kingdom Government under cover of a diplomatic note on 8 June. It is common practice in potential death penalty cases for the United Kingdom to accept such assurances, but there has never been a case in which the effectiveness of such an assurance has been tested. During the course of the present proceedings the Virginia authorities have informed the United Kingdom Government that Mr. Updike was not planning to provide any further assurances and intended to seek the death penalty in Mr. Soering's case because the evidence, in his determination, supported such action.

On 16 June 1987 at the Bow Street Magistrates' Court committal proceedings took place before the Chief Stipendiary Magistrate. On 3 August 1988 the Secretary of State signed a warrant ordering the applicant's surrender to the United States' authorities. On 5 August 1988 the applicant was transferred to a prison hospital where he remained until early November 1988 under the special regime applied to suicide-risk prisoners. The applicant, as a German citizen, is not subject to criminal trial in the United Kingdom.

According to psychiatric evidence adduced on behalf of the applicant, the applicant's dread of extreme physical violence and homosexual abuse from other inmates in death row in Virginia is in particular having a profound psychiatric effect on him. The psychiatrist's report records a mounting desperation in the applicant, together with objective fears that he may seek to take his own life.

The Virginia Code provides that eight types of homicide constitute capital murder, punishable as a Class 1 felony, including "the willful, deliberate and premeditated killing of more than one person. . . ." The punishment for a Class 1 felony is "death or imprisonment for life". The sentencing procedure in a capital murder case in Virginia is a separate proceeding from the determination of guilt. Following a determination of guilty of capital murder, the same jury, or judge sitting without a jury, will forthwith proceed to hear evidence regarding punishment. All relevant evidence concerning the offence and the defendant is admissible. Evidence in mitigation is subject to almost no limitation, while evidence of aggravation is restricted by statute.

Unless the prosecution proves beyond a reasonable doubt the existence of at least one of two statutory aggravating circumstances—future dangerousness or vileness—the sentencer may not return a death sentence. "Future dangerousness" exists where there is a probability that the defendant would commit "criminal acts of violence" as would constitute a "continuing serious threat to society". "Vileness" exists when the crime was "outrageously or wantonly vile, horrible or inhuman in that it involved torture, depravity of mind or an aggravated battery to the victim". The words "depravity of mind" mean "a degree of moral turpitude and physical debasement surpassing that inherent in the definition of ordinary legal malice and premeditation." The words "aggravated battery" mean a battery which, "qualitatively and quantitatively, is more culpable than the minimum necessary to accomplish an act of murder". Proof of multiple wounds sustained by the victim, particularly a neck wound, has been held to satisfy the test of "vileness". The imposition of the death penalty on a young person who has reached the age of majority—which is eighteen years—is not precluded under Virginia law. Age and the defendant's mental condition at the time of the offence, including any level of mental illness, are factors which can be mitigating factors in sentencing.

The average time between trial and execution in Virginia, calculated on the basis of the executions which have taken place since 1977, is six to eight years. The delays are primarily due to a strategy by convicted prisoners to prolong the appeal proceedings as much as possible. The Governor of the Commonwealth of Virginia has an unrestricted power to commute capital punishment. As a matter of policy, the Governor does not promise, before a conviction and sentence, that he will later exercise his commutation power.

There are approximately forty people under sentence of death in Virginia. The majority are detained in Mecklenburg Correctional Center, which is a maximum security institution with a capacity for 335 inmates. The size of a death row inmate's cell is 3m by 2.2m. Prisoners have an opportunity for approximately seven 1/2 hours' recreation per week in summer and approximately six hours per week, weather permitting, in winter. The death row area has two recreation yards, both of which are equipped with basketball courts and one of which is equipped with weights and weight benches. Inmates are also permitted to leave their cells on other occasions, such as to receive visits, to visit the law library or to attend the prison infirmary. In addition, death row inmates are given one hour out-of-cell time in the morning in a common area. Each death row inmate is eligible for work assignments, such as cleaning duties. When prisoners move around the prison they are handcuffed with special shackles around the waist.

The applicant has produced much evidence of extreme stress, psychological deterioration, and risk of homosexual abuse and physical attack undergone by prisoners on death row, including Mecklenburg Correctional Center.

Death row inmates receive the same medical service as inmates in the general population. An infirmary equipped with adequate supplies, equipment and staff provides for twenty-four-hour in-patient care, and emergency facilities are provided in each building. Mecklenburg also provides psychological and psychiatric services to death row inmates.

A death-row prisoner is moved to the death house fifteen days before he is due to be executed. The death house is next to the death chamber where the electric chair is situated. While a prisoner is in the death house he is watched twenty-four hours a day. He is isolated and has no lights in his cell. The lights outside are permanently lit. A prisoner who utilizes the appeals process can be placed in the death house several times.

In his application Mr. Soering stated his belief that, notwithstanding the assurance given to the United Kingdom Government, there was a serious likelihood that he would be sentenced to death if extradited to the United States of America. He maintained that in the circumstances and, in particular, having regard to the "death row phenomenon" (the length and conditions of confinement for persons sentenced to death), he would thereby be subjected to a violation of Article 3 of the Convention.

Analyze fully, as if you were writing the report of the Commission, whether Soering's extradition to Virginia by the United Kingdom would violate *Article 3* of the European Convention on Human Rights solely with respect to his being subject to the "death row phenomenon."

ANSWERS

SAMPLE ANSWER 1:

Despite Art 2(4) of the UN, the Security Council can intervene under Articles 39–42. If it determines that there is in existence a threat to peace, breach of peace, or an act of aggression, it may make recommendations and decide what measures to take. Often, however, the SC defers to a regional organization to reach a pacific settlement before it will intervene. (Art. 53) If the SC finds that the regional organization (here OAS) has failed, is incapable of doing anything or if the situation warrants it, they may even be able to intervene militarily. (Art. 42)

The UN can provide humanitarian aid if it is necessary to protect lives and to provide food and medical supplies. Humanitarian aid is not considered to be intervention to one side or the other.

At this point in the conflict it would be advisable to (1) see if the regional organization can intervene and negotiate a settlement; or (2) limit assistance to humanitarian aid. Perhaps a Council resolution calling for the cessation of U.S. and other states' involvement and covert activities would help to diminish the conflict.

Because the procedures employed may be protracted, it might be necessary for the UN to go ahead and provide humanitarian assistance if the lives or health of the people of Manatea are in jeopardy. Any country can send in food and medical supplies without risking neutrality.

Arguments Favoring UN Military Intervention

The UN is free to exercise its authority in the conflict notwithstanding the existence of the OAS. Articles 52(2) and 52(3) of the UN Charter encourage resort to regional organizations such as the OAS "to achieve pacific settlement of local disputes." The conflict cannot be properly characterized as a "local" dispute, given the intervention of the United States and the other countries, foreign nationals trapped and refugees trekking to the borders. The language of Article 52 of the UN Charter, when read with Article 103, makes clear that the UN has primary jurisdiction.

The UN is authorized to intervene on the basis of Chapter VII of the UN Charter. Although prohibiting the United Nations from intervening "in matters which are essentially within the domestic jurisdiction" of member States such as Santa Lucia and

Manatea, Article 2(7) of the UN Charter provides that this principle of nonintervention "shall not prejudice the application of enforcement measures under Chapter VII" which, per Articles 39, 42, authorizes the Security Council to undertake military action in the event of "any threat to the peace, breach of the peace, or act of aggression."

The conflict may now be described under Article 39 of the UN Charter as at least a "threat to the peace" (if not also an actual "breach of the peace" and/or "act of aggression") that warrants UN military intervention under Article 42 of the UN Charter to restore and maintain international peace and security. The intense and widespread human rights violations present in the instant case constitute a threat to the peace in and of themselves.

The recruitment, outfitting, training, supply, and direction of mercenaries by the United States in the conflict may even permit a Security Council determination under Article 39 of the UN Charter of an "act of aggression," Article 3(g) of the 1974 UN Resolution [UNGA Res. 3314 (XXIX)] on the Definition of Aggression, which is an authoritative interpretation of the UN Charter, states that "the sending by or on behalf of a State of . . . mercenaries" constitutes "aggression". The framers of the UN Charter conferred upon the Security Council, in the provisions of Chapter VII, a very broad competence both "to determine the existence of any threat to the peace, breach of the peace, or act of aggression" and to decide upon what measures should be taken to "maintain or restore international peace and security." Articles 1(3), 55, and 56 of the UN Charter, make promotion and protection of human rights one of the major purposes of the UN system, and at least implicitly authorize UN military intervention to ensure humanitarian relief and assistance.

As a lesser measure, widespread human rights deprivations in the conflict may be seen "to endanger the maintenance of international peace and security," within the meaning of Chapter VI of the UN Charter, and enable the Security Council, via Article 36 of the UN Charter, to "recommend appropriate procedures or methods of [dispute] adjustment."

Gross violations of human rights, as in the instant case, are matters of international concern and therefore beyond the reach of the nonintervention principle of Article 2(7) of the UN Charter. Also, UN military intervention for humanitarian purposes is at least implicitly authorized by Article VIII of the 1948 Convention on the Prevention and Punishment of the Crime of Genocide. The conflict presents evidence of genocidal mass killings.

Assuming that international law recognizes a State's right to military intervention for humanitarian purposes, *a fortiori* the UN, as a collection of states, is authorized to intervene militarily for the purpose of providing humanitarian relief, especially given that the achievement of international cooperation "in solving international problems of an . . . humanitarian character, and in promoting and encouraging respect for human rights" is, per Article 1(3) of the UN Charter, a central purpose of the UN system. Also, it is good policy to permit UN military intervention for the purpose of humanitarian relief because the danger of such a policy being used for abusive reasons is less likely than on the part of a state or group of states.

Arguments Opposing UN Military Intervention

The UN is not free to exercise jurisdiction and authority in the matter of the conflict without first deferring to the OAS. While the UN may be said to have primary jurisdiction as regards matters over which the OAS also has jurisdiction, under Article 33 of the UN Charter, "[t]he parties . . . shall, first of all, seek a solution by . . . resort to regional agencies or arrangements, or other peaceful means of their own choice." Article 33 of the UN Charter uses the mandatory "shall seek."

Under Article 52(3) of the UN Charter, the UN Security Council "shall encourage the . . . pacific settlement of local disputes through such regional arrangements" as the OAU. Article 52(3) of the UN Charter also uses the mandatory "shall encourage" and not the hortatory "may encourage." Except for the indirect and relatively minor involvement of a few non-American powers, the internal conflict otherwise represents a "local dispute" within the meaning of Article 52(3) of the UN Charter.

The UN is not entirely free to exercise jurisdiction and authority in the conflict on the basis of Chapter VII of the UN Charter. The conflict does not yet present a "threat to the peace, breach of the peace, or act of aggression" within the meaning of Article 39 of the UN Charter.

The indirect, minor involvement of a few powers in the conflict represents, at most, a situation that might "endanger" international peace and security within the meaning of Chapter VI of the UN Charter for the *pacific* settlement of disputes.

The recruitment, outfitting, training, supply, and direction of mercenaries by the United States in the conflict does not permit a Security Council determination under Article 39 of the UN Charter of an "act of aggression" that warrants UN military intervention. Article 3(g) of the 1974 UN Resolution [UNGA Res. 3314 (XXIX)] on the Definition of Aggression characterizes only the "sending" of mercenaries by or on behalf of a State as an "act of aggression."

Moreover, the general hortatory principles in Articles 1(3), 55, and 56 of the UN Charter, do not implicitly authorize UN military intervention to ensure humanitarian relief. UN military intervention for humanitarian purposes is not explicitly or implicitly authorized by Article VIII of the 1948 Convention on the Prevention and Punishment of the Crime of Genocide and here the evidence of genocidal mass killings is not clear.

International law does not recognize a State's right to military intervention for humanitarian purposes given Article 2(4) and the limitation of state force under Article 52 to self-defense. It is possible for UN intervention, like unilateral intervention on the part of individual States, to be selective and abusive.

SAMPLE ANSWER 2:

Part A: Extradition by Pakistan of the NLF Members to India

No duty to extradite exists in the absence of an applicable treaty. To require extradition by Pakistan of the NLF members, India must meet the requirements outlined in a standard extradition treaty. India seeks extradition of the NLF members for the carrying out of a sentence. Extradition is available for conduct which is a crime in both the requesting state and the asylum state (double criminality principle). Presumably, destruction of government property is a punishable offense in Pakistan as well as India. If Pakistan does not recognize the conduct as a punishable offense, Pakistan is not obligated to return the NLF members to India. Alternatively, the treaty may have a list of extraditable offenses.

An extraditable offense must be punishable by a maximum period, usually at least one year, or the punishment awarded must be for a specified period, usually at least several months. The Indian criminal court sentenced the NLF members to three months imprisonment.

India may assert territorial jurisdiction because the crime charged to the NLF members was committed within Indian territory. None of the accused appears to be Pakistani nationals, and there appears to be probable cause for the charge.

Political Offense Exception. Relying on the political offense exception, Pakistan may refuse to extradite the NLF members even if the conduct of the NLF members is otherwise considered an extraditable offense. Pakistan has great discretion to decide whether the conduct of the NLF members constituted a political offense. India will maintain that the destruction of the weather satellite is not a political offense because the act was not done with the purpose of overthrowing India's political regime, but was an ordinary criminal offense.

The destruction of the weather satellite is not a "pure" political offense. Only such crimes as treason, sedition, and espionage are considered "pure" political offenses.

Pakistan, however, may find NLF's crime to be a "relative" political offense according to one of the three customary approaches: the "political incidence" test, the "political objective" test, or the "predominant motive" test.

Under the "political incidence" test, the criminal offense must be committed in the course of a dispute between the government and the party with political aims. The purpose of the crime must be to further the aims of the party. Pakistan may find that the NLF members acted in response to India's refusal to effect a nuclear freeze. The NLF members acted to change the nuclear policies of India. India will argue that the NLF members did not act in the course of a dispute with the Indian government. India will also argue that NLF actions cannot constitute political offenses because the NLF is an environmental group with no aim of attaining power.

The "political objective" approach requires that the means used must relate to the political objective and a degree of proportionality exist between the political objective and the crime. India will challenge the nexus between the NLF's goal of a nuclear freeze and their destruction of a nuclear-powered weather satellite. Destruction of a weather satellite has little connection to the goal of increased security at India nuclear facilities or eradication of nuclear arms. The risk created by the NLF's actions is in fact counter to the goals of the NLF. India may also argue that the destruction of the satellite and resultant damage are not proportional to the objective of modification of government policy. The NLF members may contend that their purpose was not to destroy the satellite but rather to inconvenience the government so it would take notice of NLF's proposals. The analysis under the "political motive" would be similar but Pakistan will have to show a direct link between the crime and the political act.

Pakistan may also refuse to honor India's extradition request if Pakistan believes that the purpose of the extradition request is to prosecute or punish the NLF members for their political opinions. Pakistan may argue that the *in absentia* trial by India is evidence of India's prejudice and indifference to the rights of the NLF members. India will argue that its purpose is not persecution of the NLF members, evidenced by the light sentence given to the NLF members.

Acts of Terrorism. According to many extradition provisions for the suppression of terrorism, an act which creates a collective danger for civilians is not regarded as a political offense for extradition purposes. India will argue that NLF's offense should not be covered by the political offense for extradition purposes. India will argue that NLF's offense would not be covered by the political offense exception as an act of terrorism because the NLF's destruction of the satellite created a serious danger by the resultant shower of radioactive debris on several states. The political offense exception is based on the theory that political crimes do not threaten international public order. Although the NLF members may have directed their actions at domestic public policy, their actions clearly caused damage of an international nature.

SAMPLE ANSWER 3:

Federal Court Jurisdiction. The main jurisdictional mechanisms for bringing this lawsuit in federal court are the Alien Tort Statute and the Torture Victim Protection Act.

Alien Tort Claims Act. The federal district court may claim jurisdiction based on the ATCA, which grants original jurisdiction to U.S. federal courts of any civil action by an alien for a tort committed in violation of the law of nations. Interpretations of the prerequisites for jurisdiction under the statute are controversial, as exemplified by *the Filartiga* and *Tel-Oren* decisions. If the parties are changed, the Supreme Court has left undecided the issues of corporate liability, aiding and abetting liability, and extraterritorial applicability of the ATCA in the pending case of *Kiobel.*

Under the narrow interpretation of the statute espoused in Bork's *Tel-Oren* opinion, the federal court would not assert jurisdiction based on the statute. The Bork approach limits the scope of the statute to a narrow class of cases for which an individual cause of action for the violations is recognized in international law.

The broader view of the Alien Tort Statute found in the *Filartiga* case and Edward's opinion in *Tel-Oren* supports a finding of jurisdiction in this case. *Filartiga* held that "deliberate torture perpetrated under color of official authority violated universally accepted norms of the international law of human rights. . . ." Thus, whenever an alien is within U.S. borders, the Alien Tort Statute provides federal jurisdiction. The acts charged to Karadzic may be deemed "torture perpetrated under color of official authority." As for any other violations alleged, the court would have jurisdiction so long as the violation is one prohibited by customary international law.

Torture Victim Protection Act. The district court may assert jurisdiction based on the Torture Act, which supplements the Alien Tort Statute. The Act provides alien victims of torture with a private right of action in U.S. courts. The acts charged to Karadzic constitute torture as defined in the Act. Under the Act, Karadzic may be held liable "in a civil action for damages to the individual" victims of torture.

Genocide Convention Implementation Act of 1987. The federal district court may not claim jurisdiction based on the Genocide Act. Karadzic is not a U.S. national and the acts charged to Karadzic did not occur within U.S. territory. The Act applies only to criminal charges and would not cover the civil suit filed against Karadzic.

Justiciability and Immunity. The federal district court may dismiss the case even if the court could claim jurisdiction under the two statutes.

Political Question. The federal district court may find that the case is nonjusticiable because of the politically volatile nature of the case and its bearing on U.S. foreign policy. In *Tel-Oren,* Judge Robb dismissed as a political question a tort action based on a terrorist attack in Israel. Judge Bork's opinion in *Tel-Oren* also supports the argument that adjudication of plaintiffs' claims would require the analysis of international legal principles that are not clearly defined.

The counterargument is that the issues presented primarily involve interpretation of a number of treaties, which is the quintessential job of the courts. The doctrine does not require that all questions involving foreign affairs be considered political questions. No separation of power issues were raised, as in a clash between branches of government or with judicial usurpation of a role confined to another branch.

Sovereign Immunity. Karadzic may argue sovereign immunity as a state actor. Under modern international law, specifically the Nuremberg Charter, the Geneva Conventions, and the Genocide Convention, however, state actors may be held personally liable for international crimes such as war crimes, genocide, and torture. This principle of non-immunity is both by treaty and custom and, as such, is part of U.S. domestic law. Also, provisions of the Foreign Sovereign Immunities Act arguably deny immunity for violations of obligations imposed by international agreement.

Merits of the Case. The Torture Act provides a remedy for any alien who is a victim of torture. The plaintiff under the Alien Tort Statute must demonstrate a tort in violation of the "law of nations" or "a treaty of the United States." There is a strong consensus that custom prohibits genocide, torture, and war crimes, among other violent acts. The U.S. is also a party to the Geneva and Genocide Conventions, and the Senate has ratified the Torture Convention. Severe pain and suffering, both mental and physical, intentionally inflicted on the Serbian Moslems would meet the definition of torture under the Torture Convention and the Torture Act. Systematic rapes could also be deemed serious bodily injury or mental harm under both. The torture and rapes allegedly carried out by the Serbian forces under Karadzic's command, primarily against Serbian Moslems, have also resulted in death, serious bodily injury, and mental harm to the members of an identifiable religious and ethnic groups. Such acts, if coupled with intent to destroy the group as such, constitute genocide. The crucial issue will be whether it can be demonstrated that the acts were done with the purpose of destroying the group. Complicity in genocide or torture is also a violation of international law. Under the *Yamashita* case, an official or commander who, through reports received by him or through other means, knows that troops or other persons subject to his control are about to commit or have committed war crimes, and fails to take the necessary and reasonable steps to ensure compliance with the law of war, is responsible for such crimes. Regardless of whether the conflict is deemed a civil war or international war, the serious offenses against civilians alleged would violate the humanitarian laws of war.

SAMPLE ANSWER 4:

The question is taken directly from the facts in Soering v. United Kingdom, 11 Eur. Human. Rts. Rep. 439 (1989) before the European Court of Human Rights (a cautionary tale for students in love). The answer which follows consists of excerpts from that opinion:

The applicant alleged that the decision by the Secretary of State the Home Department to surrender him to the authorities of the United States of America would, if implemented, give rise to a breach by the United Kingdom of Article 3 of the Convention, which provides: "No one shall be subjected to torture or to inhuman or degrading treatment or punishment."

Applicability of Article 3 in Cases of Extradition

The alleged breach derives from the applicant's exposure to the so-called "death row phenomenon." This phenomenon may be described as consisting in a combination of circumstances to which the applicant would be exposed if, after having been extradited to Virginia to face a capital murder charge, he were sentenced to death.

In its report (at paragraph 94) the Commission reaffirmed "its caselaw that a person's deportation or extradition may give rise to an issue under Article 3 of the Convention where there are serious reasons to believe that the individual will be subjected, in the receiving State, to treatment contrary to that Article."

The applicant likewise submitted that Article 3 not only prohibits the Contracting States from causing inhuman or degrading treatment or punishment to occur within their jurisdiction but also embodies an associated obligation not to put a person in a position where he will or may suffer such treatment or punishment at the hands of other States. For the applicant, at least as far as Article 3 is concerned, an individual may not be surrendered out of the protective zone of the Convention without the certainty that the safeguards which he would enjoy are as effective as the Convention standard.

The United Kingdom Government, on the other hand, contended that Article 3 should not be interpreted so as to impose responsibility on a Contracting State for acts which occur outside its jurisdiction. In particular, in their submission, extradition does not involve the responsibility of the extraditing State for inhuman or degrading treatment or punishment which the extradited person may suffer outside the State's jurisdiction. To begin with, they maintained, it would be straining the language of Article 3 intolerably to hold that by surrendering a fugitive criminal the extraditing State has "subjected" him to any treatment or punishment that he will receive following conviction and sentence in the receiving State.

* * *

Article 1 of the Convention, which provides that "the High Contracting Parties shall secure to everyone within their jurisdiction the rights and freedoms defined in Section I," sets a limit, notably territorial, on the reach of the Convention. In particular, the engagement undertaken by a Contracting State is confined to "securing" ("reconnatre" in the French text) the listed rights and freedoms to persons within its own "jurisdiction." Further, the Convention does not govern the actions of States not Parties to it, nor does it purport to be a means of requiring the Contracting States to impose Convention standards on other States. Article 1 cannot be read as justifying a general principle to the effect that, notwithstanding its extradition obligations, a Contracting State may not surrender an individual unless satisfied that the conditions awaiting him in the country of destination are in full accord with each of the safeguards of the Convention.

Indeed, as the United Kingdom Government stressed, the beneficial purpose of extradition in preventing fugitive offenders from evading justice cannot be ignored in determining the scope of application of the Convention and of Article 3 in particular.

* * *

In interpreting the Convention regard must be had to its special character as a treaty for the collective enforcement of human rights and fundamental freedoms (see the Ireland v. the United Kingdom judgment of 18 January 1978, Series A no. 25, p. 90, 239). Thus, the object and purpose of the Convention as an instrument for the protection of individual human beings require that its provisions be interpreted and applied so as to make its safeguards practical and effective (see, inter alia, the Urtica judgment of 13 May 1980, Series A no. 37, p. 16, 33). In addition, any interpretation of the rights and freedoms guaranteed has to be consistent with "the general spirit of the Convention, an instrument designed to maintain and promote the ideals and values of a democratic society" (see the Kjeldsen, Busk Madsen and Pedersen judgment of 7 December 1976, Series A no. 23, p. 27, 53).

* * *

The question remains whether the extradition of a fugitive to another State where he would be subjected or be likely to be subjected to torture or to inhuman or degrading treatment or punishment would itself engage the responsibility of a Contracting State under Article 3. That the abhorrence of torture has such implications is recognised in Article 3 of the UN Convention Against Torture and Other Cruel, Inhuman or Degrading Treatment or Punishment, which provides that "no State Party shall . . . extradite a person where there are substantial grounds for believing that he would be in danger of being subjected to torture." The fact that a specialized treaty should spell out in detail a specific obligation attaching to the prohibition of torture does not mean that an essentially similar obligation is not already inherent in the general terms of Article 3 of the European Convention. It would hardly be compatible with the underlying values of the Convention, that "common heritage of political traditions, ideals, freedom and the rule of law" to which the Preamble refers, were a Contracting State knowingly to surrender a fugitive to another State where there were substantial grounds for believing that he would be in danger of being subjected to torture, however heinous the crime allegedly committed. Extradition in such circumstances, while not explicitly referred to in the brief and general wording of Article 3, would plainly be contrary to the spirit and intendment of the Article, and in the Court's view this inherent obligation not to extradite also extends to cases in which the fugitive would be faced in the receiving State by a real risk of exposure to inhuman or degrading treatment or punishment proscribed by that Article.

What amounts to "inhuman or degrading treatment or punishment" depends on all the circumstances of the case. Furthermore, inherent in the whole of the Convention is a search for a fair balance between the demands of the general interest of the community and the requirements of the protection of the individual's fundamental rights. As movement about the world becomes easier and crime takes on a larger international dimension, it is increasingly in the interest of all nations that suspected offenders who flee abroad should be brought to justice. Conversely, the establishment of safe havens for fugitives would not only result in danger for the State obliged to harbour the protected person but also tend to undermine the foundations of extradition. These considerations must also be included among the factors to be taken into account in the interpretation and application of the notions of inhuman and degrading treatment or punishment in extradition cases.

It is not normal for the Convention institutions to pronounce on the existence or otherwise of potential violations of the Convention. However, where an applicant claims that a decision to extradite him would, if implemented, be contrary to Article 3 by reason of its foreseeable consequences in the requesting country, a departure from this principle is necessary, in view of the serious and irreparable nature of the alleged suffering risked, in order to ensure the effectiveness of the safeguard provided by that Article.

In sum, the decision by a Contracting State to extradite a fugitive may give rise to an issue under Article 3, and hence engage the responsibility of that State under the Convention, where substantial grounds have been shown for believing that the person concerned, if extradited, faces a real risk of being subjected to torture or to inhuman or degrading treatment or punishment in the requesting country. The establishment of such responsibility inevitably involves an assessment of conditions in the requesting country against the standards of Article 3 of the Convention. Nonetheless, there is no question of adjudicating on or establishing the responsibility of the receiving country, whether under general international law, under the Convention or otherwise. In so far as any liability under the Convention is or may be incurred, it is liability incurred by the extraditing Contracting State by reason of its having taken action which has as a direct consequence the exposure of an individual to proscribed ill-treatment.

Application of Article 3 in the Particular Circumstances of the Present Case

The extradition procedure against the applicant in the United Kingdom has been completed, the Secretary of State having signed a warrant ordering his surrender to the United States' authorities; this decision, albeit as yet not implemented, directly affects him. It therefore has to be determined on the above principles whether the foreseeable consequences of Mr. Soering's return to the United States are such as to attract the application of Article 3. This inquiry must concentrate firstly on whether Mr. Soering runs a real risk of being sentenced to death in Virginia, since the source of the alleged inhuman and degrading treatment or punishment, namely the "death row phenomenon," lies in the imposition of the death penalty.

Only in the event of an affirmative answer to this question need the Court examine whether exposure to the "death row phenomenon" in the circumstances of the applicant's case would involve treatment or punishment incompatible with Article 3.

1. Whether the Applicant Runs a Real Risk of a Death Sentence and Hence of Exposure to the "Death Row Phenomenon"

* * *

Admittedly, taken on their own the mitigating factors do reduce the likelihood of the death sentence being imposed. No less than four of the five facts in mitigation expressly mentioned in the Code of Virginia could arguably apply to Mr. Soering's case. These are a defendant's lack of any previous criminal history, the fact that the offence was committed while a defendant was under extreme mental or emotional disturbance, the fact that at the time of commission of the offence the capacity of a defendant to appreciate the criminality of his conduct or to conform his conduct to the requirements of the law was significantly diminished, and a defendant's age.

* * *

Whatever the position under Virginia law and practice, and notwithstanding the diplomatic context of the extradition relations between the United Kingdom and the United States, objectively it cannot be said that the undertaking to inform the judge at the sentencing stage of the wishes of the United Kingdom eliminates the risk of the death penalty being imposed. In the independent exercise of his discretion the Commonwealth's Attorney has himself decided to seek and to persist in seeking the death penalty because the evidence, in his determination, supports such action. If the national authority with responsibility for prosecuting the offence takes such a firm stance, it is hardly open to the Court to hold that there are no substantial grounds for believing that the applicant faces a real risk of being sentenced to death and hence experiencing the "death row phenomenon."

The Court's conclusion is therefore that the likelihood of the feared exposure of the applicant to the "death row phenomenon" has been shown to be such as to bring Article 3 into play.

2. Whether in the Circumstances the Risk of Exposure to the "Death Row Phenomenon" Would Make Extradition a Breach of Article 3

(a) General Considerations

. . . the applicant did not suggest that the death penalty per se violated Article 3. He, like the two Government Parties, agreed with the Commission that the extradition of a person to a country where he risks the death penalty does not in itself raise an issue under either Article 2 or Article 3.

That does not mean however that circumstances relating to a death sentence can never give rise to an issue under Article 3. The manner in which it is imposed or executed, the personal circumstances of the condemned person and a disproportionality to the gravity of the crime committed, as well as the conditions of detention awaiting execution, are examples of factors capable of bringing the treatment or punishment received by the condemned person within the proscription under Article 3. Present-day attitudes in the Contracting States to capital punishment are relevant for the assessment whether the acceptable threshold of suffering or degradation has been exceeded.

(b) The Particular Circumstances

The applicant submitted that the circumstances to which he would be exposed as a consequence of the implementation of the Secretary of State's decision to return him to the United States, namely the "death row phenomenon," cumulatively constitute such serious treatment that his extradition would be contrary to Article 3. He cited in particular the delays in the appeal and review procedures following a death sentence, during which time he would be subject to increasing tension and psychological trauma; the fact, so he said, that the judge or jury in determining sentence is not obliged to take into account the defendant's age and mental state at the time of the offence; the extreme conditions of his future detention on "death row" in Mecklenburg Correctional Center, where he expects to be the victim of violence and sexual abuse because of his age, color and nationality; and the constant spectre of the execution itself, including the ritual of execution. He also relied on the possibility of extradition or deportation, which he would not oppose, to the Federal Republic of Germany as accentuating the disproportionality of the Secretary of State's decision.

The Government of the Federal Republic of Germany took the view that, taking all the circumstances together, the treatment awaiting the applicant in Virginia would go so far beyond treatment inevitably connected with the imposition and execution of a death penalty as to be "inhuman" within the meaning of Article 3.

On the other hand, the conclusion expressed by the Commission was that the degree of severity contemplated by Article 3 would not be attained.

The United Kingdom government shared this opinion. In particular, they disputed many of the applicant's factual allegations as to the conditions on death row in Mecklenburg and his expected fate there.

* * *

(c) Conclusion

For any prisoner condemned to death, some element of delay between imposition and execution of the sentence and the experience of severe stress in conditions necessary for strict incarceration are inevitable. The democratic character of the Virginia legal system in general and the positive features of Virginia trial, sentencing and appeal procedures in particular are beyond doubt. The Court agrees with the Commission that the machinery of justice to which the applicant would be subject in the United States is in itself neither arbitrary nor unreasonable, but, rather, respects the rule of law and affords not inconsiderable procedural safeguards to the defendant in a capital trial. Facilities are available on death row for the assistance of inmates, notably through provision of psychological and psychiatric services.

However, in the Court's view, having regard to the very long period of time spent on death row in such extreme conditions, with the ever present and mounting anguish of awaiting execution of the death penalty, and to the personal circumstances of the applicant, especially his age and mental state at the time of the offense, the applicant's extradition to the United States would expose him to a real risk of treatment going beyond the threshold set by Article 3. A further consideration of relevance is that in the particular instance the legitimate purpose of extradition could be achieved by another means which would not involve suffering of such exceptional intensity or duration.

Accordingly, the Secretary of State's decision to extradite the applicant to the United States would, if implemented, give rise to a breach of Article 3.

Note: Compare to the Court's holding in *Soering* and its decision in *Bankovic v. Belgium* that residents of the Federal Republic of Yugoslavia could not sue NATO state parties to the European Convention for alleged violations relating to the Kosovo bombing campaign. Application No. 52207/99 (available at: http://www.echr.coe.int). In that decision the Court distinguished *Soering* and other cases like it as involving a state's responsibility for its actions while the person is still within its territorial jurisdiction rather than a state's responsibility for the extra-territorial effects of its actions.

Appendix B

Glossary

(**AFRC**): Armed Forces Revolutionary Council; pp. 66–67

(**ASEAN**): Association of Southeast Asian Nations; pp. 93–94

(**ATCA**): Alien Tort Claims Act; pp. 139–141

(**CDF**): Civil Defence Forces; p. 67

(**CEDAW**): Convention on the Elimination of All Forms of Discrimination against Women; pp. 31–32

(**CID**): cruel, inhuman, or degrading (treatment); pp. 35–37

diplomatic asylum: the granting of refuge by a state in its embassies, ships, or aircraft in the territory of another state; pp. 39–40

dolus directus: a scenario in which the perpetrator foresees and desires the consequences of the act; pp. 63–64

dolus eventualis: a situation in which a perpetrator foresees the possibility of a harmful or illegal consequences, other than the one desired; pp. 63–64

dolus indirectus: a situation in which the perpetrator foresees certain harmful or illegal consequences as "almost inevitable"; pp. 63–64

(**ECOSOC**): Economic and Social Council (UN); pp. 20–22

(**ECSR**): European Committee on Social Rights; p. 77

(**EU**): European Union; p. 59

(**EULEX**): European Union Rule of Law Mission in Kosovo; pp. 106–107

extradition: the process by which an individual charged with a crime in one state is found in a second state and returned to the first state for trial or punishment; p. 133 (Chapter XIV, generally)

(**FGM**): Female Genital Mutilation; p. 40

(**FSIA**): Foreign Sovereign Immunities Act; pp. 139–140

(**FTCA**): Federal Tort Claims Act; p. 140

hostis humani generis: an enemy of all mankind; p. 51

(**HRC**): Human Rights Committee; pp. 20, 35

(**IACHR**): Inter-American Commission on Human Rights; pp. 6, 84–85

(**ICC**): International Criminal Court; pp. 5, 63–64, 102, 107, 116

(ICCPR): International Covenant on Civil and Political Rights; pp. 1–2, 13, 17, 19–20, 35–37, 55–56, 117, 139, 146

(ICESC): International Covenant on Economic, Social and Cultural Rights; pp. 1–2, 17, 19–20, 139

(ICJ): International Court of Justice; pp. 4–5, 59–63, 128

(ICTR): International Tribunal for Rwanda; pp. 8, 101–103

(ICTY): International Tribunal for the Former Yugoslavia; pp. 8, 101–103, 116

(ILGHRC): International Lesbian and Gay Humans Rights Commission; pp. 33–34

(ILO): International Labor Organization (UN); pp. 1, 15–16, 22–23

jus cogens: a law from which no derogation is permitted; pp. 52–53, 147

(MICIVIH): UN International Civilian Mission in Haiti; p. 100

(NATO): North Atlantic Treaty Organization; p. 106

non self-executing: only enforceable through implementing legislation; pp. 12, 144

(OAS): Organization of American States; pp. 5–6, 82–85, 87, 89, 91

(OAU): Organisation of African Unity (now African Union); pp. 5, 64, 66, 69–70, 92, 102, 158

(ONUMOZ Mozambique), **(UNTAC** Cambodia), **(UNTAG** Namibia), and **(MINURSO** Western Sahara):** refer to UN operations involving large scale government transitions in the respective countries; p. 97

opinio juris: a sense of legal obligation compelling states to follow a certain practice; pp. 10, 125, 127

(OSCE): Organization for Security and Cooperation in Europe; pp. 71, 77

preventative diplomacy: an effort to deal with potential conflict before they explode into crisis; pp. 7, 96

(RUD): reservation, understanding, and declaration (to a treaty); pp. 144, 146

self-executing: directly enforceable in U.S. federal courts; pp. 2, 12, 18, 139, 144

(TVPA): Torture Victim Protection Act; pp. 140, 143

(UN): United Nations; pp. 2–5, 7–8, 12–14, 16–23, 25–28, 31, 33–35, 38–40, 42–44, 49–50, 52, 56, 59–60, 62–63, 65, 67, 69–71, 93, 95–103, 105–107, 116, 122–123, 128, 147, 152, 156–158, 162

(UNAMID): African Union-United Nations Hybrid Mission in Darfur; p. 102

(UNAMSIL): United Nations Mission in Sierra Leone; p. 67

(UNCAT): Convention Against Torture and Other Cruel Inhuman or Degrading Treatment or Punishment; pp. 34–37

(UNMIH): UN Mission in Haiti (second); p. 101

(UNMIK): United Nations Mission in Kosovo; pp. 106–107

(UNOSOM): United Nations Operation In Somalia; p. 99

(UNSC): United Nations Security Council; pp. 7, 99, 101, 105–106

Table of Cases

Table of Treaties

Index